Managing Successful Universities

Second Edition

SRHE and Open University Press Imprint

Current titles include:

Managing Successful Universities

Second Edition

Michael Shattock

 Society for Research into Higher Education
& Open University Press

Open University Press
McGraw-Hill Education
McGraw-Hill House
Shoppenhangers Road
Maidenhead
Berkshire
England
SL6 2QL

email: enquiries@openup.co.uk
world wide web: www.openup.co.uk

and Two Penn Plaza, New York, NY 10121–2289, USA

First published 2003
Reprinted 2004, 2007, 2008 (twice), 2009 (twice)
First published in this edition 2010

A catalogue record of this book is available from the British Library

ISBN–13: 978-0-33-523743-2
ISBN–10: 0-33-523743-6

Library of Congress Cataloging-in-Publication Data
CIP data applied for

Typeset by RefineCatch Limited, Bungay, Suffolk
Printed in the UK by Bell and Bain Ltd, Glasgow

Fictitious names of companies, products, people, characters and/or data that may be
used herein (in case studies or in examples) are not intended to represent any real
individual, company, product or event.

Mixed Sources
Product group from well-managed
forests and other controlled sources
www.fsc.org   Cert no. TT-COC-002769
© 1996 Forest Stewardship Council
FSC

*The **McGraw·Hill** Companies*

Contents

Preface to the second edition

This is a second, and significantly revised, edition of *Managing Successful Universities* first published in 2003. Much seems to have happened to higher education since then – it has become an important element of globalization and international league tables have conferred a world ranking on universities operating in widely different economic, cultural and intellectual contexts; the concept of society's dependence on the knowledge economy and the universities' contribution to it has strengthened in most countries, including the UK, leading to an increased investment into university based research; student numbers have continued to grow and, perhaps particularly in the UK, there has been an increasing concern to widen participation from disadvantaged social groups; this has reinforced the recognition of universities' regional and local roles in economic terms, in their contribution to 'creative communities' (Florida 2001) and in improving access to higher education.

These pressures have widened the agendas that universities have adopted and have had an often rhetorical impact on the conduct of their core business, teaching and research, and as such are reflected in this new edition. But they have not affected the key message of the 2003 volume, and indeed the widening agenda has reinforced it, that the management of universities, the aggregation of the efforts of their component parts (Hamel 2007) represents an essential element in creating and sustaining successful institutions. These new, or perhaps it would be fairer to say, increasingly emphasized themes in higher education have been reflected in an extensive literature on which the new edition seeks to draw.

The 2003 volume was written in an economic climate which encouraged a broadened agenda for higher education. Economic growth in most countries, and certainly in the UK, was matched by increased expenditure on higher education. In the UK this included in 2006 a sharp injection of private funding through tuition fees, thus introducing a new market element into the financing of universities (although this was mitigated by the tight government control on actual student numbers). However, the worldwide economic downturn of 2007–8 and the prospect of a relatively long drawn out recovery will inevitably impact on universities, especially on those most dependent on public expenditure. A policy 'think tank' in the UK has launched a debate about university survival under the title *Sink or Swim? Facing up to Failing Universities* (Fazakerley and Chant 2009). This probably overstates the issue but underscores the fact that the economic climate has changed significantly since 2003. This new edition, therefore, gives more space to the consequences of managing retrenchment and the importance of developing new sources of income than the first edition felt the need to do. As in the university budget cuts of the early 1980s, economic downturn can provide opportunities for some universities to move up the rankings by using good management to harness the pursuit of institutional success, setting realistic targets and eliminating weaknesses; it can also penalize universities where governance and management are ineffective either because they are indecisive or because they lack internal credibility and support.

Introduction

Successful universities are successful primarily because of their teaching and research, not because of their management, but good management, including good leadership, can over time provide the conditions in which teaching and research can flourish, just as, more usually, poor management can undermine teaching and research and precipitate institutional decline. We do not give as much consideration as we should to what makes a successful university especially bearing in mind that the chief beneficiaries of such success are its students. Good teaching, good research, good academic support services, good study conditions, a well managed academic and social environment and the ability to take advantage of opportunities as they present themselves all contribute to good learning experiences and to effective education. Such benefits are long lasting and inspire affection and loyalty from students towards the institution that provides them.

Higher education would be much improved in the UK if there was a broader definition of what constitutes a successful university than the achievement of a position in a league table but we lack the differentiation of functions that we see in some countries, most notably the US where the college, usually a liberal arts college, can offer a superb teaching environment without the additional burden of seeking, institutionally, to major in research. We missed the opportunity to create such a sector in the 1970s when the rationalization of the teacher training colleges was undertaken and again in the period after 2003 when the colleges of high education were labelled 'teaching only universities' in the White Paper, *The Future of Higher Education* (DEFS 2003) and given university status but on the same funding terms as the 1992 New Universities so that they were left competing for student numbers, recurrent grant and research support on the same basis as their much larger neighbours. We should recognize that the forces and funding policies that have driven UK higher education since the 1960s have been ranged against such differentiation and that it will only take root if it is made a cardinal and continuous element in policy. The disparity between the rewards for research and the rewards for teaching in the funding regime suggest an explicit stratification of the UK higher education system which cannot confer parity of esteem between different institutional missions. Perhaps we should not be surprised by this: Codling and Meek reach the firm conclusion that unitary higher education systems, as in the UK, are much less likely to produce diversity than binary systems (Codling and Meek 2006). They also conclude that whether or not there is diversity there will always be a hierarchy of institutions. They see this hierarchy based on longevity, wealth and prestige while this book will argue (Chapter 1) that longevity and inherited wealth, important though they are, can in the modern period be replaced by other factors in the competition to identify institutional success.

Some authorities, notably the Dearing Inquiry into Higher Education in the UK (the Dearing Committee) in 1997, and David Watson, one of its members, argue that it is more important to strive for a 'world class' higher education system than for 'world class' institutions (Watson 2006; Watson and Amoah 2007). There is much to commend this view, particularly when looked at through the eyes of government. On the other hand while we may admire the University of Wisconsin System or the California Master Plan approach, it is the Madison campus, or the University of California at Berkeley, UCLA or San Diego which constitute the flagships of the systems. No one would argue, in spite of the excellence of individual components of the systems, that these were not the most successful elements. This book, therefore, while fully acknowledging the strength of the argument, remains concerned with institutional rather than system success; with those universities which are responsible for the education of a section of our most able youth, which pursue research to the highest levels of endeavour and which act as the guardians, interpreters and critics of our cultural heritage.

We need more successful universities, especially universities that have achieved success without inherited wealth or status, because of the model they present to the university system as a whole and the impact that institutional success can have on the performance of staff. This book argues that success builds momentum that can lead to further success and that effective institutional management, in its broadest sense, represents an important factor in a university 'punching above its weight' or, put less colloquially, performing better than its circumstances might suggest it could. It goes on to argue that this success does not occur as a result of a single critical decision but because the institution finds ways of getting a lot of relatively small decisions right over a long period, and these decisions reinforce one another, and because its machinery and organizational culture encourages consistency of purpose and imposes an unspoken coordination on decision making so as to concentrate rather than dissipate institutional energies. This management style addresses the processes of university management holistically relating each decision or step forward to the whole range of institutional activities and programmes so that they complement one another rather than encourage dissonance.

Such an approach relies on adopting very broad policy objectives rather than a detailed planning approach and concentrates on encouraging and seeking to stimulate success wherever it can find it whether in an individual academic's research, in a new teaching initiative, in an opportunistic idea to create a new viable source of income or in a new facility which will add institutional value. It encourages initiative and discourages control, except at the most basic system levels; it seeks to release energy around the university rather than contain it, believing that successful universities thrive on the achievements of their staff and students not on a set of carefully constructed centrally designed policies. Perhaps, above all, it is driven by ambition either to achieve or maintain so-called 'world class status', or to compete vigorously within a national hierarchy of institutions. Such a style cannot flourish in heavily hierarchical structures and top-down management styles; it works best where structures are flat, communication is quick and informal and where academic and administrator, professor and lecturer feel that their ideas will be considered on merit and not in relation to rank, status or location and where debate is open and robust. The 2003 White Paper *The Future of Higher Education* urged that institutions should be empowered to use their freedoms to be 'dynamic and self determining institutions' (DEFS 2003). We need to adopt management styles which will enable universities to realize the full potential of their staff and students, not suffocate initiative in out-dated management-speak or worn out managerialist analogies of control. Unfortunately all too many universities have reacted to the pressures of size and financial stringency by introducing additional layers of management which have the effect of pushing academic departments, which are the key units for delivering the core business, further away from central decision making and of bureaucratizing relationships which should remain fluid and direct. In a period of economic downturn these structures may seem restrictive and insufficiently robust to reshape an institution for hard times. This book is intended to offer ideas as to how management in universities can contribute to institutional success by being creative, supportive and organizationally effective. If universities are to be dynamic and self determining, however, the most important task is to give them the confidence to back initiative and respond to competition; that confidence is bred by success.

A significant question that arises out of UK funding policies and the funding differentials that it fosters is whether the funding formulae that are employed become so economically determinant that universities no longer have the chance to raise their performance, compete successfully and improve their relative position. My belief, however, is that even if the most extreme levels of research concentration are encouraged, economic changes outside higher education, innovative management and politics itself can ensure that the relative permeability of the system is retained. Ambitious institutions, with access to resources, will continue to be able to force themselves up the rankings, just as poor leadership and management and local economic decline may allow them to slip down them.

This book is intended to be both a contribution to the debate about how the higher education system should develop through its most successful universities and how those institutions should be managed to achieve and sustain success in a competitive environment, nationally and globally. As such, it is based on research but also on practical experience, and observation of institutions both in the UK and internationally. I have been very grateful over the years for the continuous dialogue I have maintained with colleagues at Warwick (particularly at Warwick) and elsewhere about what managing for success in higher education actually means. A special debt is owed to participants of the MBA in Higher Education Management and to my colleagues teaching on the programme at the Institute of Education, University of London for keeping the issues covered in this book under constant active discussion. Without this stimulus the revision of the 2003 edition could not have been undertaken.

1

What are the characteristics of a successful university?

This chapter explores the factors that define institutional success. It considers how the climate in which success can be identified has changed, how we can rank success whether through research performance or through student related measures and what conclusions can be drawn from the published league tables. It looks at contextual factors that need to be taken into account including factors which can disadvantage institutions, and whether alternative criteria can be found to measure institutional performance; along with this it reviews the special position of the post-1992 universities. Issues about the sustainability of performance are explored and the evidence in regard to company success is compared with the position of universities; it argues that performance over time can be self reinforcing in the latter except perhaps in periods of very sharp change where universities may lack adaptability to new pressures. Finally, it sums up the evidence and draws conclusions about the characteristics of institutional success and the factors that generate it.

The historical position

One of the most significant changes in the way we think about universities is how we identify success. In the years up to 1980 the University Grants Committee (UGC) operated on the principle that universities were equal or, if not actually equal, should for the most part be treated as such. In the 1950s common salary scales were introduced to ensure that richer universities should not poach staff from poorer institutions. In the 1960s the Robbins Committee sought to diminish the quality gap between Oxbridge and the rest and in the 1970s research student numbers were allocated on the basis of equality between less and more research active universities. Also in the 1970s the Universities Central Council for Admissions (UCCA) opposed suggestions that it should publish A level entry scores on a university by university basis because it did not wish to draw attention to differences in entry levels between different universities (Shattock 1994, 2001a). Few people were deceived by this egalitarian approach, least of all the research councils which were already urging the need for a greater concentration of research in fewer institutions. Indeed, not only did informed opinion accord success to some institutions but it also identified others which were failing or were about to do so: in the late 1970s, rumours abounded as to which institutions were on an alleged government closure list. Mostly these were 1960s new universities – relatively small and campus based – which had suffered from student troubles and were thought to be politically radical. Ironically one of these (Warwick) was later quoted in the media as Mrs Thatcher's favourite university, and most of them appeared high up in the 1980s research league tables. The failure to admit to differences in levels of institutional performance and to identify data that would illustrate them was damaging because it bred institutional complacency amongst some of the older universities and offered no incentive for improvement. It also encouraged too much reliance on 'informed' opinion and offered no assistance to those outside universities such as potential student admission candidates, industrialists seeking to commission research or the public at large who had a legitimate interest in selecting one institution over another.

The first steps towards change

All this was to change in 1981, not as a result of action by the Government except indirectly, but by the UGC. Facing unprecedented budget reductions the Committee chose to impose differential cuts on universities using criteria based on GCE A level entry scores, a broad perception of research quality, unit costs, the distribution of academic staff and their ages, and the relevant student numbers in the different subject areas. Because the UGC was trying to achieve three things at once – protecting science and technology numbers, preserving the unit of resource and correcting previous imbalances in resource allocations – and because London University was still a single unit for recurrent grant purposes, it is not possible to deduce from the UGC's resource allocation decisions a clear pattern of winners. A list of major losers was, however, immediately obvious: Salford, Bradford, Keele, Aston, UMIST, Stirling and Surrey, all of whose budgets were cut by more than 25 per cent over a four year period. Of these, all but UMIST were also required to cut their student numbers by 14 per cent or more. Universities that suffered budget cuts of no more than 15 per cent, and cuts in student numbers of no more than 4 per cent were, on the other hand, relative winners. They included Bath, Cambridge, Durham, East Anglia, Edinburgh, Glasgow, Leeds, Leicester, Loughborough, Nottingham, Oxford, Sheffield, Southampton, Warwick and York. The next and decisive change took place three years later when the UGC decided, under pressure from the Treasury, to review research quality across the university system and to allocate recurrent grant for research (R) differentially, and separately, from recurrent grant for teaching (T). This came into effect in 1985–6. Not surprisingly, none of the biggest losers in the 1981 cuts, except UMIST, did well in this first Research Assessment Exercise (RAE) (Shattock 1994).

These events were transitional to a new era when institutional differentiation increased as market mechanisms were given freer rein under the Thatcher reforms, but they represented a traumatic period from which some institutions did not recover easily. Twenty five years later we are in a much better position to assess university performance than we were then but the quality of performance remains a difficult and inexact process to evaluate and ways of defining success remain elusive. The RAE has shown that it is possible to distinguish between differential levels of research performance on a system-wide basis although arguments remain on methodological points. But in other areas of institutional activity it is more difficult. We feel instinctively we can recognize successful universities when we see them but there has still been little systematic research to identify what their characteristics might be, what criteria we should use to judge them and what factors can be shown to sustain success. Although traditionally universities are both research and teaching institutions, university success is often equated with research reputation alone: the 2003 White Paper, for example, referred, to the 'best' universities with research reputation apparently in mind even though it was anxious to encourage the concept of teaching universities (DEFS 2003).

Increasingly, however, there is public pressure to redress the balance and factor the teaching function into any assessment. This will increase if the system moves to a situation where tuition fees for home undergraduates are truly variable and significant differentials emerge in institutional charging policies. Newspapers and magazines, with large numbers of parents and potential university students amongst their readers, have been quick to respond to the significant public interest in the provision of ratings of university performance both in the UK and elsewhere. The failure to define university success in the post-war years had an important impact on the way higher education institutions were managed. The previous UGC system had tended to favour homogeneity rather than institutional distinctiveness and the UGC judged institutional ambition on the basis of the extent to which it matched the needs of the system as a whole: institutional performance was not compared and reputational capital rested largely on age, or seniority in the system. In a competitive environment, however, management needs to be able to define success and ensure that performance is geared to achieving it. Universities are multi-faceted, multi-product organizations which increasingly in the modern era are taking on additional roles, particularly in relation to the knowledge economy and social inclusion, although their core business remains teaching and research. This broadening of a university's role represents an important new dimension in university life, at least in Europe, and can be critical to the way universities are now regarded by their local communities and by government. It also has significant implications for the way universities must be managed. Success in this wider role, however,

should not be regarded as compensating for shortfalls in academic performance. Indeed there is plenty of evidence to show that success in the core
business reinforces performance in the wider role – major science parks,
significant industrial partnerships and impact on regional or national economic life are more likely to occur at academically high performing universities than at universities which have low academic ratings.

There is no single scale of values that can rate the value to society of a
university that scores exceptionally highly in teaching and research against
one that concentrates on a social inclusion agenda. In a mass higher education system it is important that there should be diversity of mission and that
universities should be encouraged (and funded) to play to their strengths
and to compete where they are best able to succeed. The higher education
framework report *Higher Ambitions: The Future of Universities in the Knowledge
Economy* is stating no more than the obvious when it says: 'we expect that
more universities will face up to hard choices about identifying areas where
they can really achieve excellence, and specializing in these. Very few English
universities will be able to achieve excellence across the full range of
university activity' (DBIS 2009: 96).

Equal success should not be sought, nor can be achieved, in teaching,
research and all the facets of the wider social and economic agenda. In the
modern world, however, just as we are entitled to expect that a university
which aims to address itself primarily to one or even many aspects of the
wider agenda should aim for a good performance in teaching and research,
so no university, however distinguished in teaching and research, should
ignore it.

How to measure university success?

One could seek to evaluate university success simply by measuring performance against each institution's stated objectives but experience suggests that
mission statements, at least in UK universities, have become marketing tools
rather than realistic statements of strategic purpose: the once popular slogan
'fitness for purpose' has degenerated under market pressures into rhetoric
and exaggeration and is liable to manipulation. As Birnbaum has argued
(2007) almost every university claims to be world class in something. As we
have seen in the past, reputation good or bad, unsupported by hard evidence,
can be self serving and can amount to no more than self advertisement
or unsubstantiated rumour, while statistical evidence cannot provide final
answers to what are intangible questions, and offers no more than a set of
proxies which can serve to measure the success of one institution relative to
another in the areas where statistics are available. The former Department of
Trade and Industry (DTI) produced a 'value added scoreboard' to measure
company success but the value added was entirely financial, which would
represent only one, and certainly not the most important, of the value added
factors applicable for a university. The DTI scoreboard did, however, have

one message applicable in the university world, that different sectors scored very differently – thus oil, gas and banking (then) scored well, while general retailing scored badly, with automotive and food-processing companies coming somewhere in the middle (Marsh 2002). Different kinds of universities whether different in the balance of research and teaching or in subject balance might be expected to show different results from measurement which encompassed only a single aspect of their performance.

Unfortunately all the pressures in UK higher education drive institutions in an opposite direction towards a common model. The sociological argument for institutional isomorphism was set out more than 25 years ago:

> Once disparate organisations in the same line of business are structured into an actual field (. . . by competition, the state or the professions), powerful forces emerge that lead them to become more similar to one another . . . Organisations may try to change constantly; but after a certain point in the structuration of an organisational field, the aggregate effect of individual change is to lessen the extent of diversity within the field.

> (Di Maggio and Powell 1983)

The authors define three mechanisms through which isomorphic change occurs: coercive isomorphism where formal pressures are exerted by superior organizations (national funding formulae, the RAE/REF); mimetic processes where in uncertain conditions organizations model themselves on other organizations (for example, the current fashion for institutional restructuring described in Chapter 4); and normative pressures from professionalization where the movement of professionals within an industry reduces organizational diversity (for example, the evidence of new vice-chancellors seeking to transfer the decision making model they have been accustomed to, to their new institution). All these mechanisms apply in UK higher education. However, there are also significant operational reasons which drive universities in this direction: in an under-funded system success in the RAE represents not simply a reputation pull but additional funding support; similarly a common set of funding formulae inevitably leads institutions to seek to maximize their share of the pot; a common salary spine and centralized salary negotiations drive common approaches to human resource management. There is a certain inevitability about the process and not just in the UK: Van Vught argues that the level of diversity is reduced when there is a greater uniformity of environmental conditions or a larger influence of academic norms and values, a situation which applies across most European higher education systems (Van Vught 2008).

Increased marketization, which might have been expected to reinforce diversity, has in practice reduced it because institutions have engaged in what Dill and Soo have called 'an arms race' for prestige, or Rhoades, a 'reputation race' (Dill and Soo 2005; Rhoades 1990) which is primarily based on research. This reputation competition is increasingly fuelled by international league tables which both Hazelkorn (2007, 2009) and Marginson

(2009) see as now enormously influential in institutional strategy formation. Of the two major world rankings, the *Times Higher Education* and the Shanghai Jiao Tong, the latter, which relies on statistical data (the THE scores are 40 per cent dependent on reputational ranking), concentrates solely on research. Within the UK the media have been compiling league tables since 1994. The longest running is *The Times Good University Guide* but the *Financial Times, The Sunday Times, The Daily Telegraph, The Independent* and *The Guardian* have also contributed. Since 2003 the *Financial Times* and *The Daily Telegraph* have withdrawn. The Centre for Higher Education Research and Information (CHERI) has prepared an authoritative report for HEFCE on league tables and their impact on English universities (CHERI 2008). The Report by implication directs its strongest fire on the two major international league tables. Its comments on the UK league tables are by inference more measured but make clear that with all the weaknesses of some measures being poor proxies for the qualities identified, institutions have become strongly influenced by the league tables produced. The Report summarizes in an even handed way the case for and against league tables but notes that many universities are using them as key performance or strategic targets and that some believe that they will become even more influential as higher education becomes more competitive.

The measurement of institutional success in research

The RAE, first undertaken in 1986, has been repeated in 1989, 1992, 1996, 2001 and 2008. It comprises reviews of research by subject fields (which normally cohere with institutional departmental structures) and, since 1989, has allocated a numerical score to each departmental submission offered for review. The points thus scored can be aggregated and an institutional league table created by the averaging of the scores divided by the number of departments in each institution. Each time the RAE has been undertaken there have been small variations in methodology (the largest being in 2008) but a consistent theme has been that the numerical score multiplied by the numbers of staff whose research achievements were submitted to the RAE in each disciplinary unit of assessment should serve as the basis for the calculation of the recurrent grant to each institution to support research. The most significant and controversial change was the decision in 1992, when the post-1992 universities joined the Exercise, to allow universities to make a choice as to how many of their academic staff they should include in it. This left it open to universities to take a tactical approach to the Exercise, increasingly followed thereafter by all universities, which balanced the financial advantages of high or low submission rates with the reputational advantage of achieving high scores irrespective of however few staff were submitted. This has led to considerable discussion inside and outside universities as to whether the scoring, even when qualified by indicating the proportion of staff submitted, adequately reflects the results. The change also affected the way the research league tables were presented. Tomlin is representative of the view that the omission of staff from a departmental submission changed the basis of the scoring and he suggested an alternative approach whereby all staff scored against a national average for each unit of assessment. Interestingly when he applied this the actual changes of ordering within the top 10 universities were very slight and no new institution was raised into the top 10 list (Tomlin 1998).

Table 1 sets out the placements of the leading 15 universities in the RAE in each year of assessment. Some caveats need to be entered in interpreting the table because the 2008 RAE results were presented on a different basis to those of the previous years and in particular because the proportion of the staff submitted was not taken into account. One consequence is that it is not statistically reliable to include the 2008 results in an average of all the RAEs back to 1986. Nevertheless the extent to which the 2008 results chime with the average ranking for the five previous RAEs tends to confirm the clear message from the figures that the ranking for research excellence is stable amongst the top ranked institutions. This strongly suggests that high quality research, once established, tends to reinforce itself. One or two of this group of universities have had bad years; this may have been due to variations in internal methodological approaches to submitting

Table 1 A comparison of research performance based on the RAE results 1986–2008 (top 15 universities only)

	1986	1989	1992	1996	2001	Average 1986–2001	2008
Cambridge	1	1	1	1	1	1	1
Oxford	2	2	2	3	3	2	2
LSE	3	6	3	2	2	3	2
Imperial College	3	2	5	5	4	4	4
UCL	5	4	4	6	7	6	5
Warwick	6	5	5	4	5	5	7
Manchester (joint)	n/a	n/a	n/a	n/a	n/a	n/a	6
UMIST	14	8	7	12	16	8	n/a
Manchester	9	10	14	14	18	10	n/a
York	9	8	11	9	6	7	8
Edinburgh	9	13	8	7	20	8	10
Essex	14	11	16	11	25	15	9
Bristol	6	7	25	16	14	12	12
Southampton	8	13	21	22	11	14	12
Durham	22	16	13	15	13	16	12
Lancaster	25	16	9	8	9	11	18
Sussex	17	11	10	13	17	12	28

Note: I am indebted to Rebecca Lambert and Giles Carden for the construction of this table. A note on the methodology and sources appears as an appendix.

the data but most universities seem to have performed with considerable consistency. One university (Sussex) can be seen to be slipping down the research ranking each year since 1992. Another university, Manchester, seems in 2008 to have reversed a fall in previous years. Some comment on the Manchester position in 2008 might, however, be appropriate since the improvement might otherwise be seen as an endorsement of the rationale of the merger of UMIST and the University of Manchester. In fact its higher position in 2008 was the result of a more selective approach to the submission of staff; Warwick and York, which it displaced in 2008, both submitted over 90 per cent of their staff, whereas the merged Manchester only submitted 75 per cent.

The scoring method for the ranking rewards institutions that are highly rated across a significant number of subject areas and can thus claim a general institutional excellence in research as distinct from universities which have some outstanding departments or groups of staff within departments but others that are less successful.

The table does not reflect actual funding patterns: a university with a large and research intensive medical school would win a much higher proportion of the total research funding than, for example, an institution with no experimental science departments like the London School of Economics (LSE). It also, and for the same reason, minimizes the gap between the major scientific universities and the rest: the overall depth of scientific capability at Warwick and York, for example, does not equal that of Cambridge, Oxford, Imperial College, UCL, Manchester, Edinburgh or Bristol, or for that matter the civic universities with large medical schools which do not feature in the top 15 ranking. A league table compiled on the basis of research grant income would for this reason look very different and partly explains why the table includes a number of universities that are not members of the Russell Group. But what the table does reflect is the extent to which universities, irrespective of size and subject spread, perform well in research across all the range of disciplines they profess.

The measurement of other factors in institutional success

Research rankings represent a huge reputation factor, and are by a very long way, the most sought after and respected ranking in the academic community. They are perhaps of less concern to the wider public than evidence about a concern for good teaching and other factors which contribute to universities being attractive to students, and it has been this broader spread of interest that newspapers have concentrated on. *The Times* offers the longest running and the most authoritative annual league table giving balancing higher marks for the RAE and the National Student Survey (NSS) scores and slightly lower marks to entry standards, spending on student facilities, the level of degrees awarded, student retention, employment prospects, and the staff/student ratio. Watson is less than fair in criticizing *The Times* for being 'about very little – other than about overall level of resources' if we accept that, with all the caveats mentioned below, institutional performance for the most part drives resource acquisition in the UK system (Watson 2009). The longevity of *The Times* league tables, and their broad consistency of approach, mean that they provide the most reliable long term indicator that we have of trends in that performance. *The Independent* tables, which have had a much shorter life span, generally follow *The Times* methodologies and are included only for reasons of comprehensiveness. *The Sunday Times* gives its highest recognition to entry standards but like *The Times* gives high marks to the RAE and NSS scores. The three tables contain variations in scoring levels which mean that their results, while comparable, offer different approaches to the representations of institutional performance. *The Guardian*, which developed its tables to focus on the student experience alone, omits any reference to RAE scores but includes a high recognition for value added between entry levels and degree results. *The Guardian*'s omission of any representation of research reputation marks it out as a clearly 'teaching orientated' compilation.

While none of these league table presentations would lack caveats as to the extent they represent a true assessment of institutional performance together, they may be said to offer the nearest approximation that public sources of information provide to reach some general conclusions about measures of performance. The fact that the UK possesses a well developed national university data base in the Higher Education Statistics Agency (HESA) material gives a greater security and consistency than might be achieved from international comparisons. Averaging the league table results over a period of years smooths out episodic highs and lows and enables trends to be identified more clearly.

Conclusions to be drawn from the league tables

Table 2 shows the average positioning of universities in the four current newspaper league tables, and should be compared with the rankings in Table 1 which show research excellence as defined in the RAEs. Ten universities from this latter Table (Cambridge, Oxford, Imperial College, LSE, UCL, Warwick, York, Edinburgh, Bristol and Durham) are common to the top 15 in an average of *The Times* rankings over the full 1995 period. *The Times* average rankings over this period which, of course, cover a much broader range of criteria than research alone, identify five other universities (St Andrews, Bath, Loughborough, Kings College, London and Nottingham), which have never appeared in the top 10 in any RAE league table. More significantly the six average top ranked universities in the RAE 1986–2008 are ranked as the top six in *The Guardian* league table, which emphasizes teaching and excludes the research rankings altogether. What we can see, therefore, is that the highest ranked universities for research are also the

Table 2 A comparison of published university league tables compiled on a summative basis (top 15 universities)

Published year	The Times League Table			The Guardian League Table		The Sunday Times League Table			The Independent League Table
	Average 1995–9	Average 2000–4	Average 2005–9	Average 2001–5	Average 2005–10	Average 1998–9	Average 2000–4	Average 2005–9	Average 2007–9
Cambridge	1	2	2	1	2	1	1	1	2
Oxford	2	2	1	3	1	2	2	2	1
Imperial	3	3	3	4	5	4	4	3	3
LSE	5	6	5	3	4	4	3	4	4
UCL	6	7	6	6	6	6	6	5	7
Warwick	6	7	7	7	7	7	7	7	6
Bristol	9	7	9	14	21	12	10	10	13
St Andrews	10	9	8	22	13	12	10	9	6
York	8	9	12	7	12	6	6	7	12
Edinburgh	7	11	12	22	9	14	13	13	16
Durham	11	12	9	26	19	10	12	10	7
Bath	14	8	12	18	11	18	13	11	11
Nottingham	10	12	16	10	18	8	9	11	16
King's CL	17	17	13	15	14	19	20	15	16
Manchester	16	16	24	14	20	20	19	18	29

Note: I am indebted to Rebecca Lambert and Giles Carden for the construction of this table. A note on methodology and sources appears as an appendix.

highest ranked for teaching, and that of the top 15 universities ranked by *The Times* over a 15 year period there are 10 universities who consistently have performed in the leading group of research intensive universities. It is not the purpose of this discussion to seek to establish a 'top 10' of universities – as we have seen the criteria that can be used is too varied for this – but to show that there is a group of universities that is consistently successful in the core business of teaching and research, and that research excellence seems generally to be associated in the UK with high rankings across the board in university performance.

Taking account of contextual factors

One of the difficulties about measuring success is how to assess the special factors or particular advantages that institutions may have. In any assessment of performance universities do not all start from the same position. Cambridge and Cumbria may both be universities but historically, locationally and financially their positions could hardly be more different. What then are the contextual factors that contribute to success? The first is the association of the age of the university with research prestige. In an interesting piece of research Gueno suggests that only 8 per cent of Europe's most research intensive universities were founded in the post-war period. He divides European universities into clusters according to their research performance: of the top cluster of 64 universities he finds that the majority had their roots in the Middle Ages; while the bottom cluster of 192 institutions is 'strongly polarized towards the post-war universities'. He explains this concentration of research in the oldest universities as an example of the Matthew effect:

> A good scientist is usually attracted by centres and universities of excellence where he or she finds the human and physical capital that permits development of high level research. This improves both the quality of the individual and the general quality of the institution and consequently attracts new research funds and capable researchers. In this situation there are two inter-related circles.
>
> (Gueno 1998: 265)

Merton similarly argues that those institutions that attract more of certain resources at one point develop a lead over their peers when competing for resources in the future so that over the years they accumulate a magnetic power in attracting outstanding talent and hosting the most significant research (Merton 1988). If we look at the application of Gueno's findings to the UK the picture is rather less clear: three of the top 15 research intensive universities can be dated from the Middle Ages, and seven further date from the pre-war period with three in London, but five date from the 1960s. A particular factor which affects the position of Oxford and Cambridge is the hereditary wealth of the colleges and the universities. Exempted from the enforced sale of monastic lands under Henry VIII the two institutions and their colleges retain historic endowments and buildings which give much greater force to the Matthew effect and which attract academics to Oxbridge and retain them there in a way that age and history, of themselves, could not have done. In 2001 The *Financial Times* estimated that the wealth of the colleges alone added 456 staff at Oxford and 363 at Cambridge than would have been possible under normal state funding and some £3.8m and £3.2m respectively of expenditure on libraries (Kelly 2001). Significantly, it is not possible to point to any parallel in the UK to the case of New York University which in only a decade between the mid 1980s and 1990s raised itself from being a medium performing institution into the top tier of US universities by fundraising (the stated aim was $1bn), recruiting world class faculty and raising entrance standards (Fombrun 1996).

The most noticeable absentees from the list are many of the civic universities, founded in the nineteenth century in major industrial cities, and dominant institutions in the post-war period. Only two appear in the top 15 and several languish a long way down the tables. One must conclude that they have found it more difficult to adapt to changes in the higher education system and the environment in which they have had to operate. Nevertheless, in the wider European context, Gueno's argument has great strength: older institutions can have a halo effect based on historic reputations which attract the best staff and the best students and it is the interaction of these two constituents which can create an outstanding intellectual community, generate leading research, produce excellently trained students and provide continued self-reinforcing success. Perhaps more importantly, such institutions have established over time a working environment, certain ways of doing things, an operational structure and an organizational culture which has stood the test of time and which does not need to be reinvented to cope with sharp changes in the external environment. But age is not a guarantee in itself: the tables quoted above do not list two Scottish universities with mediaeval origins. On the other hand, while none of the new post-1992 universities appears in the top 50 in any research league table, four universities founded in the 1960s appear consistently in the top 15.

Further contextual points are explored by Tight (1999) who draws analogies between university and football league tables, suggesting that location in large centres of population appears to offer considerable advantages and that elites tend to be self perpetuating. As regards the first, the data in Tables 1 and 2 offer support in regard to institutions based in London, but do not apply in the same way to Cambridge, Warwick, York, Sussex, Essex, Lancaster or Durham. The second raises interesting points because, as Tight explains, while some 'small town' football clubs have performed exceptionally well for short periods, often supported by exceptional resources, they have not been able to maintain that level of performance for very long. This might raise questions about the ability of some of the universities in the list being able to sustain their performance over long periods (the decline of Sussex might seem to be an example of this). These points are confirmed and extended by Kerr (1991) who identified locations in the US – leading centres of the professions, growing centres of economic activity, larger cities rather than small towns, rich communities, areas with effective and committed political leadership and areas of great natural beauty and good climate – as being particularly likely to see the development of outstanding research universities. While these locational points are more pertinent to the US than to the UK, location in a capital city (Imperial, LSE, UCL), in places of architectural or historical beauty (Oxbridge, Edinburgh and York), in an advantaged position from the point of view of transport access (Warwick), or having been endowed with a good coherent site with space for growth (Warwick and York) are all factors which contribute to, even if they do not determine, success. By the same token a bad location in an unfashionable town distant both from industry and from centres of social life, or in a town with a reputation for ugliness or lack of amenities, can be a disincentive to attracting good staff or students.

Factors which disadvantage institutions

Location is only one of the factors which can disadvantage an institution: by far the most important disadvantage seems, on the evidence of the 1960s and afterwards, to lie in a university's origins, whether it was created as a wholly new institution or whether it was awarded university status as an existing institution. In the former category we have Warwick, York, Essex, Lancaster and Sussex, all ranked in the highest quartile. In the latter, we have two categories of institution, the former Colleges of Advanced Technology (CATs) and the former polytechnics and Scottish Central Institutions. Of these two groups, the CATs were created universities contemporaneously with the establishment of the wholly new foundations (then called the New Universities). Twenty years later some of the ex-CATs (Salford, Aston and Bradford) featured, as we have seen, amongst the institutions whose budgets were most severely cut in 1981. Nearly 40 years from foundation they mostly feature in the bottom 10 per cent of the pre-1992 universities in the league tables. The post-1992 universities comprise the second group. It is wholly unsurprising, taking the former CATs as a parallel, that these latter universities should make up a lower tier in the league tables, only 15 years or so after their change of status. The fact that this took place at a time of very sharp reductions in the unit of resource and that they had not been previously subject to the discipline or incentive of the RAE before their transfer, created two further serious disadvantages making it difficult for them to compete with the pre-1992 universities and effectively disqualifying them from access to any significant additional recurrent grant for success in the RAE thus permanently handicapping their development.

The real distinction to be drawn between the wholly new foundations and those that have transferred from non-university to university status is that the former, while they had a slow build up, had from the beginning the ability to recruit staff motivated to the challenge of creating a university, and selected for the purpose, as well as having the freedom to design their own buildings and their own campus for full university status. In the latter, the institutions were staffed by people recruited for rather different tasks, most of whom were not recruited to do research, and had little inclination towards or capacity for it, and inherited buildings and sites inappropriate to the new mission. The evidence is that these problems take at least a generation to sort out. Of the former CATs, Bath, Surrey (both of whom moved to new sites in the 1960s) and Loughborough are now well up the tables. In the longer term, therefore, these disadvantages may not represent a permanent disability for all institutions and there is no reason to suppose that the performance of the more successful ex-CATs will not in time be paralleled by some of the former polytechnics. We should not, however, underestimate the sustained management challenge that this will involve and the length of time it may take. The 1991 White Paper tacitly assumed that if a level playing field in terms of recurrent finance could be provided that covered pre-1992 universities and former polytechnics, the market would enable the latter, or at least some of them, to compete on equal terms with the existing universities. But, the Government did not take account of the existing universities' inherited resources of staff, location, physical assets and established markets. In the marketized conditions of the 1990s these resources encouraged a widening rather than a narrowing of the gap at the extremes of the system so that we now have a greater disparity of such resources, and hence of positioning, than existed in 1992.

Alternative criteria for measuring success

The criteria for success as identified in the league tables represents the conventional and traditional ways in which university success is measured in the UK. If we were to look at some other countries where there is a much more clearly specified differentiation by mission we would find these measures to be inappropriate for various categories or groups of institutions. In the US the liberal arts college sector would score very well in all the league tables except in research, as would the very different Fachhoschulen in Germany, and the again very different Grandes Ecoles in France. The UK has no real equivalent of the US community college although the growth of higher education in further education colleges is changing the picture, but the community colleges, while a very important sector in the US, would do very poorly in the UK higher education league tables. HEFCE has made a significant effort to create a broader set of performance indicators intended to recognize aspects of institutions' social functions such as student recruitment from neighbourhoods with low age participation rates, from mature adults or from state rather than private schools, and have sought to measure institutional 'learning efficiency' by measuring completion rates (HEFCE

1999). These tend to produce predictable results: those universities which had the lowest drop out rates were those that were the most selective in terms of A level scores. But if these figures were adapted with benchmark averages for social/economic factors in the intake the league table lists would be almost reversed: the *Financial Times* (1 April 1999), using this data, put Northumbria at the top of its league table and Oxford at nearly the bottom. What the HEFCE indicators emphasized was that the conventional models do not tell the whole story and that there was a need to find ways to measure diversity. The Funding Council has refined its measurement of socially disadvantaged access to higher education but the process has not been persuasive in terms of improving other measures on which institutional success might be based. The increase in recurrent grant in respect to the admission of students from disadvantaged backgrounds goes some way towards redressing the operational imbalance between research intensive universities drawing on a national catchment of socially advantaged students, and non-research based institutions attracting mostly local students, but will not change a ranking based on public esteem.

While none of the top 15 universities in Table 2 would finish high up in the benchmarking averages for widening participation from socially disadvantaged groups because their academic reputation makes entry at the undergraduate level so competitive, if a league table could be constructed on the basis of the full spread of a wider agenda referred to above it is likely that their position would be not unlike that achieved in their core business. Thirteen of the top 20 universities have developed successful science/ research parks or incubator facilities, and all but LSE (for obvious disciplinary related reasons) have strong records of industrial research collaboration. Fourteen run major performing arts facilities or galleries with national reputations. All 20 universities make major contributions to lifelong learning/ continuing education (Oxford and Cambridge were the pioneers of university extra-mural studies in the nineteenth century).

If we look specifically at the top six universities Cambridge could reasonably claim to be the only one which has had an economic impact on its region comparable to Stanford's and the concentration of universities and colleges in the Boston area, and only LSE and UCL (for disciplinary and locational reasons) do not have very successful science/industrial park developments. According to the *Financial Times*, Cambridge contributed to the national gross domestic product nearly £9bn in 2001 (Kelly 2002). Cambridge's and Oxford's science parks are said to be the most successful in the UK with Warwick's in third place (Kelly 2002). York has led the Science City Initiative in a city not previously associated with science and technology. Four of the top six are amongst the universities with the highest concentration of industrial funded research in the UK, the other two being Nottingham and Cranfield. Four of them have performing arts facilities of major regional importance. Five of them are in the group of universities providing the largest lifelong learning/continuing education programmes. Not surprisingly in view of their academic reputation they compete extremely successfully in the international student market, particularly at the post-graduate level, and are therefore assured of a secure income from this source. Indeed a characteristic of all these institutions is their ability to generate non-government funding to support academic and other developments. What this evidence strongly suggests is that there is a coherence between success in the core business of teaching and research and success in the wider social and economic agenda: academic success becomes a reinforcing factor in success in the wider agenda. Longevity, a more favourable resource base and location may have played an important part in some cases but some of these factors could be found at other institutions. What seems to be true is that these institutions combine academic excellence with an energy in other activities. While many activities are self reinforcing there is evidence that these universities have displayed what Keynes called in another context 'animal spirits'. This energy cannot be measured but has undoubtedly been one of the components that has driven them forward. But, wrote Keynes, 'If the animal spirits are dimmed and spontaneous optimism falters . . . enterprise will fade and die' (Keynes 1936).

The position of the post-1992 universities

For the reasons advanced above it would have been inconceivable that any of the post-1992 universities could have appeared even as high as the top 25 in one of the conventionally based league tables within a period of 15 years or so. It could be argued that this offers their managements the challenge to play a greater role than would otherwise be the case in propelling their institutions up a league table where teaching is the primary function to be measured, and where the establishment of nodes of research development has, until the 2008 RAE, been largely a matter for institutional selection and investment. Table 3 uses the same data provided by *The Times* league tables to examine the progress of the post-1992 institutions in order to discover whether differences are emerging in their performance.

The identification of a leading group of post-1992 universities is much less secure and reliable than for the universities in Table 2. Comparing data year on year there are more variations in placings, suggesting that changes in statistical definitions or in the data collected may be responsible, and that the gap between the top quartile and the bottom quartile is smaller. More interesting, however, is that the gap between the pre-1992 and the post-1992 universities is being eroded to the extent that from 1998 onwards one or more post-1992 universities are listed above two or more of the pre-1992 universities but the trend has not so far been extended. There does seem to be a significant degree of stability in the rankings, whether at the top of the post-1992 table and indeed at the bottom. To what extent this consistency is simply a function of location – an especially important factor when students are largely drawn from a local catchment area and where regional economic factors may be important in the recruitment of both students and staff – is

Table 3 Comparison of the top post-92 universities, compiled from *The Times Good University Guide*, 1995–2009

Published year	Average 1995–9	Average 2000–4	Average 2005–9	Variance 1995/99– 2000/04	Variance 2000/04– 2005/09
Oxford Brookes	54.8	49.8	52.6	5.0	−2.8
Robert Gordon	62.2	59.6	54.8	2.6	4.8
Nottingham Trent	68.0	58.4	58.2	9.6	0.2
Plymouth	64.2	54.2	59.4	10.0	−5.2
Brighton	66.4	64.4	63.2	2.0	1.2
Northumbria	60.0	55.0	63.4	5.0	−8.4
West of England	60.6	61.8	66.0	−1.2	−4.2
Bournemouth	91.4	83.6	66.2	7.8	17.4
Glasgow Caledonian	76.8	74.8	67.0	2.0	7.8
Portsmouth	63.6	67.6	69.8	−4.0	−2.2
Central England (B'ham City)	75.4	89.0	70.8	−13.6	18.2
Napier	73.2	76.4	71.2	−3.2	5.2
Staffordshire	82.4	81.8	71.8	0.6	10.0
Central Lancashire	79.6	79.4	73.8	0.2	5.6
Hertfordshire	72.0	62.0	75.0	10.0	−13.0

Source: The Times Good Universities Guides for 1995–2009.

difficult to pinpoint. It is clear that contextual factors such as their origins, location, and inherited facilities have played a large part in constraining institutional performance as measured in the league tables. We may note, however, the significant rise in the rankings of the University of Bournemouth between 1999 and 2009 taking it clearly into the top group of the new universities from very near the bottom. While location may represent part of this remarkable story de-investment in less successful programmes and reinvestment in those showing real promise (for example in various aspects of media studies where Bournemouth is fast becoming a UK leader) represent a model for institutional renewal for universities from this background.

Sustainability of performance

Because university league tables are of recent origin they tell us less than we ought to know about institutional sustainability. The 1986 RAE assessed research over the period back to 1981 so it is possible to argue that we have data covering 27 years for research alone. Clark Kerr has shown that in the US over nearly 80 years from 1906 to 1982 only three institutions dropped out of the top 15 universities, ranked reputationally in respect to their graduate schools (Kerr 1991). A significant and perhaps distorting feature in the US data, so far as Europe is concerned, is that nine of the top 15 were private universities with large endowments, and all 15 had significant alumni funding, so that sustaining high ratings may have owed as much to the availability of an exceptional resource base, as to the existence of a self-reinforcing academic community. In the UK this exceptional funding strength applies only in Oxford and Cambridge where collegiate endowments and alumni support put the two universities into a different position from any other UK university. Only Edinburgh could be regarded as having remotely comparable advantages. Perhaps more encouraging is that while the Carnegie classification of Research I and Research II universities in 1973 included only 52 universities in category I and 40 in category II in 1994, the number had grown to 89 in category I and had fallen to 37 in category II (McCormack 2002) suggesting, rather like the UK research ratings, that research performance has a strong tendency to be both self sustaining and self reinforcing.

In a labour intensive industry it can be argued that university strengths lie chiefly in the quality of staff they employ. All UK universities have the same legal rights to appoint whoever they choose within broadly the same salary ranges so the differentiation comes about from universities' ability to attract staff of the highest quality. Universities wanting to push themselves up the tables from a low base may have to offer additional inducements – lower teaching loads, research facilities, support staff – to attract staff from universities with better reputations or higher standing in the particular field. Universities have a similar freedom to attract the best students but students' views are influenced by reputation of a public kind but also by the informal grapevine as to the kind of institution they are. Students are also influenced by the historical statistical evidence of how competitive a university's entry standards are. Neither the research nor the institutional teaching environment is controlled (although it is certainly monitored) by the state or by any other outside body so that organizationally the level of performance rests primarily in the hands of the autonomous institutions themselves. As we have seen, age, location and origins may play an important part – even, in the case of the latter, a determining part – but no one factor represents the whole story: the quality of institutional performance remains significantly a matter for the organization itself. As competition nationally and internationally increases these organizational factors are likely to increase in importance and it is therefore worth considering what the study of other organizations has to tell us about how performance can be sustained.

Perhaps the first, and in one sense the most reassuring, piece of information is that there is very little agreement about what constitutes sustainable success. Peters and Waterman identified 43 of the world's outstanding companies in *In Search of Excellence* (1982) and drew lessons from their mode of operation as to what made them outstanding companies. Sixteen years later, however, three quarters had disappeared or were in a seriously weakened position (Doyle 1999). The average life expectancy of a multinational company in the *Fortune* 500 is only between 40 and 50 years; a third of those listed in 1970 in the *Fortune* 500 were merged or broken up a quarter of a century later (De Geus 1997). Only one of the 12 largest US business firms in 1900 still existed in 2000 but all the largest public and private universities in 1900 exist and thrive in 2000 (Birnbaum 2000). In the UK, of the 30 largest manufacturing companies in 1955 only 11 have survived as independent companies (and one of these, Ford, is American) and some of the survivors are much smaller (Owen 2000).

Universities can, therefore, take comfort from Gueno and Kerr that their actual survival rate has so far been much greater. But even in a state dominated system such as the UK's there have been some significant fluctuations in positioning. The university scene was dominated in the 1950s, 1960s and early 1970s by the civic universities founded in the nineteenth century (Manchester, Liverpool, Leeds, Sheffield, Birmingham, Bristol, Newcastle and Queen's Belfast), by the University of London, and by the major Scottish universities – Edinburgh, Glasgow, St Andrews and Aberdeen – all mediaeval foundations. It would have been inconceivable, if league tables had been drawn up in 1970, that this group of universities would not have occupied the upper quartile of the table, after Oxbridge. The position of these universities now is noted above. In the past, Oxbridge and London were referred to as 'the golden triangle' but the University of London has now been fragmented with Imperial, LSE and UCL emerging in the leading group of universities in their own right with Kings College at their heels while some other University of London colleges are ranked much further down the list. In Scotland, Edinburgh alone survives in the leading group of UK universities in the RAE although St Andrews, in the 1970s part of a larger institution with Dundee, has significantly overtaken it in *The Times* and other newspaper league tables.

A study of corporate history offers some telling comparisons about the factors which affect the sustainability of success. Pettigrew and Whipp (1991) emphasize five interrelated factors as representing key attributes for successful companies: organizational coherence; the ability to assess the environment; translating that assessment into leading, rather than following, change; linking strategic and operational change; and recognizing human resources as assets and liabilities in the process. Increasingly, as the speed of change has accelerated with globalization, adaptability to a changing environment is seen as a crucial characteristic of successful organizations. Universities are no different and Sporn (1999) in *Adaptive University Structures* identifies five major changes to which they must adjust: the restructuring of the economy, the changing role of the state, shifting demographics, new technologies and increasing globalization.

Corporate history also offers some cautionary lessons about failure. Grinyer *et al.* (1998) suggest that the commonest reasons for corporate failure are: failure to respond to a more competitive market; lack of product market focus; not being close enough to the customer; and the tendency of top management to repeat behaviour that has been successful in the past or to lapse into inertia. Ghoshal and Bartlett (1993) on the other hand, isolate pride in past achievement – becoming so wedded to the strategic logic and organizational capability that produced previous success that they have lost the ability to re-evaluate and revise their strategy – as the most common cause of corporate decline. Failure to adapt also lies at the heart of some of the university institutional sagas of decline referred to above.

In order to adapt to change, however, universities, like companies, need organizational structures which are sufficiently flexible to respond to external stimuli. In many ways the 'tightly coupled within and loosely coupled between' structure which is said to be characteristic of university organization (Weick 1976) is well adapted to do this, and this may be one of the reasons why universities have enjoyed such institutional longevity. But we should not assume that such structures extend in the same form and in the same flexibility right through the higher education sector: the tightly managed top-down structures of many less successful UK universities, represent a significant departure from that tradition as does the increase of 'executive control' in many Australian universities (Marginson and Considine 2000). This represents a sharp contrast with the bottom heavy collegial structures described as characteristic of professional bureaucracies (Mintzberg 1979) and may tend to close off one of the strengths of the traditional university structure.

A number of studies, in addition to *In Search of Excellence*, have examined corporate histories over extended timescales to analyse the sources of their success. Thus Collins and Porras (1994) analysed 20 pre-1950s 'visionary' companies that had sustained their vigour and success into the 1980s and identified as key attributes a strong organizational culture built around a core ideology and sense of purpose, together with the willingness to make occasional and exceptional bold commitments. They did not find a demand for charismatic leadership as a necessary requirement for success but noted that companies successful over a long period seemed to rely much more on 'a stronger organizational orientation' than their competitors. While all the companies emphasized the importance of change and 'a relentless drive for progress' they did not change their core beliefs in the face of environmental changes.

> The essence of the visionary company comes in the translation of its core ideology and its own unique drive for progress into the very fabric of the organisation – into goals, strategies, tactics, policies, processes, cultural practices, management behaviours, building layouts, pay systems, accounting systems, job design – into everything that the company does.
>
> (Collins and Porras 1994: 201)

Collins, in a later study, takes the view that the secret of long term corporate performance is 'disciplined people who engage in disciplined thought, which results in disciplined action' (Collins 2001: 142). De Geus undertook a similar analysis and identified sensitivity to the environment, cohesion and a strong sense of identity, tolerance of experimentation and a conservative approach to finance as key components of success: 'Case histories repeatedly showed that strong employee links were essential for survival amid change. This cohesion meant that managers were typically chosen for advancement from within' (De Geus 1997: 6).

Ghoshal and Bartlett emphasize the importance of motivation. They quote 3M where 'By the 1990s the entrepreneurial initiative of generations of "ordinary people" had created a portfolio of 100 core technologies in 3,900 profit centres clustered under 47 product divisions' (Ghoshal and Bartlett 1993: 43). Yet despite its size 3M continued to generate 30 per cent of its sales from products introduced in the previous five years. Ghoshal and Bartlett identify the need for flat structures, information decentralization and the acceptance of 'constructive confrontation' where central policies can be challenged from below. They note that successful companies have an internally generated sense of energy, an organizational flexibility which can manage the inherent tensions surrounding change, and an institutional ambition to be the best: 'Few people', they say 'want to work for an organisation that wants to be average' (Ghoshal and Bartlett 1993: 130). Finally, Kay in *The Foundations of Corporate Success* (1993) argues the importance of what he calls company architecture in corporate success – the system of relationships within the firm and between the firm and its customers and suppliers. This architecture of relationships, he suggests, will substitute for more intrusive mechanisms for imposing cooperation, coordination and commitment. 'Architecture does not create extraordinary organisations by collecting extraordinary people. It does so by enabling very ordinary people to perform in extraordinary ways' (Kay 1993: 69). All these studies emphasize in different ways the importance of 'organizational learning', the ability of institutions to react to change and to changes in the external environment not because they are directed to by top management but because their internal structures are sufficiently open and incentivized to be mediated by contact with the external environment at all levels in the firm. Such companies are less likely to formulate explicit inflexible strategic plans and are much more likely to react opportunistically to external change, the cohesion that is necessary to succeed being supplied more by a strong organizational culture than by imposed frameworks and structures.

Not all these findings are relevant to sustaining university success but a great many of them are. Universities rely much less on a core ideology than some of the companies quoted – indeed it could be argued that the strength of a university is the presence of conflicting approaches to ideology – but some do develop organizational cultures, 'a strong sense of identity', which are strongly supportive of institutional progress, speed of decision making and internal and external competitiveness. As in business, charismatic leadership is much less important in universities than the development of an organizational orientation which accepts that external environmental change must be responded to. Universities can find common ground also in the decentralization of information and the promotion of 'constructive confrontation' where central university decision making bodies can be challenged over resource allocation policies or on strategic decision making in general: shared information makes policy making easier; challenges to central policy decisions within a self-confident academic community can invigorate policy discussion and result in redefinition of policy involving significant numbers of the academic community in the debate. Two of the studies refer to some company environments being able to inspire 'ordinary people' to perform better than their competitors: a similar characteristic can be found in some universities.

If we look at the universities that head the league tables, particularly those that perform outstandingly both in research related and teaching related activities, the qualities referred to of a strong organizational culture, a strongly competitive approach both internally and externally, an adaptability to the environment without changing fundamental identity, a willingness to take bold decisions, a conservative approach to finance in general and an open collegial approach to decision making which does not flinch from 'constructive confrontation' are all present. None have depended on charismatic leadership and when it has been tried it has generally proved to be counter productive. In particular three of them at least, in different ways, have the capacity or organizational culture which persuades 'ordinary people to behave in extraordinary ways' so that the institution 'punches above its weight': LSE because it has survived what could have been a debilitating financial downturn in the late 1980s and 1990s and exploited to the full its intellectual profile by becoming a genuinely international institution; and Warwick and York because, following quite different pathways, they have reached the top rank without the advantages of age, reputation or endowment and through all the vicissitudes of state funding of the 1970s and 1980s. These capacities and culture are not evident, or at least are much less evident, in universities much lower down the list.

Perhaps these qualities are sufficient in themselves to make success sustainable. Clark Kerr, however, offers a warning that while in the US there has been great continuity in the make up of the leading group of universities there have also been some change in periods of 'great transformation', the most recent in the US being the period between 1960 and 1980 when large increases in federal spending on research took place. He suggests that the period from 1990 to 2010 might be a similar period of transformation (Kerr 1991). If we were looking at UK parallels, the period between 1980 and 2000 when competition and market forces were first unleashed on the university system might have been a similar period of transformation. Some institutions adapted much better than others to these changes; with the economic downturn we may expect a further 'great transformation' as public funding is reduced. Our list of the most successful universities may prove to be as fragile as the companies cited in so many business texts.

On the other hand, there is evidence of a continuous upwards movement in university performance in spite of the vicissitudes in funding policies. In the 1930s it was common room gossip that serious research would be restricted to Oxbridge and one or two colleges in London. C.P. Snow, in a novel published in 1934, puts into the mouth of one of his characters:

'Universities will get more and more specialised in this generation. We shall concentrate on original work . . . in a few centres . . . the minor universities will cease to exist as research institutions' (Snow 1934: 79), yet 30 years later in 1964, Nottingham, Leicester and Reading, which would have fallen into that category, were competing vigorously with the civic universities while the next wave of new universities, including Warwick, York, Essex and Sussex, were very 'minor universities' struggling to develop research reputations. We can expect that in 30 years' time our list of successful universities will be longer and that it will contain the names of some institutions that are well below the horizon of success suggested by the current league tables.

Defining university success

This chapter has identified that those UK universities which can be identified as the most successful, using quantitative evidence, are the most successful separately in research-related and in teaching-related activities: excellence in both goes hand in hand. It also suggests that there are strong links between academic success and success in broadening the university's role in a wider economic and social agenda. Those universities with the highest levels of performance in the core business of teaching and research are generally also leading players in extending their role in society as a whole. It establishes that we can say with some confidence that there are some universities that are more successful than others and that like other organizations, notably companies, there are factors that can be identified which can sustain success.

The evidence amongst the top group of universities of continued success over 27 years in the RAE suggests that academic success can be self reinforcing. US evidence supports this. In the US the trend has on the whole been upward in that the number of institutions joining the highest Carnegie classification of Research University I has actually increased rather than that there has been a widespread changing of places. The RAEs showed a similar trend: the grade average score for all staff in the university ranked 20th in 2001 would have placed it 10th in 1996; the new methodology of the 2008 RAE identified relatively small groups of high calibre researchers located in institutions which had previously had very low institutional research rankings. All the tables highlight institutions which appear to have developed an upward curve of performance suggesting that success is dependent on creating a momentum in which success reinforces success rather than that isolated actions or sharp changes of direction can overnight alter an institution's trajectory.

As we have seen there are no absolutes in making a university successful. There are examples of universities founded in the Middle Ages which do not rank high in the RAE league table, universities with good locations which do not attract students, universities which had the advantage of being wholly new foundations gifted with large campuses which have overtaken most of their seniors while others have failed to do so and there are old civic universities in large industrial cities which have slipped from previous positions of eminence. On the other hand, there are former CATs on a rising curve of success, universities in isolated and impoverished parts of the country which are nevertheless extremely attractive to students and former polytechnics closing in on pre-1992 universities in some of the league tables. Universities with historic advantages can fail to exploit them while universities lacking such advantages can raise their performance to overtake them. Why are there such variations in performance, especially surprising in what has historically been a state funded higher education system? It is a contention of this book that, while there may be significant advantages or disadvantages to be derived from environment or historical inheritance that may help to position institutions, institutional management in its broadest sense represents an integral and perhaps in some cases a determining factor in achieving institutional success. Succeeding chapters will seek to explain those elements of institutional management which contribute most to creating and sustaining successful universities.

2

Strategic management in universities

This chapter presents strategic management as an integrating mechanism in universities. It argues that in a strongly competitive environment there are close parallels with strategic management in the private sector especially in relation to flexibility, bottom-up approaches and ensuring that strategy and direction are distributed between the centre and the operating units. It suggests that detailed planning is less effective than the establishment of broad objectives because environmental turbulence, fluctuations in the fortunes of the operating units, the need to maintain infrastructure and the criticality of day-to-day decision making demands a more flexible, and occasionally opportunistic, approach. Decisions that are mutually reinforcing establish institutional momentum which can sustain universities through an unpredictable climate. An institutional steering mechanism is necessary to channel opportunism generated by forward momentum, but a control mechanism will disincentivize initiative. Success has a cumulative effect on institutional confidence to take manageable risks.

Strategic management in higher education

A standard modern definition of strategic management is 'the art and science of formulating, implementing and evaluating cross functional decisions that enable an organisation to fulfil its objectives' (David 1996: 4). This is not a form of words that fits easily into a university vocabulary, not least because many university staff are reluctant to concede that the university as an organization has the same wider validity as a discipline or academic unit: it is a truism first stated by Searle (1972) that academics tend to be more loyal to their discipline than to their institution. A central thesis of this book, however, is that the institution and its success or failure and the way it is managed can have a critical impact on departmental success or failure and on the progress of disciplines, as well as on the student experience and the careers of academic and other staff. In an earlier age it may be that this was less the case but in the modern period where university success can have a significant impact on the institutional resource base the balance of the argument has shifted substantially towards the institution. The objective of strategic management in universities must be to achieve and sustain that success. Managing universities is a holistic process in which all the interlocking elements need to work together: for example, a concentration on academic success, to the exclusion of a concern about effective financial management, is as short sighted as a concentration on the physical refurbishment of a campus to the exclusion of continuing to refresh academic performance. At the technical, as well as the strategic, ends of the process, sustained success lies much less in dramatic new initiatives, important and necessary as these may sometimes be, and much more in harmonizing the different components of university management to be mutually reinforcing. Strategic management is therefore an integrating mechanism which pulls policies and processes together to achieve the best institutional outcomes.

Strategic planning in perspective

Much of the literature about planning and management in UK universities was either written in or influenced by a period when university finance was stable and pre-supposed that as student numbers grew, resources were provided by the state at a standard unit of resource to match the expansion (see Lockwood and Fielden 1973). The post of university planning officer tended to denote a 'number cruncher' who calculated the requirement for additional staff and facilities needed to match additional student numbers on the basis of financial and space norms prescribed by the UGC. If government funding fell short, and the unit of resource was depleted, the planning officer recalculated resource models which then redistributed the funding equitably between the different academic units on a reduced basis. Planning was primarily a quantitative exercise involving a rational distribution of resources within a government funded envelope. This approach fuelled the establishment of a strongly bureaucratic approach to management issues with a Weberian attachment to regulation and hierarchy and a reliance on elaborate committee structures. Planning was 'not normally strategic in our sense of adjusting internal activities to external pressures; and they were only secondarily, if at all, instruments of internal management' (Temple and Whitchurch 1989: 7). Many universities persisted with this approach even when government finance became more unstable and were therefore ill equipped to deal with the consequences. When this persistence was combined with an implicit belief that, however bleak the situation might be, the external political and financial situation was about to change for the better and revert to the *status quo ante* when the universities' reputation and claim on national resources would once again be recognized, the resistance to any challenge to the established orthodoxies of equity based planning and resource allocation was extremely fierce.

Lockwood and Fielden, writing in the 1970s, found few examples of 'a university creating room for development by eliminating or reducing existing commitments' (Lockwood and Fielden 1973: 110). Cambridge was one of the first universities to perceive early the need for rethinking its position and its Report on the long term development of the university (General Board, Cambridge 1974) recognized that 'as long as a university is growing it can change the balance of its activities by channelling new money into growing areas without actually cutting back the resources given to declining ones' and that in a situation of steady state funding the central problem was to devise a means of re-allocating resources to maintain the viability of the institution. Towards the end of the 1970s several universities, notably Lancaster, Southampton and London, set up *ad hoc* groups, or 'gangs of four' to determine priorities in the light of the predicted downturn in resources with the stated aim of maintaining support for academic strengths and preserving space for new initiatives, and the UGC weighed in by urging on universities the need, in the Chairman's colourful phrase, to cut out 'pallid growths' in order to 'maintain vitality and responsiveness' (Shattock 1994: 22).

But these exercises, while valuable in prioritizing academic strengths and in preparing institutions for a more robust financial climate, did not anticipate the much greater exposure of the higher education system to market forces which occurred in the 1990s. The perception that government funded unit costs would fall was amply confirmed but the growth of a mixed institutional economy of private as well as public moneys was not foreseen almost anywhere, nor was it assimilated until the rise in home tuition fees in 2006. Even now in many institutions university structures still reflect a belief that government funding is the central resource and that the function of non-government funding is simply to mitigate shortfalls in government funding. Moreover, in some ways dependence on government funding has increased in some universities because the transparency in the allocation of recurrent grant has meant that the basis on which the grant is calculated, academic department by department, is now exposed to the gaze not only of the public and the wider political process, but also inside universities. What was once a 'black box', to be unpacked by a few numerate experts, has become public property to every competent dean or head of department. Desirable though this may be from the point of view of accountability, it has had the effect of weakening the central decision making powers of many institutions by dissuading them from allocating resources according to their own strategic judgement. Funding formulae for each discipline, created for the purpose of a national division of resources, have too often become the currency for resource allocation within institutions: it has become too easy for central decision making bodies to abrogate their responsibility for strategic management by simply replicating the judgements of the funding councils irrespective of whether the basis of the formulae correctly reflect their own activities or, indeed whether the funding council's overall judgement about resource levels is appropriately arrived at.

This kind of approach can produce the worst of both worlds: the university allows itself to accept not only that government funding is the core resource and that the funding council is essentially a monopoly purchaser, but also that the funding council's priorities as demonstrated by its funding allocations must necessarily be the institution's own even though the allocations are designed to meet system-wide priorities rather than the priorities of any single institution. The passive acceptance of funding council funding formulae turns the leadership of an institution into an apologist for the formulae and drives a wedge between the leadership and the academic units so that the centre of the university takes on the appearance of being a creature of an external authority rather than being responsible for providing strategic direction to an autonomous and self governing community. The negative effect on institutional culture is profound, even in institutions where academic units are capable of generating significant external resources, and inevitably leads to a top-down management culture where those at the top are for the most part seen merely as a conduit pipe for resource allocation decisions taken elsewhere.

Universities have changed greatly since the 1980s and the most successful universities are amongst those that have adapted best to the new environment. Instead of receiving around 80 per cent of their funding direct from the state, universities as a whole now receive only about 40 per cent of their income in this way. Government recurrent funding is differentiated between research (R) and teaching (T), with the most research active universities receiving a grant of around 50:50 between R and T, reflecting their performance in the RAE, while the ratio for the least research active can be something more like 5:95. The strategic priorities of the former group of universities are therefore inevitably very different to the latter's: since student recruitment generally follows research reputation the former are much less concerned about the recruitment process and much more about the recruitment of staff and the maintenance of research excellence while the latter, particularly after the introduction of higher tuition fees and income contingent loans, are primarily concerned with maximizing their student recruitment profile. Of course, there are many universities that fall wholly into neither category, which have strong, but not across the board, research excellence and which have mixed recruitment profiles. These universities naturally have to tailor their strategies to their strengths and weaknesses. The most significant change, however, is the diversity of funding sources and the extent to which non-funding council money deriving from research, student fees, short courses, the sale of services, and from residences and catering has transformed universities' balance sheets with some universities generating more than 70 per cent of their funding from non-funding council sources. The impact of rising levels of tuition fees has had an important impact here. Because universities are labour intensive organizations and because research and institutional infrastructures are so dependent on financial support, funding structures and the availability of finance for investment in new developments are key factors in university success: even mathematicians, once renowned for requiring only paper and pencils for their research now require extensive computing power, and students in whatever field need sophisticated IT support in addition to whatever else their discipline demands. In general, the more successful a university the higher its cost structure, and the more it will be driven to look outside the government funding envelope for support; and in a competitive university system, where an institution wishes to recruit and retain the best people, any sign of a significant diminution in the resource base will be destabilizing and will lead to the loss of key staff to competitor institutions.

Strategic management in the modern firm

This broadening of the institutional financial base, the diversification of income sources and the intensification of competition provide much closer parallels with private sector organizational objectives than would have been true in the past. This is not because universities are, or should, become more business orientated in a strictly managerial sense, or because they have simply entered a market situation and are driven by the need to sell a range of products in a commercial environment, or because they should now be measured for success on the basis of financial criteria, but because some of the organizational characteristics and strategic management required for success mirror best practice in progressive private sector organizations more closely than used to be the case. This new financial climate may demand new styles of strategic management in universities but it does not, or should not, change their fundamental objectives. The key criteria for success remain success in the core business of teaching and research even though the routes by which it is achieved may have changed. Entrepreneurial universities as described by Clark (1998, 2004) and Shattock (2009) are not universities which have sacrificed academic excellence for a new commercialization but universities which have become entrepreneurial in order to generate funds to enable them to maintain and enhance their academic position.

If we look at the key strategic characteristics of successful companies operating in the 'new competitive landscape' where traditional, efficiency-orientated, vertical structures have been rendered anachronistic and where 'the search for new organisational practices in which flexibility, knowledge creation and collaboration are essential characteristics' (Volberda 1998: 12) one is struck by the parallels with university management in a period when the certainties of the bureaucratic model of development within a public sector framework have broken down.

These strategic characteristics can be summarized as follows:

- Scepticism about the value of processes which result in the production of a fixed strategic plan. Hayes (1985: 114) for example, argues that

  when you are lost on a highway, a road map is very useful; but when you are lost in a swamp whose topography is constantly changing, a road map is of little help. A simple compass – which indicates the general direction to be taken and allows you to use your own ingenuity in overcoming various difficulties – is much more valuable.

Most university strategic planning documents are very like road maps – too prescriptive and too detailed to be useful when the external environment is so changeable. Moreover they take on a life of their own and become fixed points to be clung to by the adherents of previous arguments deployed to construct the plan.

- Belief that the best strategic plan is evolutionary rather than directive. Mintzberg and Walters (1985) urge that managers should respond to an evolving strategy 'rather than having to focus on a stable fantasy', and remind us that strategic management is messy and disorderly. Collins suggests that strategy has to be based on incremental change and momentum: 'If you want to build a meaningful track record over 15 years or more, the last thing you want is revolution' (Collins 2001: 169). Volberda (1998: 35) describes an 'adaptive model' where strategy is *ex post* and bottom-up and where improvements are expected 'to bubble up in an entrepreneurial fashion from lower levels in the organisation'. He contrasts this with 'the methodology of formal strategy planning and even worse the organisational attitudes and relationships that it often cultivates [which] can impair a company's ability to compete' (Volberda 1998: 34). Kay (1993) argues that successful companies' strategies are opportunistic and adaptive.

- Acceptance that strategy is formed more by bottom-up methods than top-down (Ghoshal and Bartlett 1993) where the role of senior management is more as the 'retroactive legitimiser' than the charismatic leader (Quin 1985) or, as Hayes puts it, 'top management's job is less to spot and solve problems than to create an organisation that can spot and solve its own problems' (Hayes 1985: 116). Strategic management must therefore be organization wide not located only at corporate headquarters, and horizon scanning activity must be a shared responsibility between corporate headquarters and the operating units. This requires considerable organizational flexibility so as to respond effectively to environmental pressures, and strategic capability that is located in the operating units as well as in corporate headquarters, to ensure that new opportunities can be explored and exploited effectively. Individuals need to feel a sense of ownership.

- Recognition of the critical importance in developing a business strategy of understanding and adapting to the environment and to environmental change: the concept of the 'dynamic fit between the organisation and the environment' (Volberda 1998: 42). This puts a heavy reliance on effective two-way communication and mutual trust and confidence between corporate headquarters and the operating units to encourage a learning organization which is 'skilled at creating, acquiring and transforming knowledge and at modifying its behaviour to reflect new knowledge and insights' (Garvin 1993: 80) and which emphasizes the need 'to formulate strategies to take advantage of external opportunities and to avoid or minimise the impact of external threats' (David 1996: 34). Strategy creation should be seen 'as emerging from the way a company, at various levels, acquires, interprets and processes information about its environment' (Pettigrew and Whipp 1991: 135).

- These approaches to strategic management necessarily lay stress on the capabilities of the company's staff. Ghoshal and Bartlett (1993: 241–2) argue that

  At the heart of the emerging concept of the Individualised Corporation is a fundamentally different belief that companies can and must capitalise on external and even the ideosyncrases – the eccentricities – of people by recognising, developing and applying their unique capabilities.

  Hayes suggests that companies should adopt means-ways-ends rather than ends-ways-means approaches: the latter emphasizes leadership from the top, adopting a plan and adapting the company to achieving it, while the former encourages investment in people who will themselves, through their entrepreneurial and other skills, drive the company forward. Bryan and Joyce advocate creating formal networks where professionals can 'build and exchange both personal and collective knowledge in defined areas of mutual interest', and the creation of talent and knowledge market places where the 'mind power' within companies can be mobilized (Bryan and Joyce 2007: 64–5).

- At the same time companies need coherence and integration. Milgrom and Roberts (1995) argue that a key to success is the complementarity of a company's activities and that superior performance is achieved not by piecemeal changes of individual parts of the operation but by combining all the elements together in such a way that the overall contribution is stronger than the sum of the various parts. High performance organizations do not just do the right kind of things: they combine more of them and they integrate them differently and by doing so they outperform their competitors. Milgrom and Roberts describe how the implementation of a system of 'mutually enhancing elements' can be shown to raise performance in a very competitive business. Whittington *et al.* (1999) and Pettigrew *et al.* (1999) endorse its effectiveness in wider organizational settings. Hamel writes: 'the goal of management is first to amplify and then aggregate human effort – to get more out of individuals than one might expect by providing them with the appropriate tools, incentives and working conditions, and to then compound those efforts in ways that allow human being to achieve together what they cannot achieve individually' (Hamel 2007: 250).

- Financial management which is conservative in its relation to matters of expenditure but not in relation to matters of control. The more financial management emphasizes integrity, frugality, a concern for the pennies rather than the pounds, and a reluctance to borrow, the more it will command internal respect and provide a secure finance base for acting opportunistically and responding quickly to environmental change (De Geus 1997). Conservative financial control mechanisms on the other hand can create unnecessary layers of hierarchy and bureaucracy and can choke initiative. Ghoshal and Bartlett (1993: 45) describe how 'front line managers' frustration began when they saw their creative thinking and careful analysis regimented by standardised reporting formats and homogenised by a consolidation process that abstracted and agglomerated information as it was rolled up for top management review'. Fiscal conservatism of this sort can stifle entrepreneurial activity in companies as well as in universities. Bryan and Joyce (2007) argue that companies should place greater weight on returns and talent than on returns on capital and that profit per employee should become the primary metric of profitability. Some universities maintain comparable data about research grant and contract income or publication records per members of staff on a year by year basis for similar strategic reasons.

As higher education has itself become subject to market pressures and to depend less on government sources for its finance there are many lessons that it can learn from the performance of private sector organizations. There remain, of course, important differences between companies and universities not only in ultimate goals – profits, rewarding shareholders and avoiding takeovers – but also in legal structures. Even in the most progressive companies staff are employed on a less secure, more flexible basis than in universities, and private sector bodies are not bound by the traditions or legal requirements for corporate decision making that universities must employ through their senates/academic boards and governing bodies; the issue of ownership also differentiates companies from universities. Yet the emphasis on flexible evolutionary strategic planning, encouraging bottom-up approaches, ensuring that strategic thinking and capabilities are distributed between the centre and academic departments, investing in people, environmental scanning, an emphasis on the complementarity of processes and on mutually enhancing elements, and a style of financial management which incentivizes performance and not control are all approaches to strategic management which sit well within the university culture.

By contrast many universities have adopted structures that seem to owe a great deal to an earlier industrial age where top management teams, answerable to external boards, adopt a strongly top-down, non-participative, non-empowering style of management. While this may be justified as a short term defensive reaction to acute financial stringency the longer term impact is likely to reduce the prospects of recovery because it imposes an inappropriate framework for achieving academic success. In the most successful universities, while the actual process of decision making may be streamlined in various ways, the commitment to collegiality and participation represents an essential element in the achievement of organizational goals and a key strength, not a weakness, in a competitive environment.

The strategic framework

In an age of growing demands for accountability and when state controls are increasing it is not surprising that bodies like funding councils demand formal and fully documented institutional strategic plans to reassure them that institutions have a planning process in place. In so far as such plans involve financial forecasting over a period of years they can be valuable but any attempt to produce detailed, line by line, plans for academic development over a three to five year timescale is fraught with difficulty and can have a negative impact if they become, as they easily can, a straitjacket which inhibits incremental or opportunistic change. It is much more important that a university should establish some broad objectives as long term but realistic goals to be achieved over an unspecified timescale. These objectives should be primarily directional in nature and should be designed to give academic departments, faculties, deans and administrators a firm steer as to the medium term lines or priorities for institutional development. They should not be specific about the timescale of achievement unless absolutely necessary because the myriad of activities which are involved in significant strategic shifts within a university – the provision of funds, the appointment of appropriate staff, the attraction of students, the assembling of space – can all make detailed programming a constraint rather than a stimulus to achievement and can close off innovation elsewhere.

The essential element in establishing these broad objectives or goals must be to provide a framework within which a wide variety of individual innovatory ideas, some spontaneously welling up from academics or departments on a bottom-up basis some emerging from the centre or out of dialogues between the centre and the departments, can be considered. It is the realization of these ideas and plans which will ultimately determine the shape and reputation of the university rather than major central strategic initiatives, but since no university can be successful without concentrating and prioritizing its resources, such ideas and plans need to be considered within an overall framework of prioritized goals. Typical of such goals might, for example, be: re-balancing the university between one set of academic areas and some others (which may involve a reduction of staff in some subjects and an investment in new staff, taking special steps to attract students in the areas to be invested in, and providing additional support in terms of space or equipment, refurbishing of laboratories, etc.); growing its graduate research population (which may involve the creation of graduate awards, the enhancement of library and other academic services, providing incentives to departments through resource allocation mechanisms, building new graduate residences, etc.); refurbishing the building stock (which may involve cutting back on other capital programmes, holding back on student number expansion in areas likely to be temporarily out of commission, looking for alternative short term space, restricting some academic activities to secure best fit in the refurbished premises, etc.); or increasing the university's contribution to the regeneration of the local and regional economy (which may involve the identification of new staff, the creation of new internal incentivizing mechanisms, the establishment of closer links with external agencies, the setting up of new funding vehicles for particular activities or developments, etc.). All such goals, therefore, require action – but it is action which will involve a significant range of people, organizations and activities within the university; they must be understood and endorsed by the whole university before they become effective drivers of achievement. If they are not they will be stalled or frustrated by competing objectives that appear adventitious because new opportunities have for some reason arisen. Successful universities either corral these opportunities within existing directional frameworks or they say no. For universities that thrive on opportunism, this is one of the most severe tests for strategic management.

These objectives reflect much more the need for a compass in a swamp, to use Hayes' analogy, than a road map on a highway (which is the kind of document that a government department normally seeks). They should emerge or evolve out of discussion over months if not years as the broad set of directions in which the institution should be moving, not simply constructed after debate and adoption as part of a formal process extending over one or two meetings of a committee or a chance discussion at an 'away day'. Such a framework, of perhaps three or four key objectives, needs to be endorsed through the appropriate governance structures as laying down guidelines within which other decisions will be taken but it will not constitute a fixed plan; it will evolve as the institution or its environment changes but, within the constraints of funding, the timescales of re-balancing academic areas, and the inter linkages of one set of decisions with another. The expectation must be that the framework should serve the institution for some years: it should not be of the character or superficiality that it will alter year by year although it should certainly be reviewed annually to test its continuing relevance; it should represent the settled conclusions of an institution that knows where it is going but that is willing to give itself the latitude to adopt various different routes to meet its objectives depending on the options that present themselves on a year to year basis.

There are four important reasons for this approach to strategy:

- *Environmental turbulence*
  This can include the following: sharp changes in the funding policies of the state (a sudden change in a funding formula may remove £1m from the annual budget without replacement); downturns in non-government moneys; new external research initiatives for which the university must bid and which require matching institutional investment; a sudden volatility in particular overseas student markets on which an institution may be dependent for funds; changes in the national economy affecting the salary bill, the exchange rate of the pound or changes in borrowing requirements; the collapse of a major industrial partner; some piece of adverse publicity which may affect the perceptions of student applicants; or simply

the loss of key staff to another institution. Keller calculated that three quarters of all change at most universities in the US is triggered by outside forces such as directives from the state board of higher education, economic recession, changes in migration patterns, changes in politics and shifts in job markets (Keller 1983).

- *Fluctuation in departmental fortunes*
  A university depends for the success of its core business on its academic departments and research centres/institutes, and a change in the fortunes of any of them – a loss of key staff, or a gain of significant new staff who wish to launch new initiatives – may affect an institution's plans. Monitoring the progress of departments by retaining and recruiting key staff members including meeting their legitimate demands, giving support to applications for external funding for research or other activities, trying to meet departments' voracious demands for space (sometimes involving putting up whole new buildings to house new equipment or additional staff) and other resources, constitutes the major and most fundamental task for the central management of a university. It places an absolute premium on good communication, mutual trust and respect between academic departments and the centre and calls for the exercise of sophisticated academic judgement and tactical and strategic skills in human resource management in the centre working with and through a network of contacts and decision making processes. A university which fails to give priority to the competitive position of its departments relinquishes the prospect of itself being competitive. This must be an ongoing concern: departments face decline as senior colleagues lose their research edge or their enthusiasm to engage the interest of students, or the discipline as currently taught may fall out of favour with students so that student numbers decline, or key staff may leave, and reinvestment has to take place. Often this will occur just at the point when other departments find themselves on a rising curve of performance with younger staff reaching academic maturity and demanding additional resources to capitalize on their success. The extent to which these requirements can be met and the right choices made represent a significant variable in year to year strategic planning.

- *Maintaining the infrastructure*
  The third significant variable is the preservation of a university's infrastructure including the academic support services such as libraries, IT systems, the administrative services, the student-related services (such as residential, social and sporting facilities), and the maintenance of premises and equipment. It is all too easy for this infrastructure to be neglected: it is expensive to maintain, it will generally lack powerful advocates until particular services have deteriorated to the point of collapse and in a competition between individual academic departmental priorities and services the directly identifiable academic priorities will appear to offer best value for money. If infrastructure is 'owned' by anyone it is by the

centre, and calls for re-investment in these areas can be seen as self interested, appeals for feather bedding, or simply a sign that the centre is
insensitive to the needs of academic departments. Yet one of the major
causes of academic inefficiency, low academic morale and the low public
esteem in which higher education is often held is the extent to which
institutional infrastructure has been allowed to decline. In many universities core services and systems simply do not work, campuses look
down at heel, student residences are run down (but demand high rents),
food services are poor and maintenance backlogs have been allowed to
build up. The effect on students and staff is to reinforce a sense that
higher education is not at the cutting edge of modern society, that it lacks
the tangibility of success that can so easily be transmitted by the modern
private sector corporation, and that even if it can produce high individual
research performance, it is in spite of, not reinforced by, a structure that
seems to derive from an outdated public services model. Yet the efficiency
and effectiveness of such structures are as necessary to make universities
work well as they are in the private sector. Effective teaching and learning
cannot be delivered when libraries are badly run, computer systems
break down, and teaching room facilities are inadequate. Research time
will be wasted if administrative and financial systems are unreliable. If
student social and other facilities are run down students will treat them
accordingly and their quality will decline yet further, and be very expensive to restore to an appropriate standard. A low quality infrastructure
can affect an institution's credit rating with banks and finance houses and
can therefore impact on its ability to borrow; no external donor wants to
give money to campuses which are poorly maintained and attract litter
and graffiti.

University services should not only be run with snap and purposeful
effectiveness but require constant and regular re-investment. Maintaining
or enhancing infrastructure, while it should be operationally predictable,
is often not; its components can malfunction, simply wear out for unexpected reasons or be subject to the pressures of technological change.
Infrastructure and services which are allowed to deteriorate require
abnormal, and probably undeliverable, resources to be brought back to
effectiveness and an injection of new staff and ideas that are difficult to
find. Infrastructure and services that are well maintained can add value
to an institution in often unmeasurable ways but the costs of such maintenance can seem high when the most obvious measures of institutional
competition can be demonstrated elsewhere.

- *Managing the day-to-day*
  Managing universities on a day-to-day basis, by the very nature of the
  enterprise involves more individual and unrestricted decision making
  than in most organizations whether private or public sector. As Birnbaum
  (2000: 239) writes:

  > every time an institution hires or dismisses a faculty member, starts a

new programme or curtails an old one, decides to recruit students or staff in one way or another, it is creating a strategic plan through its actions. The greatest influence managers have over their institutions is through the daily choices in what Baldridge and Okimi (1982) once called 'jugular vein decisions', which 'build their institution's internal strength and condition it to respond favorably to opportunities or threats. Cumulative, every-day decisions can have a lot more impact on an institution's destiny than any master plan.' These decisions ... create 'emergent strategies' (Mintzberg 1994) that 'converge in time in some sort of consistency or pattern' (Hardy *et al.* 1983).

The value of the Hayes' 'compass' and the establishment of a limited number of broad objectives is that it encourages decisions which fall into the 'consistency or pattern' which Hardy *et al.* are seeking, but which in practice may be hard to achieve in a university context. The university which can manage to structure its decisions so that they are mutually reinforcing, not through control machinery but because it has achieved a general consensus on goals and objectives, will find itself developing a direction and momentum that is denied to an institution where decision making is internally contradictory and where the reconciliation of decisions taken in different parts of the institution is necessarily a major preoccupation and leads inevitably to compromise and fudge.

An alternative approach adopted by at least one UK university is the Balanced Scorecard Methodology (Donaghue and Kennerley 2008). This draws on Kaplan and Norton's work (2001) which sees strategy as 'one step in a logical continuum that moves an organisation from a high level mission statement to the work performed by front line and back office employees' (Kaplan and Norton 2001: 72). The difficulty with this in a university context is the implied lack of flexibility and the absence of freedom for departments and disciplines to develop their own approaches within a common framework: it emphasizes the top-down as compared to the bottom-up. It also risks conflict with Mintzberg's dictum that: 'No amount of elaboration will ever enable formal procedures to forecast discontinuities, to inform managers who are detached from their operations, to create novel strategies. Ultimately the term "strategic planning" has proved to be an oxymoron' (Mintzberg 1994: 321).

Universities are what Habermas, in a slightly different context, called 'bundle institutions' (Habermas and Blazek 1987) which resist being corralled into a single mission statement unless it is so general as to be almost meaningless. Universities, on the other hand, flourish best when their heterogeneity is seen as a strength and when they give the freedom to their operations units to respond to their own disciplinary environmental pressures within a common broad understanding of the university's overall objectives.

Annual strategic review

Such variables determine two essential features of university strategic management: the first is that the establishment of broad objectives must be supported by an annual strategic review, and the second that for strategic management to be effective a holistic view must be taken of the institution and its activities so that the different elements (or 'complementarities') of a university's activities can be harmonized to reinforce rather than conflict with one another. Universities are pluralist organizations which perform best when their activities can be focused and when the various interactions can be organized to strengthen institutional operations as a whole rather than dissipate them.

The construction of an annual review and a concurrent revision of the medium term financial plan needs to be built into the fabric of an institution's management. It must start with a revision of the previous year's financial forecasts for the following five or six years and should offer options for investment (or budget reductions) in each of those years. It can be argued that to begin with a financial scenario places too much stress on the non creative side of strategic management but in a period of financial stringency there are greater dangers from destabilizing the core academic business by having to make unanticipated and perhaps dramatic cuts in an institutional budget in order to restore a bottom line running into deficit than in accepting the principle from the start that the budget must remain in surplus at a given level every year and that new proposals or ideas must be forced to compete for support. There are many examples of universities investing to achieve academic success in the next RAE, gambling on higher ratings bringing higher rewards but taking insufficient account of the risks of doing so from an insecure financial position. There are others which have borrowed from the financial markets to refurbish buildings or catch up on maintenance against speculative estimates of the increased revenue that might result. (Cardiff in 1986, in respect to a new telephone exchange, and Cambridge in 1998, in respect to a new financial system, both embarked on major capital expenditure against optimistic cost benefit analyses which promised pay back savings which would outweigh the original cost. See Shattock 1994; Shattock 2001b.) Universities that have attempted to spend their way out of difficulties have invariably courted disaster when misjudged optimism has led to sharp retrenchment and loss of morale. Budgetary discipline is a key component of academic success.

Discussion of investment options should take place openly and freely and not be contained within a small group of managers or technical experts. Although from a practical point of view, only a group of a certain size can in the end discuss and reach conclusions on all the options, communication both formal and informal across an institution is both desirable and, in the long term, efficient. The most sensitive issues will often centre round the competing claims of the academic and the infrastructural sides of the institution and the extent to which capital programmes (which will generate longer term recurrent commitments) conflict with recurrent academic needs. Investments in posts or facilities which are intended to generate new sources of income in the future must be justified by business plans showing how and at what level the new income is to be generated. These discussions represent the heart of the strategic process: to be effective they require an element of 'constructive confrontation', of robust argument, and the interplay of strongly worded opinions; they need to be backed up by data and statistical evidence; and in autonomous and self governing institutions they should not be settled by the exercise of rank or administrative fiat. When decisions are reached they should be explained to the university community in a way that the arguments for this or that policy can be understood by those affected by them.

Unpredictable strategic decision making

Not all critical decisions will fit neatly into an annual strategic round; indeed far more will come hurtling out of a clear sky when least expected. Should the university bid for such and such a research initiative which if the bid is successful will involve capital expense? A donor is willing to invest so much in a project providing the institution matches the gift. A strategic alliance is proposed with some other body which will require up front investment. A planned development has fallen behind schedule and needs reinvestment and new leadership. The prospect of attracting a professor from another institution can only be realized if new laboratories or transferred research teams can be provided for. A promising course proposal needs investment now to persuade departments X and Y to commit themselves to it. The new climate requires decision making of a different order from the past, that is machinery able to turn round an issue of strategic importance within a week, that does not flinch from being opportunistic and that is prepared to take risks. The recognition that 'time has become the competitive strategy of the firm' (Schoenberger 1997) is as true for universities as the private sector, the more 'agile' they become the more they can win a competitive edge.

Universities can no longer afford the leisurely decision making of the 1960s when Ashby could describe the stately process where ideas floated upward from the lower rungs of a committee hierarchy and decisions flowed back down from the committee systems' upper reaches some months later (Ashby 1963). Universities that cannot respond quickly to events, to external indications that a bid for a new project which could have significant internal policy implications would be welcomed, if made immediately, or to invitations to collaborate with external bodies, or to come up with a complicated package to attract or retain key people, will inevitably lose out in a competitive climate. To do so, however, requires two key elements of university management to be in place: the first is the ability to assemble quickly the appropriate skills to analyse and assess the position – these may be administrative, financial, legal and even physical planning as well as academic skills – and the second is a process of consultation and decision making, which does not exclude the academic community, and which is consonant with the institution's statutory or other decision making process.

Burton Clark (1998) has described 'the strengthened steering core' which institutions need if they are to balance entrepreneurialism with legitimacy, a machinery which combines strategic capability and executive powers but which also contains a collegial and representational character and the capacity to exercise independent judgement. Decision making must be speedy but must have legitimacy in an academic community or it will generate negative reactions which will make each opportunity more difficult to grasp than the last. More important, decisions taken on the basis of individual authority, while perhaps easier to make in the short run, are in the long run more risky because they are less likely to be subject to the critical interplay of a range of academic decision makers. For the steering core to act there must be mutual trust between the decision makers, high levels of skill, a willingness to cut through bureaucracy and an institutional ability and professionalism to go the extra mile in checking facts, re-working data, consulting internally and presenting a case. Above all such machinery must recognize the importance of time constraints and the consequent need for 70:30 decision making, that is taking a decision on the basis of judgement and instinct without quite all the supporting data being available. This is more difficult in universities than in some other walks of life because the basic instincts of an academic community is instinctively to want to weigh all the facts and to be prone to over analysis when out of the ordinary decisions have to be taken. To carry through such decisions, therefore, requires there to be considerable confidence in the process and in the decision makers themselves. More often than is realized, even in the university world, success is achieved, not by presenting the best case but by being quickest on the draw, by being able to mobilize opinion and reach a decision faster than one's competitors in the confident knowledge that it will command retrospective institutional support.

In a competitive environment decision making is likely to be both opportunistic and involve risk. New prospects and possibilities more often in the current climate, emerge unexpectedly and on a timescale divorced from a tidy institutional planning round. They arise out of timetables generated by external bodies like government or international agencies, or from the competitive activities of companies or from pressures in the global economy which have no relationship with university decision making cycles, and they occur often because someone inside the university is willing to invest time and energy into turning a half possibility into a full opportunity by following an idiosyncratic timetable entirely of their own. In a financial environment where traditional recurrent funding is declining but where the processes of allocation are highly structured the sources of non-traditional funding are proliferating but in a highly differentiated way. To take advantage of these new opportunities successful universities will adapt their machinery, reinforce their managerial capacity, and recognize that ultimately institutional success is built in the modern era on an accumulation of one-off individual academic successes each of which adds to the capacity of the institution to achieve further success within a broad framework of agreed objectives rather than, as in the past, on formal planning and on lengthy deliberative processes.

Risks

In *Built to Last*, Collins and Porras (1994) identify the ability to take, on occasions, significant risks as a characteristic of what they describe as 'visionary companies'. On the whole universities are less risk averse than risk unaware in their dealings with the external world, a weakness which derives as much from their history of long term reliance on state funding and their anxiety to find a short term replacement for it than from any inherent weaknesses of university structure. Unfortunately, this has led to an over compensation in the regulatory framework prescribed at national level the efficiency of which in the private sector can be judged by the recent performance of the banks. This demands that universities exercise stringent safeguards against risk; the requirements for published investment appraisals and for risk audits represent a significant official disincentive to institutional risk taking (although not intended as such) at a time when international competition places a higher than ever premium on the need to take initiatives in situations where long term success or failure is impossible to predict with accuracy.

One cannot ignore the dangers of weak institutions taking risks and the need to protect them and, ultimately, the public purse from the consequences of such risks being realized, but the situation can be altogether different in strong institutions: first as universities get used to accelerating their decision-making processes they develop a momentum that carries them through from one decision to the next giving them renewed confidence in the process itself, and second, confident universities are better at implementing decisions than less confident ones. Confidence comes from developing a forward momentum. A university that has a corporate self-confidence will expect to be able to manage risks, to bend circumstances to fit the framework it wishes to establish, to motivate entrepreneurial individuals and thus carry through developments which would probably fail at other institutions. Risk, therefore, must always be assessed, but well managed and confident institutions will have a better chance of bringing inherently risky developments to a successful conclusion than those that are not; universities that are used to attacking problems and overcoming them are more likely to succeed than those that seek first to defend themselves from possible failure. And where the risk turns out to be reality universities that have many initiatives in train are more likely simply to admit failure and write off the cost and move on to the next project than universities that only have a few, and where a single failure can have an overwhelmingly discouraging impact.

But this atmosphere of quick decisions, opportunism and willingness to take risks needs to be underpinned by two important managerial characteristics. The first is that initiatives or projects must be consistent with an institution's broad objectives, with the directional points of its compass. Universities that chase every opportunity, irrespective of their strategic objectives, will endanger the rigour of their decision making process and will spread themselves too thinly across too broad an area of expertise. Universities cannot major in every field and a concentration of strength produces much higher and more reliable performance. The establishment of a limited number of broad strategic objectives provides the essential framework within which to consider such opportunities and the decision making process must be sufficiently robust to reject those that fall outside them. The second is that assessing such an opportunity must be undertaken from a holistic point of view – does it reinforce existing academic strengths or buttress weaknesses? Do the various necessary investment components represent a reasonably secure forecast of longer term institutional commitment? Are there financial, physical planning or human resource implications? What, if any, demand will it have on the university's infrastructure? Will it be exploitable in financial terms? Does it offer opportunities for further development? Will it enhance the university's reputation? This holistic assessment is essential if the university is to respond effectively to external opportunities; but responding effectively also requires mechanisms of internal coordination – academic, administrative, financial and property led – which can only be achieved in an institution where communication lines are short, where management is closely integrated and where generalist professional skills of a high order can be deployed quickly.

Strategic management and institutional culture

It might be argued that such coordination and emphasis on timing requires exceptional leadership skills at the top. There is plenty of evidence from other fields, however, and from higher education itself, that it is not charismatic leadership that is the prerequisite of effective management. Jarzabkowski, for example, argues convincingly in a study of managerial contributions to strategy in three universities that in 'distributed activity systems', that is systems such as you find in universities where decision making is dispersed, 'managerial agency . . . is less about heroic leadership than about social skill and competence in managing the emerging activities within an organisation towards purposive and persistent outcomes over time' (Jarzabkowski 2003). Individualized leadership is less critical to success than an organizational culture that encourages a sense of common purpose, welcomes the need for rigorous and disinterested debate and accepts that decisions have to be taken and implemented within an appropriate timescale. The central steering core may initiate policy but its more important task is to coordinate and react to proposals that are fed to it from below. 'Strategies happen in environments that encourage new ideas' (Birnbaum 2000: 63). Strategy in high quality universities is much less a formal process as old style public management approaches demand but more a matter of working within an institutional culture:

> Successful organisations seem to be good at continuous adaptation, seem to have strong cultures, and seem to enjoy well developed communication skills (both internally and externally). They form strong internal value systems that serve as compasses and filter information from a wide variety of sources through that value system. They do not make 'strategic decisions' in the old linear/rational way but sense and flow in a continuous process of growth, change and re-imagining.
>
> (Leslie and Fretwell 1996: 109)

The essential academic vitality of a university must lie in its academic departments; the role of the central steering core is to sustain that vitality, support their ambitions within a framework of strategic objectives and manage the processes that bring their ambition to fruition. Departmental initiatives will often be launched by individuals and not by the department as a whole, and sometimes they will be initiatives that elements in departments are uncomfortable with; it is the responsibility of the central steering core to decide who to support and to what extent, and in a way that offers continuous encouragement to others to bring forward new ideas. Strategic management is about fuelling and winnowing this process and ensuring that the ideas that should be supported are consistent with the framework of institutional objectives already established.

Strategic management which is seen as a control mechanism will act as a disincentive to initiative just as formal structured planning reduces institutional vitality. Good universities encourage a climate of innovation and development, where new ideas are supported and initiative is rewarded. Success has a cumulative effect and drives up performance across the institution; optimistic universities can take contested decisions without leaving lasting scars within the academic community because the momentum that success brings enables an institution to move quickly on to the next decision. Strategic management must be driven by institutional ambition, by the competitive urge and by the recognition that in a competitive climate there must be losers as well as winners; it works best when it operates in a very open environment where debate is at a premium and legitimate argument and challenge is never far from the surface but where pressures of time and resource compel speedy decision making. It works least well when it is overfed with data and where the participants in the process are unwilling to risk failure. In a competitive climate strategic management is about creating success not about propping up the *status quo*.

Successful strategic management is highly dependent on a supportive institutional culture which is sustained not by glossy newsletters or electronic interventions in the form of state of play messages from the head of the institution but by shared understandings about what the institution is about and what its ambitions are. Tierney defines this as 'the manner in which individuals work with one another, the way they decide issues, the formal structure of governance, and the like provides clues about the culture. Indeed more often than not, individuals find meaning not from broad sweeping statements or events but from the routine, microscopic aspects of everyday life' (Tierney 2008: 170). In other words institutional cultures can be negative as well as positive factors. Academic departments which feel that they have been pushed a long way away from the centre of decision making may not be supportive of new initiatives; academics who no longer feel that they have opportunities to participate in governance may feel disinclined to participate actively in new policy departures; the loss of a sense of 'shared governance' may lead to negativity and cynicism about decision making (Birnbaum 2004).

A key element in the creation of a positive institutional culture is what the management jargon calls human resource management. Too many universities have permitted the critical interface between the institution and the individual academic to be mediated through a professional office which has been trained in the regulation and the enforcement of employment relations. This may be unavoidable in the interpretation of employment law but too often it becomes dominant in essentially trivial but personally aggravating areas of academic activity where commonsense and an understanding of academic work is more important than a mastery of the application of the rules relating to human relations in an institution. Nowhere is this more important than in the conduct of the processes of academic performance review. An academic community wants to believe in the integrity of the process, that it is securely in the hands of its academic peers, that promotion to a professorship is adjudicated upon by other professors who understand and are competent to evaluate the criteria of academic performance that is required. Trust in and a respect for these processes are integral to the creation of a positive institutional culture where the appointment or the promotion of youthful talent is accepted and where the academic criteria is uncompromising. The best incentive to excel in performance in the core business of teaching and research is that it will be rewarded by promotion to seniority in the institution; successful universities are forcing houses for talent.

If we were to analyse major universities that have slipped down the league tables we would find ossified departmental structures, a failure to recognize the dynamics of a changed environment, hierarchical and conservative decision making processes, a reluctance to recognize individual talent and an unwillingness to compete. In the private sector, companies would be punished more quickly for these shortcomings, but in the university world, persistent failure leads to slow decline, increasing financial stringency and a tendency to grasp at short term solutions. But as the decline takes root the problems crowd in, and just as a university which has established a momentum of positive decision making will take difficult decisions in its stride, so universities in decline will find that the decline process instils a weary pragmatism where problems are not addressed and new initiatives can be stifled by internal scepticism or by an unwillingness to see others succeed.

The gap will widen between universities where good strategic management is firmly embedded and those where it is not, those that spend too much of their effort on detailed forward planning and insufficient on responding to the new environment and those where previous failures have led to an over cautious approach to decision taking.

3

Managing university finance

Financial management in universities is inevitably placed under strain by the competitive environment. Universities' financial profiles and the complexity of their operations vary greatly from research intensive to teaching intensive universities but five principles of good financial management apply to all universities. This chapter argues that no university and particularly no research intensive university can maintain competitiveness by relying on state funding alone and it seeks to define the state managed and the private sector markets in which universities now must compete for funds. It goes on to describe the steps involved in generating non-state income, the importance of creating machinery for this purpose and outlines seven key principles for success. The chapter emphasizes the importance of budgetary planning, monitoring and strategy, and the need to integrate state and non-state funding in a single forecasting and resource allocation process. Strategic management must, in the current period of financial stringency, be resource led and the allocation process should translate strategic priorities into effective expenditure. The chapter concludes with a statement of the essential characteristics of a financially healthy institution.

Financial stability

Success in a university's core business of teaching and research is underpinned by financial stability and good financial management. Academic work is bound to suffer in conditions of financial instability. Conversely, the availability of resources at the right time, even if they must be competed for, and the existence of a well understood process of financial reporting and administration, provides a secure financial basis from which programmes of teaching and research can readily be launched. Although there are examples of individual scholars and even full academic departments achieving significant academic reputations in institutions facing serious deficits or where financial management has broken down, it is difficult for them to be insulated from the impact on the institution as a whole. It is no accident that the two most successful universities in the UK are also the richest although the record of Cambridge's financial management (in spite of its wealth) in the late 1990s led to concerns being expressed there as to the effect this might have had on its academic standing (Shattock 2001b). It is a truism that while all universities are costly the best universities are more costly than the rest.

In fact there are substantial differences in the size of the financial management task between different universities. Primarily these differences arise from the level of the research commitment. The more research intensive a university the more individuals and departments develop a multiplicity of short term income streams, which may involve a variety of risks, require different reporting mechanisms, and bring with them commitments to staffing, equipment, running costs and demands for space and other facilities (which need to be balanced against overhead contributions), not to speak of safety and other considerations and the need to consider the various commercial exploitation routes. Implicitly or explicitly a research intensive university will also find itself committed to collaborate with other institutions so finding itself forced to share financial controls with other bodies, whether universities, research council institutes, government departments or companies. Universities that have a major commitment to research in science, technology or medicine have financial management issues to deal with that are out of scale from those that occur in non-research active institutions. While the extraordinary courage that Manchester showed in backing the radar telescope at Jodrell Bank in the 1950s to the point of putting the whole University at risk (it was rescued by the Science Research Council after the telescope's success in tracking Sputnik) is fortunately not required too often, it remains the case that universities can sometimes need very strong nerves when their staff are engaged in research that demands investment in major research facilities. Inevitably this brings with it requirements for performance and accountability and for robust financial systems which can both analyse financial performance but also provide the requisite data to satisfy funding bodies, VAT and other regulatory bodies.

Research intensive universities also attract historic assets such as research libraries, museums and research collections, art galleries, botanical gardens, observatories, farms, hospital research facilities, animal houses, marine research stations and so forth, and a network of research relationships with both private and public sector bodies all of which add greatly to the financial complexity of a university's operations. Research therefore can be an important determinant of financial policy. Since the disaggregation of R (research) and T (teaching) monies by the funding councils these differences have widened with some institutions receiving around 50 per cent of their total state income from research while some universities receive less than 6 per cent from this source and over 75 per cent from teaching.

Since research is assessed through the RAE/REF (Research Effectiveness

Framework) and research funding has to be vigorously competed for, R funding cannot be regarded as necessarily recurrent and the R component encourages the need to invest, whether in people or in facilities, to maintain or enhance institutional positioning, in a way that the T component does not. Research intensive universities will have more favourable staff/student ratios, will spend more on libraries, IT and on research infrastructure and, in order to recruit and retain the best researchers, will pay more people on higher salaries than non-research active universities. The Bett Report indicated that the ratio of senior lecturer posts and above in the pre-1992 universities was 49 per cent as compared to only 27 per cent in the post-1992 universities (Bett 1999) and even with the greater willingness to reward teaching in the last decade that situation has not much changed. The more research intensive a university the larger the staffing component of the budget will become. Success in the RAE will be matched by further income from research grants and contracts from research councils, charities and industry, especially in universities with large medical schools, thus further distinguishing between the budgets and staffing of research and non-research intensive institutions.

These differences between research intensive and teaching intensive universities encourage different organizational structures for financial management and dictate different financial strategies. But five broad principles of successful financial management remain common:

- That financial stability makes a key contribution to successful academic work. Nothing can be so destructive of academic time, the ability to innovate, or the maintenance of good morale as a financial crisis: negative decisions about financial support for deserving academic initiatives, taken in the heat of the moment, rarely offer a good basis for policy and can be corrosive in terms of future initiatives. On the other hand, academic progress whether in research, publication or teaching can be significantly enhanced when financial conditions in a university are relatively stable and when good cases for new investment can be expected to be judged on their merits and not ruled out automatically on grounds of financial stringency. Once financial stability has been disrupted, a series of new hurdles, procedural and otherwise, must be overcome in order to justify investment: the financial climate becomes cautious, non-entrepreneurial and overladen with negatives. Such discouragements can stifle innovation and destroy the momentum of promising academic initiatives. A financial climate of acute stringency may have an intensively discouraging effect unless it is managed in a positive way. Many successful universities have achieved financial stability because they have been entrepreneurial in attracting funds from different external agencies. Good financial management ensures that the risks inherent in such activities do not result in recurrent deficits and volatile sets of accounts.
- That financial management, and understanding financial indicators of performance are too important to be regarded as the sole prerogative

of the central finance office (or the finance offices of devolved structures). Financial literacy needs to be widely distributed through the
institution; administrators and academic managers outside the finance
office should be free to challenge financial assumptions and academics
need to understand and participate in financial discussion or they will be
unable to contribute effectively to decision making over policy either at
institutional or departmental level. The finance office itself needs to contain financial managers as well as those professionally qualified to carry
out a strictly accounting function; and finance staff need to be encouraged to take part in policy discussion, rather than, as is often the case,
being tacitly excluded. An understanding of finance and a respect for its
disciplines needs to run throughout the institution.

- That a conservative approach to institutional spending at the top sends
  a message throughout the institution. De Geus describes in the context of Shell (De Geus 1997) how this has an important impact on
  institutional culture. Senior university officers who do not assume special
  travel privileges, do not claim named parking places on the campus
  and have modest lifestyles can set a tone for economy and plain living
  which translates well into university decision making, just as heads of
  departments who watch the pennies in their departments and avoid
  going into deficit set a tone for their academic colleagues. A culture that
  is concerned about petty excesses can sometimes be tiresome but institutional thriftiness emphasizes that financial probity and transparency
  represent traditional characteristics of university life and sit well with
  the moral standards of scholarship which the academic community
  aspires to. Ostentatious expenditure – institutional cars for all senior
  officers, lavish offices for central staff when teaching rooms are poorly lit
  and furnished, or institutional perks for senior staff that are not available
  to others – destroys a commitment to institutional economy.
- That risks should be examined carefully but when accepted the investment should be generous to ensure a successful outcome. A conservative
  approach to financial management will be concerned to set proper procedures in place, ensure that the essential financial fabric of the institution is secure and that the management has a firm grip on the main
  financial drivers. This does not mean that it should set its face against
  innovation and occasionally take large risks. Indeed institutions should
  only take risks from a conservative financial base because, in a university
  context, a financial risk that is realized, leaving significant losses and/or
  debts, will produce just the kind of financial instability which damages
  the institution's core business. Risks, however, can be much reduced by
  the development of implementation skills; a risk too far in one university
  may represent only a modest risk in another for this reason. A conservative
  approach to finance will discourage borrowing except against projects
  that will in themselves recoup the loan; when the institution loans itself
  funds from its cash flow to put up a new building, it will lay down a firm
  target date for repayment. It will punish departments that overspend their

budgets and will discipline individuals whose conduct conflicts with the requirements of the university's financial regulations.

- That good financial management requires that where adverse financial messages are apparent such as a failure to meet financial targets, shortfalls in particular areas and over-expenditure in others, these should be acted upon in an alert and effective manner. Financial analysis and efficient accounting will only take you so far in a university environment unless they are backed up by decision making processes which command respect, by effective implementation skills, and by a management style that can be interventionist when things have gone wrong. Every time a university fails to act when a significant over-expenditure has occurred the chances of it happening again are multiplied. A university can learn from occasions where financial control has been lost and by doing so can achieve real long term benefit, but a university that regards them as so typical that they can be ignored is storing up future trouble for itself.

Making up shortfalls in state funding

It is impossible nowadays for a research intensive university to maintain national, if not international competitiveness, by relying on state funding alone. With significant falls in their unit of funding from the state since the late 1980s (only partially recouped by the tuition fee regime introduced from 2006), UK universities, like universities in the rest of Europe, have found that funding has fallen far behind the growth in student numbers. Whereas in the mid-1970s universities were complaining about a worsening of the staff/student ratio to 1:10, universities midway up *The Times* league table now admit to staff/student ratios of 1:20, and some of those at the bottom of the table are closer to 1:30 in many departments. Moreover, the framework of state funding is unusually inflexible because it is formula driven. Universities can be deterred from taking risks to adapt to changing students markets by the threat of a 'clawback' of funding if they undershoot their target student population in any year or, in some years, being fined if they exceed their overall target. Fluctuations in RAE methodologies, in funding levels for individual subjects or formulaic changes which reflect national policy initiatives can all impact unpredictably on individual institutions.

These conditions have increasingly encouraged universities to look to non-state (or at least to non-Funding Council) sources of funding to make up the shortfalls. The generation of non-government funding for universities has a long tradition in the UK. Indeed, it could be argued that present trends reflect a return to the 1920s and 1930s when universities' funding support came one third from student fees, one third from other private sources (mostly income from endowments and investments), and only one third from the state through the UGC. In the 1920s Leeds ran eight separate external appeals for non-state funding suggesting that private capital donations were used extensively to pay recurrent costs. Such approaches cannot easily be employed today. Industry has become globalized and the relationships between a company and its local university have been broken as the company headquarters have moved to London or abroad. Companies themselves are also more constrained by the wishes of their shareholders from making substantial capital donations unless a donation can be seen as directly contributing to the company's interests. Post-war tax regimes have prevented, until very recently, the build up of significant private fortunes so that alumni fund-raising, except at Oxbridge, has tended to be on a relatively modest scale.

Increasingly, therefore, universities have looked to earning non-state income rather than hoping to supplement their income with solicited donations. The 1980 government decision that non-EU international students should be charged full cost fees opened the door to an increasingly marketized approach to funding higher education. Some institutions have adapted to this much better than others. Inevitably the better endowed universities have benefited most because of their advantages of reputation, research standing and history, but as we have seen, there have been some examples of newer institutions breaking into the list of successful universities perhaps primarily because of their ability to compete in a more market orientated system.

This market can be divided into two types, one which is managed by the state under various headings and is therefore in large part artificial, and one which draws entirely on non-state sources, which is non-directed and more 'commercial' in character.

The state managed market

- *Competition for UK (and EU) students*
  Formula funding for home students within the limitations described above might seem to discourage the idea of a market, but in fact almost nowhere is the competition more intense, because a strong application field not only ensures that an institution meets its fee income target but also protects a university from the possibility of a 'clawback' of funds, and provides a platform for bidding to a funding council for additional 'funded' student places. It also provides a secure basis for taking advantage of any flexibility offered by the funding council for exceeding targets and so achieving a year by year expansion and therefore a more flexible budget. (It is easier to respond to external change from an expanding than a contracting budget.) Exploiting this flexibility can be a way of financing new academic posts and strengthening individual academic departments.

- *Competition for research funding through the RAE/REF*
  The market here is more to do with recruiting and retaining research active staff in competition with other universities and providing the support that

encourages them to be productive. Recruitment and retention go far beyond questions of salary and status, though these can be of great importance, but extend to the availability of research infrastructure, laboratory and other space for research teams, sabbatical leave arrangements and the continuance of collaborative research partnerships with colleagues.

- *Competition for research grants and contracts from research councils*
  The market here is very diverse ranging from individual applications for grants or for research studentships to bids for programme grants (i.e. up to five year research support), to institutional bids, e.g. the JIF (Joint Infrastructure Fund) and SRIF (Science Research Infrastructure Fund) competitions or competitive bids to establish designated research centres. Most of these major competitions require subventions from the universities themselves or support in kind or cash from industry. Since success in such competitions can have a decisive impact on departmental RAE results, winning or losing them can have lasting effects on institutional development. Sensible institutions and departments maintain budgetary flexibility so that they can respond quickly to demands for matching support.

- *Other competitions run by the funding councils or the research councils*
  In recent years the state has increasingly used competitive bidding to determine the allocation of funds for developments in which it has an interest. Such bidding might be for something as large as for a new medical school, or for resources for building renovation, or for exceptional capital projects. A qualification for entry to the competition may well be the provision of matching funds from the institution itself.

The private sector market

- *Fees charged to international students*
  This represents a £13bn market (of which the UK has a £5.5bn share) in which every institution competes not only with other UK universities but with universities from other higher education systems. It is a market which demands investment to succeed, and high levels of professionalism. However, success is also heavily reinforced by academic success, as demonstrated by published league tables, and by historic reputation. Like any commercial market it is also affected by factors over which universities have no control such as the level of exchange rates, movements in the global economy, and political and other events.

- *Fees for home and EU undergraduate students*
  It was the clear intention of the 2003 White Paper that the introduction of variable tuition fees supported by income contingent loans was to open the prospect of an institutional market in fee levels. The fact that UK universities (outside Scotland which rejected the introduction of

tuition fees for undergraduates), with only a tiny number of exceptions, opted to charge the maximum obviated that possibility, although a subordinate market in bursaries for economically disadvantaged students has been created. The prospect of permitting greater flexibility in fee levels in a period of economic downturn (strongly hinted at at the time of writing) will reinforce not only the differential reputation pull of various institutions – a genuine marketization – but also the vocational value that can be placed on various disciplines. Decisions surrounding higher fee levels have the potential to redefine the UK higher education system.

- *Fees for home and EU postgraduate students*
  Since there is no state control over fees payable by UK students for postgraduate study, Master's and PhD programmes have become part of a significant new market particularly in vocational Master's degrees (most notably the MBA) or for the PhD, in areas of high research distinction. Postgraduate fees for home and European students approximate perhaps the most closely to a pure market where the level of fee charged reflects an institution's or a department's reputation with higher fees charged for highly rated institutions or departments. In some areas like the MBA there is evidence that candidates appear to regard the level of fee charged as itself an indicator of the quality of the product. They emphasize the growing marketization of higher education.

- *Competition for research funding from industry and commerce*
  This is not a new market but with the state emphasis on encouraging Mode 2 (or near market) research, research council and industrial support can be interrelated or mutually dependent.

- *The exploitation of research*
  This can cover the level of overheads (or indirect costs) charged on research grants and contracts, money earned from patents and licences, taking equity in companies to exploit research, direct consultancy or commercial research partnerships. Some of these activities may be organized into separate university-owned or spin-out companies.

- *Short courses for industry and other bodies*
  This is a well established market in certain disciplines, fuelled by the knowledge society and the general interest in lifelong learning and by a recognition that Mode 2 research depends on building partnerships at all levels with companies. While the organizational forms vary between departmental leadership (e.g. in a business school executive short course programme) and central leadership of programmes (e.g. through a central marketing unit), the essential characteristic of the programmes is that they are undertaken primarily to generate additional income. In many programmes there are close links with vocational Master's programmes where short courses can be linked as modules leading to a qualification. When they are given overseas, they can also form part of the international fee market.

- *The exploitation of university facilities for commercial purposes*
  Universities have considerable opportunities to exploit their facilities to generate income. The most obvious and the most clearly profitable is the utilization of university residences, catering and teaching facilities in the vacation for the benefit of the conference market, but sports facilities, swimming pools, language centres and scientific test equipment all offer possibilities for earned income. Some universities have invested in special facilities such as executive training centres, available all the year round, with the prime object of generating income but with the added benefit of using the facility itself. Standard university services such as printing, binderies or photographic services can, in effect, be privatized so as to provide a better service within the institution but also to generate profits from external customers, the broadening of the range of activities bringing benefits to both sides of the business.

- *The sale of goods and services*
  Universities are increasingly entering the retail business. Traditionally universities, or their students unions, have sold T-shirts, proprietory clothing and souvenir items but a large student market in universities some distance from commercial shopping venues can generate a significant retailing business. Some universities own and manage their own bookshops, while others rent space to established commercial booksellers. Universities run food stores, post offices, stationery stores and gift shops and provide other student related services, as well as letting space to banks, pharmacists, opticians, hairdressers. Oxford and Cambridge run major publishing houses whose significant profits are covenanted back into the institutions as integral parts of the two universities' budgets. In addition Cambridge owns UCLES, its examination board, which offers school examinations including A levels under its name on a worldwide basis and covenants an element of its profits into the University.

- *Fund-raising and endowment income*
  According to a report by the Higher Education Policy Institute the combined value of the endowment and investment assets of Cambridge, including its colleges, amounted to £4.1bn in 2006–7 providing an income of around £130m; the next richest university (after Oxford) was Manchester at £15.6m (Chester and Bekhradnia 2009). Increasingly, following the success of Oxford and Cambridge in fund raising, other universities have moved to establish development offices for fund-raising purposes although significant success is patchy. Many universities have recognized the importance for the future of alumni giving and have set up operations to stimulate alumni support. However, alumni support is dependent first on the extent to which an institution is willing to invest in a lengthy period of re-establishing its relationship with its alumni ('friend raising') and second on the actual memory of the institution which the alumni retain – good or bad. Once again the successful university which has delivered an excellent undergraduate education and has engaged

with its alumni in a generous spirit will be more likely to receive a long term reward, than institutions that simply seek a quick pay back.

Generating non-state income

Although it cannot be said that every university is equally well positioned to generate 'earned' income the key assets which are necessary remain the same. These are: managerial capability, academic reputation, location, staff and buildings. Many of these assets are interdependent: an institution may have the management capacity to market itself well but unless its academic reputation is strong its flow of students may be short lived or may be of a quality that imposes costs through heavy teaching or supervisory requirements; a university may have architecturally attractive and flexible academic and residential buildings but if they are located in an inaccessible part of the country they may be much less of an asset for income generation than if they are situated in or near main centres of population; an institution may have the most distinguished staff but if they are in fields that do not have an external earning capacity, their contribution may be limited to attracting international students. A university may have reputation, location, distinguished staff and attractive buildings but if it lacks the managerial capacity to exploit them these assets will not be utilized to the full to generate income.

Clark (1998) has identified the development of a diversified income base as one of the key characteristics of his model of the 'entrepreneurial university'. This concept, in spite of the ambiguities of the word 'entrepreneurial', is discussed more fully in Chapter 10 but attaching it simply to the process of generating income from non-state sources does not do justice to Clark's ideas which envisage much more the integration of the process of income diversification with entrepreneurialism that is primarily academically led.

Academic and financial entrepreneurialism usually go hand in hand and successful universities find ways of harnessing the two sides of the activity in new specially created organizational forms such as 'centres', 'groups', 'institutes' or 'programmes' that lie outside the standard constitutional arrangements. But in the modern era, especially in institutions where such activities proliferate, entrepreneurialism of this kind must be accompanied by a clear understanding of the academic and financial benefits and of the underlying contributions and costs to the institution. Academic 'intrapreneurs' can have a strong propensity to be optimistic about the former and to give little attention to the latter with the result that innovative initiatives can often be stalled at too early a stage through a lack of financial realism.

Activities which are part of the state managed market and activities which fall under the private sector market are in practice closely interrelated. As we have seen industrial research contracts are far more likely to go to universities which are research leaders in the particular field and are already in receipt of substantial research council support; international students are much more likely to come in large numbers and pay high fees to institutions that have an international reputation for excellence; UK students are attracted to universities that can combine academic excellence with high quality facilities which may have been paid for out of private sector activities; student residential accommodation which is brought to near hotel standard to attract the conference trade is likely to be much more attractive to students than facilities that are never offered to external customers; industry will buy short courses from highly rated departments that have available high quality teaching facilities that may have been built out of short course income surpluses; alumni are more likely to contribute to universities in which they can take pride. Success in some activities will, therefore, naturally reinforce success in others. But the real benefits to be achieved are where different activities can be consciously used to reinforce others. For example, the university with a large conference income which uses part of that income to defray the cost of residences for students is laying down a competitive marker to attract students in a period when student finances are under great strain; a university which builds postgraduate residences will both encourage a growth in its postgraduate population and will also increase its fee income. Integrating short course programmes with Master's programmes can grow both and provide sufficient income to pay for capital investment in new buildings or equipment primarily to assist research. Income generation, and the need to invest to generate it can transform university campuses by providing the drivers for extensive building and refurbishment programmes which significantly affect their ability to recruit and retain outstanding staff.

But universities must bear in mind that additional income, of itself, is of little value unless it can be shown that the activity generating it is providing a useable surplus. The old commercial adage that 'sales are vanity, profits are sanity' applies strongly in universities. Universities often regard non-government income as automatically a positive performance indicator when they do not know whether the activities are loss-making or profitable: there are obvious long term financial dangers in undertaking research contracts for industry if the overheads paid are such that the university is subsidizing the company concerned, just as there are dangers in letting out sports centres and swimming pools to outside users at charges which do not cover the additional staffing and building wear and tear involved. In the conference trade it is necessary to know the profitability of each of the components – the residential accommodation, the catering, the conference facilities, the staffing, etc. – or the business cannot be run effectively. There are well attested cases where universities have spent more on their fund-raising office than the funds actually raised. So a crucial step in entering these various markets must be to create machinery and a financial system and awareness that will ensure that institutions know what their costs are and how they are distributed. Some earned income activities may add value in other ways but a crucial first question should be whether they generate surpluses or can be managed to do so in the future, or whether they represent an unfocused diversification of activity which actually directs money away from the institution's core purposes.

Generating a surplus on earned income activities is a great deal more difficult than simply generating income, and universities need to devote special processes to the task. An important first step is to establish a special board or committee to take ownership of the process. The various earned income streams need to be identified and the accounting machinery created which can enable the board to assess, at stated intervals through the year, how each stream is progressing against forecast both in terms of income and likely surplus. This will enable the board to 'manage' the income, in the sense that it comes to understand each income stream or 'business' and can intervene to ask questions if the figures do not match the forecasts. Such questioning may expose internal obstacles to performance – a slow down in the admissions office in respect to processing international student applications, a conflict between priorities for minor capital works, the lack of easy access to retail outlets, or staffing shortfalls in a particular activity – which the board may be able to remove. Management at this level may seem to have more of the character of fire fighting, although it keeps the board in close touch with the various activities and ensures that those responsible for them feel able to communicate difficulties in the expectation that something will be done about them, but it is an essential task for the board because in any public sector/private sector organization the most significant difficulty in launching private sector initiatives is overcoming internal procedural log jams.

Of equal importance, both for the success of the activities and for overall university planning and strategy, is a five year planning process, updated each year, where the person responsible for each activity reviews and rolls forward the business plan for the activity detailing expected surpluses and those investments in capital or people that are necessary to achieve them, and is subjected to a challenge meeting by the board, where the plan may be accepted, rejected or referred back for amendment. This process inevitably throws up important strategic questions: to raise the surpluses on the conference business it may be necessary to re-conceptualize catering and dining arrangements requiring significant capital investment; to maintain the profitability of retail outlets major refurbishments may be required (again requiring capital investment); to reinvigorate the short course programme of a particular academic department there needs to be a reconfiguration of staffing arrangements because conflicts between research commitments, teaching and executive programmes are emerging; to open up a stream of well qualified students from country X the institution needs to invest in an office there and send out a high level delegation to talk to the relevant minister. The board will not be able to solve all these issues itself – questions about major capital works, even when paid for by the activity itself, will need to be assimilated within wider university considerations about institutional cash flow and campus planning; academic issues will need to be looked at by academic bodies; personnel matters need to be integrated within wider institutional policies of evaluation and remuneration – but at the end of the process the board should present an updated five year plan which can be integrated into the institution's five year financial forecasts, detailing the financial contribution that each activity is required to make to the overall resourcing of the university.

To be successful the board should recognize seven key principles:

- *The need to monitor earned income streams closely and individually*
  Managing earned income effectively and making it profitable requires the kind of application and attention that would be necessary in running a business; it is at least 90 per cent perspiration and 10 per cent inspiration and requires a process which at regular intervals concentrates the board's mind on what is actually happening with each income stream. The board should therefore monitor income, expenditure and surplus closely against forecast on at least a quarterly basis as well as at year end. This places a real responsibility on the 'manager' of the income stream to understand how the 'business' operates over the year in order to produce the necessary forecasts at each two monthly point at the beginning of the year. Where there are significant variations from the forecast the board should seek an explanation in order to establish whether there are internal reasons why the forecast is not being met. The board's monitoring role is crucial to the whole process because it ensures that it remains close to the activity and that the 'manager' of the activity is aware of his/her accountability for meeting the forecasts. Process is more important than unstructured entrepreneurialism.

- *The need for constant investment and reinvestment*
  The board needs to be able to operate like a venture capital agency to invest to achieve results and stay ahead of competition. The board does not necessarily need to have delegated powers for this: there is advantage in the board having to present a case to a higher body like a university finance committee because of the wider financial or other considerations that may be involved. But the principle of the need for investment must be established, and the higher bodies need to be encouraged to take a balanced and long term view particularly where the claims on cash flow for capital purposes may put academic investment and income generation projects into competition. The higher body will have to make a judgement between the long term financial needs of the institution, which may be affected by a failure to invest in an earned income activity where high levels of profitability are forecast, and the need for investment in an academic activity which may be important for academic development. The board must insist that activities build up contingency funds so that they can themselves constantly invest back into their 'business'. 'Cash cows' which can generate income must not be starved of resources to bail out the rest of the institution or those responsible will be demotivated and the activity will depreciate by comparison with its competitors.

- *The need to develop pricing policies as part of an institutional 'business' strategy*
  Universities are often resistant to charging high market prices, for example, for short courses or conference bookings, either from a residual caution or diffidence or because of a reluctance to compete with a wider commercial market. But high charges not only produce larger surpluses, they generate higher performance from staff and demand better facilities to match the price. They not only reinforce the external market position but impact on the standards that apply in internal university operations. High quality teaching facilities in executive training centres soon find themselves replicated in undergraduate seminar rooms.

- *The need to consider a vertical integration of 'commercial' activities rather than outsourcing them*
  Conventional business management approaches will encourage the outsourcing of as many activities as possible outside the core business. This may make good business sense in a tightly focused private sector firm but is much less satisfactory in a multi-product university set of operations where interrelationships between activities are strong and where outsourcing introduces rigidities when flexibilities between term and vacation needs, understanding the different requirements of different academic customers, or of working within the confines of a university environment represent characteristics which commercial businesses find difficult to match. Moreover, vertical integration into the institution means that the institution retains the surpluses for future investment in its own integrated strategies rather than someone else's.

- *The need to share earned income and surpluses between the university and its departments*
  Universities must strike a balance between retaining surpluses in the centre and allowing them to be retained wholly in departments; the former offers no motivation for departments to generate resources, the latter gives the institution centrally no stake in the process, reduces the capacity to make significant investments and can create significant inequalities between those departments or institutional activities which by their nature can generate resources (e.g. a business school) and those that cannot (e.g. a classics department). The right balance needs to be found which provides a motivation to generate resources at the departmental level but which enables the centre both to retain a significant share for future investments and to ensure that significant differentials between departments do not arise. This balance may vary between the different elements of an earned income budget: thus international student fees might be split on the basis of 60 per cent going to the centre and 40 per cent to the academic department; overheads on research might be split on a sliding scale to encourage departmental negotiation with external bodies for high percentages; for short course income the overhead might be kept low but the profit sharing between department and the centre might be 50:50. Such arrangements need to be approved on a university wide basis

and incorporated in financial regulations to eliminate constant attempts to renegotiate them. Inevitably over time these arrangements become increasingly sophisticated as experience, the differential growth of particular income streams and the dispositions of departments change, but where variations are negotiated to take account of special local factors, such decisions should be transparent and should be taken through established machinery and not behind closed doors.

- *The need to maintain academic trust in the process*
  In earning income the university should not be seen to go down market, that is to employ stratagems which are not consistent with the university's character or to enter into activities which could lower the university's reputation; even more important, the proceeds must be seen to benefit the university's core activities of teaching and research. In other words a university should not be thought of as generating resources simply for financial reasons but because the resources are necessary to build a more academically successful university. In particular the academic community will want to be sure that the process reinforces academic values and does not reward differentially non-academic sectors of the institution. While the board should concentrate on the process of generating funds, and should not try to second guess the senate/academic board on academic matters, the academic community will want to be sure that the board retains a sensitivity to academic or student concerns.

- *The need to develop professionalism and managerial capability*
  Earning income and generating surpluses in a university context require a high degree of professionalism not just amongst the financial and central managerial team that reports to the board but in the various academic departments and other activities where external income is being generated. It demands both a high degree of financial literacy from all involved as well as social and political skills in interfacing centre and departmental perspectives. The board might be expected to comprise a mixture of administrative, managerial, academic and lay members and to be served by a team of academic and financial administrators who can maintain close links with the actual 'managers' of the earned income activities and help them with their business planning. But some key players will need to be brought in from the private sector, for example as managers of retail outlets or to run a conference business. Here the task must be to help them succeed in a university environment while not losing their commercial edge. Building this team, maintaining its professionalism and ensuring that its activities reinforce one another and do not conflict with the institution's core activities is critical to achieving success.

Figure 1 describes the development of the finances of one research intensive university over a 27-year period. What it illustrates is the extent to which this university has moved from a reliance on state funding through recurrent grant to a diversified income base. While this university may not be wholly

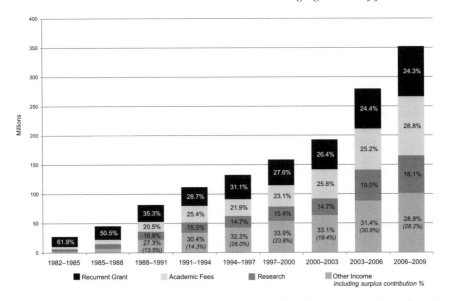

Figure 1 Growth in recurrent grant income in one university as a proportion of total university income in one university over a 20-year period.

Note: I am indebted to Tracy Grant and Rosie Drinkwater for providing this chart.

typical of universities listed in Table 1, where universities are ranked by RAE performance, because its HEFCE funding was augmented from 2000 by the build up of a new medical school and because of its exceptional drive from the beginning of the period to generate income from non-state sources, nevertheless it is not untypical in other ways. First it demonstrates a volume growth in the size of its financial base (£25m in 1982–5; £350m in 2006–9). Second, it shows how the tuition fee element in the budget (home and international) has increased (from 6 per cent to over 30 per cent) emphasizing the forces of marketization and the importance of reputation in a market led funding system. (In universities that do not benefit from a substantial research income the percentage would, of course, be higher.) What it also shows is the revolution that has taken place in the funding of universities generally and, at least for this kind of university, a return to a balance of funding more like conditions in the 1920s and 1930s, before the state took over the funding of universities. The striking difference in this university's case is the substitution of earned ('Other') income for endowment income and the extent to which this income produces considerable surpluses (shown as a percentage of 'Other Income' in Figure 1) which are available to invest back into the institution. This additional source of income, if the earned income activities in the university are managed effectively, represents a more reliable income stream than could be produced by the interest on endowments realized by universities in the 1920s and 1930s.

In practice the successful adoption of an earned income approach to university finance achieves much more than simply making up a shortfall from state support because it encourages the university to be outward, rather than inward looking, and it ensures that the university pays attention to its outward face – its building maintenance, its landscaping, the effectiveness of its services, the quality of life it can offer – all of which reinforces its attractiveness to staff and students and creates a better environment for the pursuit of teaching and research. In particular it opens the university much more to public use. This can have a reputational advantage as well as simply integrating the institution more securely with the wider world. There is no reason why a bookshop or any other retail outlet on a university campus should not be run at least as effectively as one outside, or a conference venue provide facilities and service at least as good as those of its commercial competitors, or have car parking arrangements which are not as visitor friendly as any other organization, but it is sometimes surprising how universities can exempt themselves from such comparisons on the grounds that they are academic institutions and therefore *ipso facto* they can be excused for being less than efficient, down at heel, or unresponsive to the public, failing to understand that in modern society the public are much less charitable in their views than they once were about state supported institutions which underachieve.

Earned income should not be seen as an alternative to seeking donor support either through a general appeal campaign or from alumni. Ambitious universities will not restrict themselves to any one route to generating non-state resources but in the cultural climate of the UK only a few appeal campaigns can possibly succeed in the way Oxbridge's have done. Moreover, the costs of launching an appeal, the burden it places on the vice-chancellor and the risks of failure are such as to discourage most institutions not founded before the First World War from even trying. Where an appeal is launched, however, it should be treated as an earned income item for monitoring purposes simply to ensure that the costs of the exercise can continuously be measured against the funds raised; appeals can be slippery operations where the costs are lost sight of in the euphoria that accompanies external gifts. Most universities may find that the steady cultivation of and relationship building with alumni provides a more reliable long term fundraising platform for creating scholarship and bursary endowments that relate directly to the university's core finances than welcome but 'one off' donations for facilities which have only a peripheral impact.

Budgetary planning and strategy

Following the Cardiff affair (Shattock 1994) most universities have taken steps to monitor their income and expenditure regularly throughout the financial year. Good practice suggests that an expert budget group accountable to the finance committee should be established so as to ensure that divergent figures can be questioned and investigated in a way that is not possible when a monthly financial report represents only one item on a long agenda. Too often this process is seen as a matter of accounting rather than as a matter of management – a set of aggregated figures that provide an overview but conceal internal fluctuations of performance. Divergent figures, potential overspends, and, in the maintenance and minor works areas, even underspends, require active intervention to explain variations from forecast figures. Regular budgetary reviews by a group established for the purpose enables an institution to keep a firm grip on its finances and to identify issues which senior management might not otherwise be aware of. Chief amongst these may be the monitoring of debtor levels, of cash flow generally, the costs of utilities, particularly energy, and the progress against budget of the capital programme. Debtor levels are rising as universities become more dependent on non-state finance: debt levels on student fees, on industrial support or on income from short courses requires a much more managed approach than in the past and much tougher and more robust action if cash flow and investment income is not to be insufficient to support institutional policy goals.

As universities have expanded and their stock of post-1960 buildings has grown, maintaining their capital plant has become increasingly onerous. Many universities have economized on their maintenance budgets during periods of financial stringency in order to give priority to their academic function (or because they are unwilling to cut their salary costs) and are left with maintenance backlogs which require significant injections of capital to remedy. These requirements in their turn then compete with important new projects. Managing the estates function in these circumstances has often become a professionally thankless task, as the condition of many university campuses bears testimony. Organizationally, estates and buildings offices have become detached from other central management functions to the detriment of the integration of a concern about the physical conditions of a university with other strategic policy issues. A close monitoring of the maintenance budget can simultaneously provide a progress check on the performance of the estates and buildings office and have the effect of bringing the estates function more closely into touch with central management issues. Large economies can be achieved in the field of energy (and are now required by Government policy) and water conservation and institutions have no choice but to invest in the technologies involved in controlling their costs. University capital programmes may be the responsibility of a senior committee of the governing body but such a committee will normally meet too infrequently to exercise detailed policy control. A budget monitoring group meeting at regular intervals provides a forum where a detailed examination of expenditure on a university's estate can take place.

A budgetary group can therefore be a key management tool in the coordination of university activities. From a financial point of view knowing where the institution is positioned against its budget at predetermined points in the year provides strategic information of great value because it enables the institution to respond effectively to external events. If an under-spend is likely or earned income is more buoyant than forecast it can respond more confidently to invitations to submit bids where matching funds are required, or mid year, it can bring forward projects planned for a later year to give itself a head start on a new development: opportunism needs to be underpinned by a secure and up-to-date understanding of an institution's financial position.

Effective financial management in the mixed economy mode of university finance depends on accurate forecasting. Forecasting has become more difficult because far more variables have been introduced into the financial picture. Financial planning can, therefore, never be precise but it can be improved by rigorous reviewing of the quality of forecasts made in the past. Universities that plot the variances to past forecasts of income and expend-iture under various key headings in a structured way, subjecting each five year forecast of the main lines of income and expenditure to scrutiny at the end of that period, will not only improve their forecasting over time but will give themselves greater confidence in the financial room they have to take developmental decisions.

If an institution has effective machinery to monitor its budget through the year and to understand its own biases and prejudices and the balance of its own optimisms and pessimisms in financial forecasting, it is able to engage in five year forward financial planning with some confidence. Such exercises can be seen as purely financially driven and undertaken mainly to satisfy external authorities but in modern conditions it is through the medium of a financial plan that university strategy is best decided. As we have seen, in the past, strategy was largely a function of student number planning against the expectation that the state would fund the student number target within the framework of a given unit of resource but, in modern conditions, the process leading up to the rolling forward of a five year financial plan should be the occasion for the most searching examination of university expend-iture over the previous year. This is not a technical exercise, though it will depend on the input of high levels of technical expertise, and cannot be regarded simply as the responsibility of a finance office alone, because such an office will not necessarily be aware of the policy implications of all the many lines of institutional expenditure. It would be surprising if, in any year, this review did not throw up some lines of expenditure which could be discontinued. Such an exercise represents the essential backdrop to the annual strategic planning exercise referred to in the previous chapter (Annual strategic review). An important issue in this review is the integra-tion of state funding and earned income so that the five year forecast takes full account of the five year earned income plan giving it equal weight to forecast levels of state funding. In practice experience may suggest that a well managed earned income portfolio can be more securely forecast than state funding which, over any five year period, may be more volatile because it is dependent on the vagaries of government policies and the fall-out from the decisions of the public expenditure round.

Performance indicators and comparisons

It is a bold and foolish university that does not take a close interest in the financial performance of its competitors if only because, if they are genuine competitors, the institution is likely to learn from them. The UK HESA publishes financial profiles for all universities and these provide the basis for indicators of financial health. These performance indicators offer useful measures to compare the diversity of funding sources for individual institutions, short term solvency, the retention of reserves, the proportion of expenditure directed towards the estate and the management of long term debt.

Perhaps the most interesting lessons to be drawn from these tables are the benefits of financial stability and the threats posed by financial instability. If we look at the top group of universities which perform best in teaching and research all have good records in terms of short term solvency assets and the numbers of days of total expenditure which could be met from general funds, and all but two have a low ratio of borrowing to total income. Moving down the list the position is much more variable and it is easy to see how financial constraints can inhibit some institutions from reacting quickly and effectively to external opportunities. All but two of the top group of institutions, one of whom is developing a new campus and the other has severe site restrictions on capital expansion in central London, would seem to take a relatively conservative view of finance – they do not borrow much, their reserves are adequate, their expenditure on staffing does not constrain the institution's flexibility even though staff/student ratios are favourable, and they are not over dependent on international student fee income.

Conventional wisdom argues that institutions should only borrow against projects which will themselves generate income so that the debt can be met from the project itself. Some universities, however, have borrowed against unspecified future income or taken out bonds, presumably against an anticipated expansion of student numbers or some other expectation of increased income. (Rowe 1997 and Armstrong and Fletcher 2004 provide telling examples of where this has occurred.) Inevitably this borrowing will exercise a constraint on expenditure policies in the future, not just because the interest and repayments will represent a first charge on income but because the higher the level of borrowing the less favourable borrowing terms the institution is likely to obtain in the future; a high level of borrowing may impose restrictions in the future over borrowing against income generation projects that could be financially beneficial to the institution.

Borrowing for projects which cannot themselves repay the costs involved is dangerous because the impact can be unpredictable over an extended period of years. Some universities have even borrowed or taken out bonds to cover backlog maintenance costs, a line which should always be firmly built into any budget. Such borrowing is seductive and, unless there is very clear evidence of future increases in income, must be regarded as likely to worsen rather than improve a university's financial position over time, not least because it offers no encouragement to the university's leadership to exercise tight budgetary control over other items. Those individuals who take responsibility for the decision to borrow in such circumstances will usually have left office before the longer term consequences are felt; there is a danger that what might seem a positive decision at the time may represent a significant liability to their successors. The financial health indicators published by HESA show in how many cases universities' current liabilities exceed current liquid assets or where over time there has been a deterioration of net liquid assets to total expenditure both of which offer pointers to financial vulnerability. Universities have much less flexibility than companies in dealing with long term debt because of the constraints under which they operate; they should therefore exercise great caution in seeking to solve problems in this way. The relief felt after an injection of borrowed cash may be matched by the future problems of repayment that will be faced by their successors.

Developing a predilection to solve problems in this way rather than taking the more difficult decision of prioritizing the competing demands for capital expenditure within a fixed financial envelope can all too easily become a way of life for some university managements so that an institution finds itself imprisoned by decisions taken in previous years. There can be no doubt that there are a group of universities whose future rise up the league tables may have been foreclosed by borrowing decisions. With the increase in borrowing, universities have entered the commercial world of credit ratings. The standard bases on which a major bank would rate a possible commercial borrower would be the quality of their brand or reputation (see Chapter 9), income diversity, operating cash flow, quality of management, location and prospects. It is not difficult to fit universities into this rating framework or to see how universities may be advantaged or disadvantaged by their position in the league tables. Standard and Poor's have actually issued a statement on university credit ratings. It assesses universities under: government support and the regulatory framework, academic standing, demand risk and competitive position, asset quality, operational performance, business strategy and governance and it looks carefully at income and expenditure ratios, revenue diversity, debt and liquidity, and cash flow analysis. It considers 'a strong and experienced senior management team to be a positive credit feature' and argues that management quality 'can be measured by its ability to consistently achieve targeted goals and its ability to manage budget shocks' and it makes clear that it 'evaluates management's track record of achieving forecasts and its degree of consistency in applying its financial strategies' (Standard and Poor's 2003: 19). Only a few UK universities have sought a credit rating from Standard and Poor's so we lack comparisons with like institutions in other countries, for instance universities at the top of the UK league tables with the US Ivy League. But there is comfort for the UK system in a comparison of Standard and Poor's university ratings with company ratings carried out by the *Times Higher Education Supplement* (*THES*) showing Sheffield, for example, at AA–, apparently above many

UK household business names like Thames Water, Sainsbury's, Cadbury Schweppes and Boots, and only one point behind Microsoft (Jobbins 2002).

The allocation of resources

In times of financial stringency almost any internal allocation of new resources has strategic importance. In planning its finances over a five year period a university is implicitly if not explicitly deciding what kind of university it wants to be, whether it wants to change its profile over the period or reinforce it. Does it want to improve its research ratings? If so it will allocate funds both to improve its staff/student ratios and to buy some non-research active staff out on early retirement. If its aim is to redress maintenance backlogs it may have to cut staffing budgets to find the necessary investment. If it has particular capital projects it wants to complete in the period, it will have to allocate the cash to build them, remembering that the recurrent costs of servicing the buildings when they are built must also be included in the plan. These major strategic decisions represent the essential framework of the university's development.

But, unlike most organizations, university strategy in regard to its core business is determined as much by a myriad of detailed micro-decisions as by the macro-strategic decisions of which examples are given above: academic departmental performance can rise or fall on the basis of one or two decisions a year about new academic appointments, research reputations can be made or broken on whether particular grants are won or on how a book is received. Getting the major strategic decisions right is only part of the route to success because academic success is built up cumulatively on the back of many much smaller decisions, arising out of how resources are allocated at a detailed level. As universities have grown larger there has been an increasing tendency to devolve detailed decision making about resource allocation for the core business downward. In times of acute financial stringency the principle of every barrel standing on its own bottom becomes increasingly attractive to senior university management because it devolves first line responsibility down to operating units, but this does not necessarily lead to academic improvement. From the point of view of financial accountability there is much to be said for giving faculties or departments devolved budgets, which they may allocate from according to their own best perceptions of future success. In addition, most universities, following the Transparency Review Assessment of Cost Recovery exercise (TRAC) have introduced systems whereby departmental (or faculty) budgets must demonstrate a notional fixed financial return to the central budget to cover the university 'overhead' for the funding of central services. However, there are dangers in an absolute devolution of budgets. The first is that resource allocation becomes primarily financially rather than academically led and the demonstration of an appropriate level of financial return to the centre becomes a determining policy issue. Departments or faculties that are unable to achieve this are considered to be 'in debt' and are required by higher authority (often by governing bodies unaware of the academic implications) to 'get out of debt' irrespective of the academic damage that will be caused. Financial viability becomes the prime criteria for resource allocation – departments that can make the return are 'strong', those that cannot are 'weak', ignoring the fact that, for example, a small but 'uneconomic' History of Art department may invigorate a humanities programme through its optional courses, that some academic disciplines are simply less economic in an accounting sense than others or that academic policy considerations might justify cross subsidy from economically strong to economically weak areas providing that an overall financial balance could be achieved.

A second danger arising from the absolute devolution of budgets is that it does not take sufficient account of the comfort factors that can intrude at the faculty or departmental level – the tendency to allocate resources equitably to reduce teaching loads rather than to reinforce recognized research strengths, to preserve areas of the curriculum in spite of student disinterest rather than force staff to teach in areas in which they are not expert or to produce a mathematically equitable division of resources between different subject groups or departments as a substitute for the inability to reach clear academic judgements. In some universities the drive for excellence is so engrained that departments are themselves willing to make hard choices but for the majority of universities there is great advantage in such a decision being shared with some body outside the department even where the department has budgetary authority to fill a vacancy on its own initiative. The opportunities to fill academic vacancies or create new posts are so infrequent that each one becomes a strategic decision and value for money is best obtained by a close scrutiny of each case by academics from outside as well as inside the department rather than by adopting automatically the department's view of its own priorities. Under this model academic development monies, or savings targets, or perhaps both together, should be allocated as part of the five year plan to a specialist academic resource allocating body which assesses and evaluates bids from departments so as to ensure that an overall institutional strategy is translated into detailed resource allocation decisions. Any such process must take account of areas where performance has fallen or where resources need to be reallocated from one area to another. Where institutional size or complexity makes full devolution unavoidable it is imperative that resource allocation at the central university level is based on a severe retrospective review of decision making as well as the operational units' forward planning or the university may find itself in a perpetual catch up process of investing resources to re-establish academic strengths which have previously been dissipated by a dominance of parochial over strategic criteria in faculty/departmental decision making.

If robust 'constructive confrontation' is a necessary feature of macro institutional budgetary decision making so it should be in relation to academic departments. Departments need to have sharply defined strategic priorities and the central academic resource allocation body should be equally direct in commenting on them. This kind of dialogue and argument represents an essential background to good decision making: too easy an acceptance of departmental priorities implies an absence of central strategic awareness but ready departmental acceptance of a central strategy over academic priorities reflects an absence of academic self-belief. Jarzabkowski suggests, arising out of an investigation of three quite different resource allocation models, that the models reflected primarily the 'contextual characteristics of culture, history and structure' of the institutions investigated and that resource allocation models are 'less a matter of best practice, neatly transferable between institutions, than one of internal fit' (Jarzabkowski 2002: 29). The conclusion implies that the model is determined by an institution's organizational culture rather than itself being one of the determinants of the culture. This is bad news for vice-chancellors and others who want to tighten the focus of resource allocation and make a given model more strategic. If we accept that, in a period of scarce resources, decisions about academic resource allocation assume a greater significance than in a climate when resources are expanding, then how such decisions are taken, by whom and to what strategic end become critical to success in the institution's core business.

An essential component of academic resource allocation is the need for an annual review of departmental expenditure including overspends, the size of departmental reserves and the consideration of any audit reviews by the internal financial audit team. Universities are much more than a federation of departments and a tradition of good financial practice at departmental level has an impact throughout the university and will condition the discussion of financial priorities. Heads of departments, particularly experimental science departments with large external portfolios of research grants and contracts, need financially qualified administrative support and should expect to receive some financial awareness training. Financial administrators should expect to be accountable to the university finance director on professional matters and to see such relationships as one of partnership not mutual antagonism; they should always be represented when the university is discussing financial systems or technical matters which bear on their own responsibilities. By the same token heads of departments (who may have financial responsibilities equating to that of the managing director of a small company) need to be fully informed on macro-university financial decision making since, as some of the biggest spenders, they have an interest in seeing the university well managed, and can, if necessary, bring a day-to-day experience of academic financial management to the institutional decision making process. Angluin and Scapens' (2000) study finds that pre-1992 universities tend to operate 'high transparency regimes' which enable departments to challenge resource allocation decisions but 'new universities ... seem particularly likely to operate non-transparency regimes and these are associated with perceived unfairness. Fairness in contrast is associated with transparent regimes' (p. 31). If departments do not feel there is integrity in the process they will not feel committed to the strategy which drives it.

The essential characteristics of a financially healthy institution

If financial stability is an important constituent of ensuring sustainable success in a university's core business we need to ask what are its essential characteristics. The list is, of course, not very surprising:

- *Short term solvency*
  A university must consistently and year by year aim to maintain itself in credit (and must always plan to do so in the last year of its five year financial forecast). It must have the ability to meet its short term financial obligations, and retain sufficient liquid funds to cover exceptional items. A university that needs regularly to rely on bank borrowing during the year is living too near the edge and reduces its ability to respond to external opportunities. Maintaining a sufficient level of financial liquidity is important. Institutions should seek to be able to cover at least 90 days of expenditure to be secure.

- *Retention of reserves*
  A university must build up and retain reserves that can buffer and absorb unexpected shifts in its external funding environment, respond to market changes, or renew its assets. A university will not be able to act opportunistically unless it can draw quickly on cash to support the action. Achieving at least a 5 per cent surplus at year end (assuming no capital support from state sources) should represent a normal expectation.

- *The effective management of long term debt*
  Increasingly universities are having recourse to medium to long term borrowing for capital purposes. In a period of low inflation the interest rates may be low but the capital repayment burden must be borne by their successors in a period far enough ahead when it is not possible to forecast the state of the financial environment. The Lancaster case (Rowe 1997) demonstrates that the complexity of the financial arrangements necessary for a bond issue can produce a short term financial crisis. Institutions that borrow for projects that cannot be relied upon to cover the capital interest repayments are putting themselves at long term risk.

- *The effective management of the estate*
  The record of the 20 years of financial stringency between 1980 and 2000 is that the first item on which universities economize is building maintenance; evidence from the private sector suggests that the mismanagement of capital assets often lies at the heart of medium sized companies' financial difficulties. Universities that do not invest appropriately in building maintenance are laying up long term risks for themselves. Such risks are multiplying with the need to comply with legislation in regard to the size of an institution's carbon footprint. Perhaps the single most important indicator of financial health may be the size of a university's budget for long term maintenance.

- *The ability to generate non-state funding*
  It is essential to establish a diversified funding base both to match the shortfalls in state funding and to provide support for innovation and new initiatives. The ability of the state to sustain effectively both the development of a greatly expanded higher education system and the increasing costs of institutions that want to be internationally competitive is limited. Universities that wish to remain successful in the new mixed economy mode will have to develop sustainable strategies to do so.

- *Consistency of budgetary strategy with mission*
  In a competitive world where resources are scarce institutions need to align their budget at the macro-level to their ambitions, and allocate their resources accordingly. Getting best value out of the resources allocated will be a key factor in achieving success. Deciding what is best value should remain the heart of the institution's strategic debate.

- *The maintenance of financial sustainability*
  The concept of financial sustainability has been enhanced by the introduction of full economic costing (FEC) in relation to UK research council grants which recognizes formulaicly the need to cover indirect costs and estate costs in addition to the direct costs of a research project. This has been of considerable assistance to research intensive universities. However, sustainability goes much further and is, in effect, embodied in all the characteristics of a financially healthy institution listed above. Its application, however, comes under severe stress in times of acute financial stringency.

Good financial management is not a function of one set of offices in a university but is a characteristic which should run right through the institution, through academic departments as much as through central offices. While the best guarantee of financial security is probably to be an academically successful university which attracts students of high quality in large numbers, teaches them well and is good at research, good financial management can enhance the academic function by providing stability, making available resources for investment and renewal, and ensuring that the institution gets best value out of the deployment of the resources it has. In a competitive and increasingly marketized higher education system good financial management can give an institution an initial competitive edge over those that have restricted their options through over commitment and are therefore unable to respond effectively to opportunities as they arise.

4

The academic context: organization, collegiality and leadership

If universities' core business is teaching and research then the organizational framework in which it is delivered represents a key variable in factors that contribute to success. But there is little modern research into academic organization which can be said to offer clear pointers to a transferable successful model. If we look at universities that are recognized to be successful there is no consistent organizational pattern although McNay's model of internal cultures embodied in four quadrants – collegium, bureaucracy, enterprise and corporation – represents a helpful way of describing different styles of exercising control over policy and practice (McNay 1999). The most useful piece of empirical research into organizational models was conducted for the North Commission on the governance of Oxford, and this concluded that the governance of the UK's most successful university, Cambridge, was so complex that no one in Cambridge understood it (the North Report – University of Oxford 1997). Shortly afterwards there was widespread criticism of both the governance and the management of the University in official reports (Shattock 2001b) and within the University. While this criticism has concentrated on the more formal aspects of governance it inevitably touched on aspects of the University's organizational framework itself. Cambridge's success should, therefore, be seen as perhaps occurring in spite of its organizational framework rather than because of it, a point readily conceded by Johnson in his introduction to Cornford's *Microcosmographica Academica* (Johnson 1995).

This chapter examines the determinants of academic organization and the forces that have driven structural change and assesses the effectiveness of academic organizational structures quoting examples of where piecemeal changes have weakened rather than strengthened institutions. It then outlines the key principles of academic organization noting the key role of the department, faculty and/or college relationships with the centre and with departments, and the ambiguities in the roles of deans. It places emphasis on the maintenance of short lines of communication and of face to face contact rather than extended decision making systems and the role of the centre in a centre:department matrix. It discusses historical and more modern approaches to collegiality and managerial direction and emphasizes how that impacts on leadership styles. It reviews the contribution of students and emphasizes the importance of the provision of comprehensive academic data to assist decision making.

The determinants of academic organization

University structures are critically affected by an institution's age, disciplinary mix, physical location and size: collegiate universities, particularly where teaching is the responsibility of residential colleges, inevitably have organizational structures that differ fundamentally from universities that are entirely departmentally based but this only arises at Oxbridge (where other factors apply) and, to a lesser extent Durham; the organizational model that works well at LSE, a relatively small institution located in the inner city, and primarily social science based, would not be appropriate in universities with medical schools and a major commitment to science and technology or in universities of 20,000 students or more. The dispersal of a university over several distinct sites will also have a significant impact on its academic organization just as will the concentration of a university on a single out-of-town campus; big universities create structures which would be intolerable in much smaller and more intimate institutions, while small institutions rely much more on informal processes to make strategic decisions (McNay 2002). An ideal academic organizational structure cannot, therefore, be neatly defined and offered as a prescription (although this has not stopped a great number of attempts by universities in the last decade to re-structure towards some other universities' perceived model).

The absence of research evidence on the effectiveness of particular structures has led university organization to be driven as much by fashion or by received ideas deriving from industry or the public sector, as from coherent thought about organizational fit: it is very rare in fact that organizational change is driven by a convincing set of educational ideas. Much more frequently, organizational change is based on unresearched ideas about management. One important driver can be institutional lack of success and a belief that a particular academic model, associated with a more successful university, can provide solutions to persistent underperformance in another with little analysis being undertaken of the precise contribution that the particular model has made to the former's success. In others, changes may be a reaction against organizational changes introduced a generation ago, to which some groups of staff were never reconciled, or may simply reflect the wish of a new vice-chancellor to replicate the model of his/her previous university.

According to Hogan (2005) of 81 universities reviewed between 1993 and 2002 74 per cent undertook at least one significant reorganization and, in a separate analysis of 68 universities between 1994 and 2002, 51 had changed their structure of faculties or schools. But this mania for structural change showed no predilection for a given pattern except in general to reduce the number of units in the structure by various means: by simply reducing the number of faculties or departments, by removing faculties altogether and merging departments into schools or by replacing schools with faculties. On the other hand, 12 universities in Hogan's first group and 11 in the second actually increased the number of faculties/schools. 'Managerial rather than academic concerns', Hogan suggests, have been the dominant factors behind most reorganizations (Hogan 2005).

Some universities seem to have become serial reorganizers. Thus one pre-1992 university, over a period of 12 years and two vice-chancellors, has changed from five faculties, elected deans and a central resource allocation body to budgetary devolution to elected deans, back to central resource allocation and finally to a four college structure with budgetary devolution to externally appointed college heads who carry the title of pro-vice-chancellor. Another, over 15 years, has moved from a devolved structure of eight faculties, to the abolition of faculties in favour of some 30 schools made up of merged departments and finally to a devolved five college structure headed by externally appointed college heads. It is clear from the case histories of many universities that centralization, decentralization and recentralization have become recurrent themes, with centralization being associated most often with periods of acute financial stringency and decentralization with periods of growth and more generous financial support. Reorganization has begun to take on the character of a 'management fad' (Birnbaum 2000).

In the 1980s and 1990s, dominated by the pressures exerted by financial stringency, most of the organizational change that took place was associated with how best to allocate resources or distribute budget reductions and to whom, how to secure accountability for the distribution so that it added value to the institution and how best to control costs and eliminate deficits. The Jarratt Report (Committee of Vice-Chancellors and Principals 1985) first popularized the benefits of devolving financial authority downwards to faculties, schools or departments, a structure already introduced at Sussex under the influence of the management consultants, McKinsey. The devolved structure was already widely used in industry either as a reaction to growth in organizational size or as an attempt to revitalize monolithic organizations by devolving centralized decision making down to operational units. Devolution of financial decision making also became a key element in the New Public Management reforms in the NHS and elsewhere in the public sector in the 1980s (Ferlie *et al.* 1996) and offered a solution to many pre-1992 universities struggling to balance their budgets in the wake of the 1981 cuts. Several vice-chancellors of pre-1992 universities chose to avoid a great deal of personal unpopularity by devolving their deficits to academic units and encouraging them to manage themselves out of it.

Lockwood offered a more positive rationale for devolved structures:

The more individual units are held responsible and accountable for what they do, the more they are likely to exercise responsibility. It is a matter of liberating their enterprise and initiative within a framework of quality controls and institutional assessments of the futures of each unit.

(1987: 105)

Devolution, in his eyes, was qualified by central management controls. Of course the devolution process raised many questions – should devolution be to a faculty or to a department? What exactly should be devolved? In a situation where over 50 per cent of a university's expenditure was on academic staff salaries should decisions about filling academic staff vacancies or creating new academic posts be devolved? And bound up with decisions on this, could posts of dean of faculty or head of department remain elected when the institution was vesting in them such power and responsibility? On this last point Jarrett strongly recommended that they should be appointed by the governing body on the recommendation of the vice-chancellor and not left to the whim of an electorate or to a 'buggins turn'. Jarratt's view envisaged appointments from within the institution, in other words selecting the best person in the eyes of the university's senior management from within the list of people available. But fashion in Australia where these developments went much further and faster suggested the value of publicly advertising deanships and making appointments from other universities thus reinforcing a sense of deans being part of a management hierarchy deriving its legitimacy from the top rather than being any kind of representative of academic opinion at a faculty level. It is no coincidence that in the increasingly marketized 'enterprise' universities in Australia this practice took root and spread first to the UK post-1992 universities where student recruitment represented a dominant issue; it has now become more common across the whole university sector.

Organizational changes may very appropriately be prompted by questions of institutional size, and also by institutional mergers. The merger of three medical schools with Imperial College, for example, reinforced the significantly devolved structure that already existed at the College. It is no coincidence that as Imperial College deans have migrated to vice-chancellorships at other universities they have sought to introduce similar structures to Imperial's at their new institutions. At Manchester also the merger between UMIST and the University, combined with the size of the new institution, drove the introduction of devolved faculty structures. Such devolved structures raise important policy issues. If the dean is the budget holder what is in the budget? If the dean has power to decide on creating new academic posts, filling vacant ones, imposing vacancy freezes or seeking early retirements from existing staff, to what extent has the central authority placed itself at risk if inappropriate decisions are made? How are deans made accountable and to whom? If accountability is primarily financial, and if the devolved structure is seen essentially as a means to ensure financial control, as it has been in many post-1992 universities, then the vice-chancellor, as the institutional accounting officer, is the natural line manager. This reinforces the chief executive model. If, on the other hand accountability is much more academic and dominated more by considerations of improving performance in the RAE as it has been in many pre-1992 universities, devolving effectively 75 per cent of a university's budget to a group of deans means that staffing decisions which constitute key elements in an institution's RAE strategy, with implications for its recurrent grant and position in various league tables, are being taken away from the centre, and the university's central bodies can only monitor the results. Even accepting that university statutes may require formal confirmation by the governing body for some of these actions and that budgeting controls may prevent major fluctuations in staffing, such a university is, in effect, transferring key policy tools away from central decision - making bodies to substantial faculty 'baronies' whose interests may not always coincide with central perceptions of the university's best interests.

Another important area of devolution relates to the provision of services. At Sussex, in the high flush of the McKinsey report, decisions were taken to decentralize budgetary responsibility for some essential services to the extent that schools could prioritize various items of expenditure and deprioritize others. This led to some significant losses in the perceived coherence of corporate management: uneven expenditures on portering, for example, led to the abandonment of common policies about opening academic buildings. In some Australian universities where the devolution of services is common, wealthy or impoverished faculties can be identified at a glance by the standards of decoration, cleaning and equipment of their buildings. In many reorganizations the centre can find itself dismembered as registry, finance and even estates staff are transferred to faculty administrations on the general ground that decisions affecting academic life are best taken at the coal face rather than in head office, ignoring the counter argument that coal face workers have proved to be singularly bad at closing their own pits or at proposing effective strategies for surviving sharp downturns in demand. At best such devolution of administrative functions can affect an institution's manoeuverability under pressure – the loss of a strategic capability to produce a quick analysis, on a common basis, of student numbers or of financial forecasts or even of long term building maintenance plans; at worst it can escalate administrative costs, and divide an institution into well defended bailiwicks which erode flexibility and build up significant barriers to change.

Tradition and academic discipline also play a substantial role. In some subjects, most notably medicine, dentistry, agriculture and veterinary science, the combination of the need to manage significant facilities such as hospital services, farms or estates, with the need to coordinate separate departments' contributions to single degrees which carry professional status, requires the deans' powers to be of a different order of magnitude to what might be expected in, say, a humanities faculty. Business schools also seem to demand a powerful decanal structure though business school deans rarely command the same authority inside their own schools as medical deans because of the greater employment mobility of business school staff.

Disciplinary culture may also be important in defining a dean's powers.

Kekale (1998, 1999) has shown that different disciplinary fields produce different leadership styles with, of the four subject areas he researched, physics being at the higher end of a spectrum of respect for individual authority and history at the other. Becher and Trowler group disciplines into hard and soft and pure and applied profiles. Thus they categorize the pure sciences as 'hard pure', humanities and pure social sciences as 'soft pure', technologies as 'hard applied' and applied social science as 'soft applied' (Becher and Trowler 2001). It is not difficult to align these profiles with styles of academic organization: faculties in the pure sciences and the technologies tend to be more streamlined and business-like, more willing to 'get on with the job' and to permit the dean to wield real authority, while faculties in the humanities and social sciences tend to be more discursive, less willing to cede authority to a dean, be reluctant to accept policies laid down by central authority without question and be much more willing to challenge the *status quo*. A prime reason why the Imperial College structure would not work, for example, at LSE is the very different disciplinary base of the two institutions. There are serious managerial risks in trying to transplant one set of organizational structures to another institution where the disciplinary cultures are different. One size fits all rarely works. As Ramsden has written in relation to Australia: 'The basic error which many universities have made is to believe that structures are superordinate to cultures. But no structure can be effective unless the culture also "works" ' (Ramsden 2000: 262).

Assessing the effectiveness of academic organizational structures

One of the difficulties of assessing the effectiveness of organizational change in universities is the often random nature of what has produced it and the easy assumption that a change in the decision making framework is fundamental to improving performance. Taylor provides an interesting account of four pre-1992 universities which have restructured for a variety of reasons: improved administration, the prospect of disciplinary change brought about by new multi-disciplinary groupings, the need to be more 'fleet of foot', and the pressure of market forces and competition. In each case the universities reduced the number of faculties (in one case establishing colleges) and merged departments into schools where, although departments often continued to exist in more or less shadowy form, the head of school was responsible for strategic planning, leadership and the delivery of teaching and research. Taylor found that staff welcomed the shorter executive decision - making procedures and 'passively' accepted the resulting erosion of the consultative powers of bodies like the senate. But in each case he found that the university was 'treading a tight rope between the need for strong, authoritative central direction and a desire for devolved responsibility and incentives'. He also found that devolved decision making did not always ensure a quick response to external pressures (Taylor 2006).

In many universities changes in organizational framework do not replace but are superimposed on the last set of organizational changes. Thus in the Taylor account the decision making chain could actually be lengthened if the natural point of reference remained the disciplinary focus of the previous departmental structure. The experience of one university (not included in Taylor's study) may illustrate this. This was a university which had a traditional faculty and department structure where the heads of departments were accountable to the vice-chancellor. The latter was concerned about the number of academic officers that thus had a direct reporting relationship with him and a school structure headed by deans was therefore introduced, which was intended to merge departments under schools, but which in practice left most departments operating as separate subject groups within the school structure. A few years later even this seemed too flat a structure and the deans and their schools were grouped under a further tier of four provosts (or super deans). But the first reform remained in place when the second was introduced leaving subject groups still operating within schools which were headed by deans who were now answerable to provosts. Neither reform, unsurprisingly, produced an improvement in academic performance, nor did they reduce the number of subjects submitted for assessment in the RAE. On the contrary they created extra levels of decision making, extra layers of bureaucracy, longer lines of communication and extra links in the chain of command. A new vice-chancellor concerned about weak performance in a variety of subjects found he could only intervene to produce change at the subject level by negotiating first with the relevant provost then with the dean and only then with the subject head. The command chain was too long and there were too many layers in the structure, each of these layers serving to protect subject groups that were performing inadequately. Instead of one structure in which department heads reported direct to the vice-chancellor each structural reform had superimposed a new structure without subtracting its predecessor.

Since the late 1990s there has been a mounting pressure for organizational change but there is no hard evidence that it has had any significant impact on academic performance. There are few, if any, universities that can claim that such changes have been responsible for better RAE scores, an improved level of recruitment of international students or raised teaching standards. Indeed the contrary seems often to be the case. As Hogan points out: 'No matter what direction [a] reorganisation takes, it is bound to involve a period of disruption or uncertainty as the previous structures are replaced' (Hogan 2005). Too often re-structuring represents a distraction from the tough business of managing academic performance, a kind of 'moving the deckchairs on the Titanic' rather than grasping the nettles in the centre of the university about underperformance, the need for reinvestment or the re-direction of resources from one part of the university to another. Extensive devolution of decision making may be necessary to cope with increasing size but it can also reduce flexibility, restrict opportunism and actually slow down decision making over big issues. Too often academic restructuring is a palliative, to satisfy impatient governing bodies, rather than providing a clear path to more competitive academic performance.

The principles of academic organization

Experience suggests that while there may be no 'right way' to organize academic structures and that no structure in itself can provide guarantees of university success, certain principles need to be observed.

The key role of the department

Becher and Kogan (1992) and Becher and Trowler (2001) argue that departments represent the essential university building block. Becher and Kogan (1992) point to their resilience within the institutional structure and the importance of their command of subject expertise in their field: the department 'embodies a cluster of activities which depend strongly on intellectual ability, technical training, individual creativity and the motivation to exercise all these to the full' (p. 102). Zempski *et al.*, writing in the much more marketized United States system, argue similarly for the centrality of the academic department and urge that 'The way to reform lies not in circumventing the structure endemic to academic institutions across the globe' (Zemski *et al.* 2006: 204). The sense that every department is unique within its university because of its disciplinary authority has sometimes in the past resulted in institutional inertia because it could be used as a protection against arguments for change but the effect of RAE peer review ratings has been to make institutional judgements on the comparative research standing of departments both easier to make and easier to justify. It is undoubtedly the case that the concept of the disciplinary based department has been weakened both by the creation of multi-disciplinary schools and by the adoption of modular degree programmes which can loosen a student's ties with a given academic discipline but Taylor's claim that we are seeing 'the demise of the department as the main unit for the delivery of teaching and research' (Taylor 2006), on the basis of his four case studies, goes too far. Multi-disciplinary schools may fit notions of streamlined resource allocation systems, may serve to reduce criticism of the continuance of small, apparently non-viable departments by sweeping them up into larger subject combinations and may produce a more 'manageable' academic structure but disciplinary groupings still survive both as a key intellectual point of reference and, as in Taylor's case studies, as a tool for student recruitment. Indeed, they are reinforced by the RAE and the state's requirement to measure research excellence. Most importantly the disciplinary based department imposes an academic rigour on both teaching and research, and in practice seems to offer no hindrance in high ranking institutions to interdisciplinary teaching through joint degrees or to collaborative project based research over several disciplines. If we believe that successful universities must be both research intensive and teaching intensive the department, its performance, the way it functions and its reputation are crucial to a university's success.

Departments need to be nurtured and supported. Their leadership, their succession policies and the way they encourage their younger staff should be of continuous interest to a university's central authorities; their success should be celebrated, their disappointments sympathized with. Any resource allocation process should seek, within the constraints available, to ensure that departments are equipped as best they can be to meet their research and teaching responsibilities. Departments themselves need to have confidence in that process even if it does not always deliver the resources they feel they should be allocated. The relationship between the departments and their senior staff and the central authorities need to be regularly monitored and kept refreshed; difficulties should be addressed immediately and not allowed to fester. Strong departments can sometimes act as a constraint on the initiative of some of their members, particularly younger staff, who wish to challenge departmental orthodoxies. Universities should, therefore, be sensitive to discordant ideas within departments and sympathetic to calls that they become involved in settling internal departmental disputes rather than permitting such disputes to disrupt academic work and lead to high profile departures or difficulties in staff recruitment. This does not mean that departments should be monolithic. However hospitable and accommodating a department may be to ambitious staff members who are successful in attracting external research support, such staff will want to develop a sense of greater autonomy over their research programmes and generate greater external recognition. Universities should encourage not discourage this and should put only minimal hurdles in the way of permitting them to set up their own identifiable research centres or institutes to serve as vehicles for attracting further support. Some safeguards against academic anarchy, however, are important, the first that there should be a regular review of the justification of the independent structure to prevent it becoming ossified after external research support has dried up, and the second that the head of department should remain formally accountable for the financial and other operations of the research centre because such activities cannot be effectively monitored at the centre without a disproportionate increase in administrative costs. The existence of a penumbra of identifiable research units, centres and institutes in a university is good evidence of individual research ambition and the willingness of the institution to back it.

Good departments will be the main training ground for young academics, establishing codes of academic behaviour, acculturating them into what constitutes good performance, providing them with the professional equipment to succeed in an academic career, and giving them an identity in the 'invisible college' which ensures that they make their mark in the wider world of scholars in their field. This is not to disparage the work of centrally appointed staff development/teaching and learning teams but simply to emphasize that able young academics learn faster from and carry a stronger imprint in their later careers from colleagues in their own discipline within a departmental framework, than they do from more formal institutional attempts to prepare them for future progression. The department plays a vital role in sustaining institutional academic success because it provides the nursery for academic talent and creates the next generation of academic leaders by nurturing their early research successes. These, as a consequence, may in time grow to become the dominant foci of the department's research programme and the areas of work for which the department is best known. By the same token a department has an enormous impact on its students, undergraduate and postgraduate, not just because of the rigour and professionalism of its teaching but because of the social and intellectual atmosphere it provides. Universities seeking financial support from their alumni soon come to accept that however excellent the university may consider itself to be it will be the alumnus' memory of his or her teachers which will exercise the strongest influence on whether that support is given willingly or at all.

Faculty relationships with the centre and the departments

Except in professional areas like medicine, dentistry, agriculture, veterinary science or occasionally engineering or business studies, faculties (or colleges which are faculty look-alikes) do not command the same levels of intellectual collegiality and ideological coherence as the department; effective deans or college heads will only very rarely be regarded with the same academic or intellectual respect as effective heads of departments, and their very effectiveness may be the subject of suspicion in respect to those on whose behalf they are being most effective. Faculties as administrative units risk becoming a bureaucratic layer which buffers and sometimes acts by design to seal off relationships between the centre and departments. In addition where they have resource allocation powers they are much more likely than central bodies to take parochial decisions which fail to take account of wider strategic considerations and the external environment. A faculty resources committee will usually comprise representatives of all the main bidders for support and, whatever formulae are used to assist distribution, will be influenced by the internal politics of the faculty. The dangers of insularity and the impact of personalities and departmental rivalry is even greater where faculties play a role in the annual review for the promotion of academic staff. Where deans or college heads are given decision making powers they inevitably lack the standing and strategic authority of the vice-chancellor and will always be at risk of being suspected of horse trading by their senior colleagues or of excessive loyalty either to the centre or to individual colleagues or disciplines within the faculty. Externally appointed deans or college heads on fixed term appointments can even more easily become isolated. Because they have no departmental base and no defined teaching and research role that binds them to colleagues they risk being thought of as external agents pursuing an agenda laid down in the centre. In a crisis, externally appointed deans and college heads can be outvoted by their faculty boards or heads of department grouping without the prospect that, like internally appointed deans, they can return to their departments of origin. On the other hand, if the internal pressures become too great they can abandon the central university strategic perspective for which they were appointed and become the faculty's most diehard defender against the centre, in which case they lose the confidence of the central authorities. Even in medicine, where traditionally it is accepted that deans must have substantial powers, deans can be undermined by powerful professors whose research standing enables them to exercise their right to open up direct channels of communication with their vice-chancellors.

A prime motivation for devolving central powers to deans of faculties or college heads has been, in large universities, to unclutter the desks of senior officers in the centre and to introduce a more strategic management style where targets and performance measures set centrally can take the place of a more detailed involvement in the day to day issues. In very large universities this may be a necessity but even in such cases the institution that relinquishes an interest in the performance of individual departments is tacitly conceding that its size has outrun its ability to manage its key components. The problem is that the performance measures that can be identified as devolved targets are necessarily simplistic and can have a distorting effect on overall performance. A faculty which has overshot its admissions target may have met one target but may have created conditions where it has tacitly abandoned another, namely, to improve its research rating, or by accepting too many poorly qualified applicants, may have lowered its academic status in the eyes of future applicants so its student number target may be more vulnerable in the following year. Faculty targets for external research income may be met but may conceal telling variations in departmental performance. At the faculty level itself the act of simply passing on the target pro-rated for each department may ignore disciplinary differences in the name of equity of performance.

Targets and performance measures tend to assess specific activities only, whereas university performance needs to be viewed holistically. To raise the performance of a failing department intake quality, course quality, staff quality, research quality, physical resources, staff student ratios and personal relationship issues need to be addressed all together. It is rarely the case that a dean or college head has the freedom or the resources and powers to do this so that only partial measures, often palliatives, tend to be employed; a central authority not only has the ability to make the critical strategic choices but the necessary legal and other powers to implement them. In the end it is the university's performance that will be judged by the public, not the faculty's. Devolution to faculties may seem to simplify academic organization but it may also make it more difficult to raise a university's performance.

There remains an important role for faculties in course approvals, teaching arrangements and maintaining course quality, and for representing academic opinion to the senate/academic board. Departments need a wider forum in which to discuss academic issues, and issues which span the academic interests of several departments. A coherent 'science' view or a 'humanities' view can represent a significant input into university policy. Faculty boards are more appropriate than mono disciplinary departments for providing the machinery to conduct course reviews because they represent a wider span of academic expertise and opinion and, by bringing together departments from conjoint disciplines, they provide a first sift for new course proposals or for considering new research-based centres or institutes. Because they share a common interest in a group of related disciplines they also offer the best machinery for reviewing teaching arrangements, student progress and academic performance within the departments that they represent. In general academic matters faculties make an important contribution. However, where they obtrude between the essential mechanisms for university management in the centre and for the academic operations on the ground in departments, which together give the university its academic cutting edge, they can represent an organizational weakness. Any intervention between these two elements carries costs in terms of decision making which risks being slowed down, made more diffuse and less genuinely strategic. Institutional size is often put forward as the argument for devolution to faculties but the organizational impact of student number growth can be mitigated if it is contained within a framework of existing departments which themselves will grow stronger as they increase in size. If, on the other hand, the growth in numbers is accommodated by allowing departments to bifurcate or by creating wholly new departments round new disciplines then there is a danger of growth being spread too thinly and of departments remaining too small to be internationally competitive. (No actions can be more destructive of internal relationships than the closure of small departments simply on the grounds of their size.) Where a devolved resource management system works best is in medical, dental, veterinary, agriculture or business schools where departments or academic disciplines combine to contribute to a single or to a homogenous range of undergraduate programmes. Where it works worst is where faculties have a mixture of strong and weak, and large and small, departments and where deans or provosts or faculty resource allocation committees have the task of restructuring the departmental mix but are too close to their constituent departments to do it effectively and where, in any case, the decision making bodies hold only a partial grasp of the levers that are required to produce change.

Deans

It has, as we have seen above, become the fashion since the late 1990s, even in some research intensive universities to make external appointments to full time executive deanships and to reinforce the role by establishing so-called colleges and according the dean the title of college head, and often with the rank of pro-vice-chancellor. It is too early to assess the effectiveness of this as a model. On the one hand, in very large universities, it may offer an inescapable substitute for the traditional management role of a vice-chancellor in a sector of the institution. On the other, in universities of medium to large size, it risks introducing a costly, managerial approach which in practice may offer no greater level of effectiveness than a dean elected or appointed from within the faculty who may retain academic links with the faculty through teaching or research and who carries the faculty's confidence. External appointments may offer the prospect of short term gain but no longer term advantage, and the disadvantage that they may lack the implicit sense of colleagueship which the internal appointments bring.

If it is necessary (as this book argues) for a dean to be firmly located within the academic fabric of a faculty, to be an academic colleague, fellow teacher and researcher and member of an academic department in order to be effective as dean in relation to the interests of the faculty, so it is also important that the dean is not isolated from the central decision making of the institution. This is often the case where there is a high degree of financial devolution to a dean when it can be argued centrally that deans should be measured on the basis of the performance of their faculties. In such circumstances central management's task is to incentivize the dean, not the faculty, and to act, in business terms, as the strategic control or financial control group at corporate headquarters (see Campbell and Goold 1988 below). Deans who are external to the central decision making process, however, lose much of their value to the university because effectively they can only transmit messages in one direction, from the faculty to the centre. Where elected deans are not part of the central institutional management process or, for example, are simply members of a deans committee whose remit is limited to coordinating faculty business, their vision all too quickly narrows to an interest in protecting their own faculty in competition with other faculties, and in arguing for their own faculty interests above those of the university. Such a position can be destructive of good university management and can reduce all consideration of institutional issues to a negotiation about the self interests of the institution's constituent parts.

It is, therefore, just as essential for a dean, even in a university with well articulated and direct centre/department relationships, to be part of the central management decision making process. The deans must be part of the 'steering core' because without them the steering core can become detached from the institution's essential business of teaching and research and dominated by central administrative business, or by strategic thinking that is not adequately rooted in the academic interests of the institution; it can rapidly lose touch with what is happening in departments. By the same token, particularly in the more complex mixed economy of the modern university, deans need to understand the constraints of institutional decision making and feel responsible for the central management of the university by being part of it. Only if they can legitimately claim such a role are they in a position to exercise authority at faculty level by helping to determine priorities and initiating or supporting innovative new activities. Under such a structure deans come to act as a crucial interface between central and departmental interests, transmitting messages in both directions and ensuring, through their membership of key central decision making bodies, that the faculty voice, the academic interest, remains at the heart of the process. Elected deans may not be 'executive' in the sense that they have not been appointed by an authority outside the faculty and not been given formal managerial powers over their faculty colleagues, but they can certainly be executive in the sense that they are part of a corporate decision making structure; because it is recognized that they have to balance corporate and representational responsibilities, they can develop considerable executive authority. Effective service as a dean in such circumstances can represent an obvious first preparational step to becoming a vice-chancellor.

Maintaining short lines of communication

The point has already been made in Chapter 2 that an essential characteristic of the modern successful university is the speed of communication that is necessary between different parts of a university. Nowhere is this so true as between academic departments and the centre. In Chapter 2 it is emphasized that good academic performance is made up not of a series of isolated processes but of a closely interrelated network of activities which combine to produce an effective, academic product. In an inter-university competitive environment, how a single staff vacancy is filled or whether a particular allocation of equipment grant is made can have strategic importance for a department and, therefore, on the department's, and on the university's longer term performance. The recruitment of a single professor may transform an under-performing department into becoming almost overnight an exceptional department because of the way the professor's research interests integrate with other departmental interests in teaching and research or releases and encourages research interests latent in a department. At the same time the loss of an individual professor or even, in a small department, an individual lecturer, may be a potential blow to a department's future so that the university has to take steps, outside the normal rules, to try to persuade them to remain. What these examples illustrate is the importance of maintaining short lines of communication between the centre and departments. In the past the concept of the vice-chancellor's or the registrar's door being always open to academic colleagues was a euphemism for being readily available for informal consultation. Now, the need to move quickly, the ability to be available for a meeting within 24 hours on matters of academic priority, the willingness to communicate out of hours in the evenings or at weekends and the requirement to take decisions sometimes involving significant expenditure within a week or less, marks a necessary acceleration from the more leisurely processes of the past.

But channels of communication must necessarily be wider and deeper than this. Senior people, academics or administrators, working in the centre of a major university should know their senior colleagues in academic departments individually, and the social life of the institution should be so organized that people meet frequently and informally in conditions that encourage them to talk freely. Visit any successful university and you will find that at lunchtime there are places where people eat together whether it is a senior common room, a university restaurant or bar, a college dining room, or a faculty snack bar. Drinks after public lectures, drinks before university events, coffee before senate/academic board or in breaks during senate meetings, social events in departments are all necessary adjuncts to the pursuit of university business. Universities comprise a series of networks, academic, physical (in terms of a building or a floor), social or linked to the conduct of university business. The speed with which information (and gossip) travels round these networks is a good indication of how effective a university's internal communication is when there is an issue to be settled or a problem solved. Of course universities will have formal communication systems, both electronic and paper based, but in successful universities, where interest in what is going on in the institution is widespread, it will be the personal networks that are the most important at critical times.

The kind of university decision making that builds success and raises performance is much more to do with getting a myriad of quite small decisions right within an agreed strategic framework and an appropriate timeframe than big fundamental decisions that require major shifts in resources. Success is cumulative, not normally achieved by taking a single decision, or in a single event: new staff members are appointed, they attract research grants and research students, they need more laboratory space and it has to be found, they need an equipment allocation and it has to be made, they need conference fees and travel money to present their research, they win more research grants, attract more research students, need more space, need more equipment and before anyone realizes how quickly time has passed they are being headhunted for readerships or chairs at another university and the university must act quickly to protect its investment, which may mean fast tracked promotion and the provision of more space and more equipment. (Parallel stories can be found in the humanities and social sciences where library support or study leave can be substituted for laboratory space and equipment.) Building success and sustaining it is achieved only by a constant sensitivity to the process of academic performance, and taking the right decisions in a timely fashion in a way that conforms with the grain of academic behaviour. University success is predicated much more on achieving the most effective outcomes on a host of relatively small but individually critical issues than in lengthy debate over large ones. These issues can only be decided effectively at the crucial moments if the department and the centre are in close and regular communication: in two of Jarzabkowski's three sample institutions, both ranked in the top seven in Tables 1 and 2 (see pages 11 and 14 respectively), 'face to face interaction is a key negotation technique for maintaining coherence within the system' (Jarzabkowski 2003). Intermediary structures not only slow down the process but cut into the communication cycle.

As universities grow larger, maintaining this degree of connection between the centre and the departments becomes more difficult and makes greater demands on the energy of both, but particularly on the centre. Pro-vice-chancellors and other senior professors become more important as intermediaries; new structures may have to be invented to encourage dialogue about departmental and institutional objectives; the roles of heads of departments and deans grow in interpreting departmental needs and in explaining university priorities to their departmental colleagues. At some point size may indeed determine that the connection no longer exists in any real form but good universities seem to postpone this for as long as possible, because they have established so many channels of communication both formal and informal that providing there are not unexpected large scale changes in key personnel the essential links survive. Change can be precipitated when some significant alteration in the academic structure occurs, for example, as a result of a merger with another institution, the founding of a large and wholly new activity like a medical school or the decision to develop a new campus. But it remains the fact that the strong centre: strong department matrix appears to offer the most effective organizational structure for modern conditions because it provides direct and speedy communication between the critical action points and clear, quick and unambiguous routes to decision making in a way that a strong centre: strong faculty organization does not. Academic issues do not often come in tidy parcels but in loose bundles trailing secondary and even tertiary issues in their wake. Re-packaging them and finding the right solutions is rarely achieved most effectively by faculty organizations not only because they lack the necessary authority in all areas and the university breadth of vision but because their communication systems are less direct and are too often cluttered with conflicts of interest which slow the process down. The retention of the strong centre:strong department relationship in delivering academic success should be regarded as a key strategic issue in any consideration of new academic developments which might weaken it. Universities need to consider very critically any departure from a structure that contributes so much to success.

The role of the centre

The decision making centre of any university will be personalized as revolving round a few key individuals but in practice the effective centre should incorporate the significant number of colleagues from academic departments and from faculties who form central resource allocation committees, strategy committees (which will also have some lay membership) and academic committees. Some of these bodies will be chaired by the vice-chancellor and some by pro-vice-chancellors, who themselves, by retaining an academic presence in their departments, provide one of many bridges into the academic community. But these bodies will also contain variously deans and other nominees of senates/academic boards and governing bodies or of faculties. It should not be possible to describe the centre as presenting a monolithic view of the university's affairs. But the centre must also include the senior administrative officers, the registrar and the senior staff responsible for academic matters, finance and the estate and their senior colleagues, who may in some people's eyes be thought of as likely to present a monolithic view, whether or not they do so. A centre which only comprises administrative, that is non-teaching, officers will certainly be regarded as monolithic by those outside it even if it has the appearance of being effective; a centre comprising only part-time members, that is academics, will find it hard to be effective and may become factionalized over particular issues. For this reason the centre should include a mixture of academics, elected or appointed to serve as members of particular committees working in close consort with a vice-chancellor and full-time professionals in the field. The latter, though influential, may not be formal decision makers much of the time. For some issues the 'centre' will be joined by senior lay members from the governing body in order to bring a wider perspective into discussions. Such a centre will have some important characteristics – it will create the 'strengthened steering core' (Clark 1998) which meets regularly and has decision making powers; its academic members will take a university not a departmental view of the business in hand; there will be close and supportive relations between administrative and academic members; and it will work within a common culture which, because most of its members are from academic departments, will be transmitted back into departments.

One of the most important features of the steering core is how it is refreshed with new faces and new attitudes. There are serious dangers for institutions when senior appointments such as pro-vice-chancellors or deans are made on a permanent basis or when the 'senior management team' comprises permanent appointments only. Not only do such individuals become identified irrevocably with certain policies but they can too easily lose touch with the academic culture within which they must work; they become managerialist because they lose the patience to persuade and argue, and take the short cut of imposing solutions on unconvinced colleagues. A centre that is made up of personalities most of whom change every three or four years and who come out of departments and return to departments, ensures that central thinking becomes diffused around the institution and, when a crisis has to be resolved, a core of former office holders may be available to be drawn in to give their views. New faces bring new views; while the learning curve about university policies may seem to be disrupted by regular turnovers within the steering core, and less efficient than permanent appointments, the new faces bring new experience to the top table which can dissipate any fixed mindset about a range of issues that may have taken hold of the senior management team. At the professional levels it is also important that the centre does not ossify and that there is movement in the senior positions with people moving onto posts elsewhere to be replaced by younger but equally able people from within. Succession planning makes a critical contribution to preserving an effective central steering core. While it is sometimes hard for academics recently appointed to a central academic resource allocation body to divest themselves from taking a faculty or even a departmental view the effort of doing so, especially when, round the table, the more experienced members can provide a good example, represents the key realization of the ideal of university self governance. And the decisions that such a group will produce will be better because they have been arrived at after discussion, and be more respected and less challenged than those taken by individuals holding permanent positions whose attitudes have been hardened by long exposure to similar issues.

Even when it is agreed that a centre:department matrix is the most desirable of the models, the character and mode of the central steering core must be examined. Campbell and Goold suggest that in companies, relationships between the centre and business units (for which read academic departments) can be defined as falling under the descriptions: strategic planning, strategic control and financial control (Campbell and Goold 1988). While in a company it is possible to ask whether a business unit would perform better as an independent company, in a way that is much less feasible in the university context, it remains the case that it is possible in both types of organization to ask how much value the centre itself adds to the organization or to the business unit or academic department. Campbell and Goold identify a series of tensions in the centre:business unit relationship, all of which are relevant in universities: strong leadership in the centre which gives clear directions as to product and markets *vis-à-vis* the desirability of releasing energy and entrepreneurial commitment in the business unit; coordination from the centre and accountability from the business unit *vis-à-vis* cooperation between the centre and the business unit; a shared responsibility, thorough analysis and planning *vis-à-vis* entrepreneurial speed of response; long term strategic targets *vis-à-vis* short term financial targets; and tight financial controls *vis-à-vis* flexible strategies. Even in the most relaxed of the Campbell and Goold headings, strategic planning, the danger is that planning takes up too much time and inhibits the freedom of the business units, while in the least relaxed, the tight financial control model, business units can be discouraged from being adventurous because they are required to meet short term financial targets to satisfy shareholders.

Very similar considerations apply in universities. A university's position, however, is compounded by the need to satisfy the demands of an extensive regulatory framework while at the same time observing a market orientation and practising private sector style innovation. Many universities tend to follow Campbell and Goold's coordination and accountability model with varying degrees of rigour in relation to faculties and departments because of the pressures exerted by these demands, while others, certainly the more successful universities, encourage the more entrepreneurial models where a great deal of initiative is left to departments. It is unwise to load responsibility for all central decision making onto one body be it a governing body, a vice-chancellor or a senior management team but to disperse it: the steering core then becomes a network of bodies which are coordinated via cross membership and the involvement of a small group of university officers. Thus while the strategic control function might be located in the central steering group, strategic planning would be the function of a strategy committee and the financial control function would be the responsibility of the finance committee with delegation to a budget monitoring group or to an academic resource allocation body. Woodfield and Kennie (2007) provide an interesting analysis of top management teams in universities and categorize four different types each having a different role: the academic/administrative committee (advisory and consensual), the vice-chancellors' advisory group (advisory and directive), the executive board (corporate and consensual) and the chief executive officer's (corporate and directive) while conceding that not all research intensive universities would claim to have what they call a 'top management team' at all. It is clear that the first and third of these models fit more closely with the research intensive university but the corporate model carries the danger that an over dominant vice-chancellor might exercise too forceful an influence on decision making without the possibility of challenge within a decision making network.

Much more than a private company of similar size a university's 'strengthened steering core' should have a high 'buzz' factor: it should be permeable to individuals with new ideas because universities encourage individualism much more than companies but, because universities are much more subject to external controls, their financial controls need to be at least as tough as those to be found in the best companies. The two fatal positions, both of which can be found without difficulty in universities, are either to believe that all the good ideas emanate from the centre or that the nature of universities determines that ideas essentially come from academic departments and that the role of the centre is simply to wait for them to emerge. The great strength of the centre:department matrix is that the communication, networking and decision making required to make it work effectively, is faster and more direct than other models and incentivizes creativity and a sense of corporate endeavour.

Collegiality or managerial direction

In 1966 a distinguished vice-chancellor wrote:

It is clear that the optimal distribution of responsibility for academic management is not the most economical of time and effort. A much smaller and more authoritarian oligarchy, with a tight hierarchy of subordinates could reduce the size and complexity of the committee system. It would, however, be unacceptable for the valid reason that under it academic freedom would be restricted and academics would carry out

research and teaching less well. The academic does not produce best
performance to order.

(Aitken 1966: 77)

He went on to condemn the notion of 'making deanships into full time
appointments'. Times have changed, the Jarrett Report was not yet written
and the pressures of financial stringency, growth in student numbers and
accountability have tightened the way that universities must be run from
the more relaxed mode of the 1960s. Whether or not vice-chancellors in the
pre-1992 universities are really chief executives in the 'business' sense that
Jarratt used may be open to question (Shattock 2002) but they are certainly accountable for their university's financial management under public
finance rules and, even in the most collegial of institutions, they carry formal
and legal responsibilities for the dismissal of staff and the discipline of students. Universities also require more management now than in the past. The
translation of the polytechnics into universities brought a new model into
the UK university system where the board of governors was given a much
reduced academic membership, the academic board was not given the statutory powers over academic and related matters or the role in strategy that
remains the characteristic of senates in the pre-1992 universities, and vice-
chancellors were designated as chief executives and were given individual
responsibility for advising their boards on the educational mission of their
institutions. Serious questions have been raised about the efficacy of this
model (Knight 2002) but it is also worth bearing in mind that it is not out of
line with the constitutions of US universities where, nevertheless, a long
tradition survives of 'shared governance' (Shattock 2006). Much depends on
the way the constitution is interpreted in practice. Nevertheless if we wish to
polarize positions in respect to collegiality and managerial direction in the
modern university world two statements from the North Report (University
of Oxford 1997) can be used to do so. The first comes from an account of
Cambridge:

> People at Cambridge see the University as a largely self governing 'com-
> munity of scholars' with relatively little outside lay advice – not a top
> down managed institution. The academics work very hard – but 'would
> be unlikely to have the same motivation' under a regime of the latter
> type. 'The present system works well and it would be absurd to change it'.
> The problem is to keep this ethos while meeting the demands of the new
> world for which the University must be well organised.

The second from DeMontfort University, a post-1992 institution, where the
University has

> a compact structure with a small Board of Governors working closely
> with a Chief Executive ... who really is the Chief Executive and has
> considerable delegated powers; the Chief Executive runs the institu-
> tion with the Senior Executive including four Pro-Vice-Chancellors,
> two Associate Vice-Chancellors, the Director of Finance, the Academic

Registrar, and the Director of Personnel . . . There is a matrix management structure.

These statements represent the opposite ends of a broad spectrum. The weaknesses of the Cambridge structure have been exposed in the Capsa Inquiry but the report recognized both the University's position as 'academically the most successful University in the UK' and the need 'to retain its all important tradition of academic self-government while at the same time preventing it from lapsing into cosiness and injecting into its governance a set of more rigorous and self-critical attitudes' (Shattock 2001b). But the report identified as serious weaknesses the 'tradition of suspicion if not hostility' between the central administration and the departments, and the undervaluing and underfunding of the former, and the lack of external lay involvement in the financial governance of the University. Cambridge's success cannot simply be ascribed to collegiality and its adherence to the notion of a university as a 'community of scholars' but must also be attributed to its inherent advantages of history, wealth and what Gueno describes as the Matthew effect (see p. 15). Nevertheless while a collegial style of university management and the close involvement of the academic community in all key decisions may not, as Aitken said, be 'the most economical of time and effort' it is nevertheless a characteristic of the management of all the top seven group of universities.

Hardy in *The Politics of Collegiality* (1996) defines the collegial, political, the 'organized anarchy', bureaucratic and technocratic approaches to decision making. In her analysis of how Canadian universities coped with retrenchment in the 1980s she ascribes characteristics to them which draw on these definitions. Thus Toronto operated as a 'federal bureaucracy', where power was devolved to deans who had a distant line authority relationship with the central administration, which itself worked closely with the governing council. Montreal, on the other hand, had a technocratic style run by 'a cabinet of president and vice-presidents', in which the deans were relatively powerless to influence institutional decisions because of the centralization of decision making, with cuts being determined by the central administration according to productivity formulae leaving the deans powerless to challenge the decisions which were implicit from the application of the formulae. At British Columbia on the other hand a more political style was employed with deans confronting one another as well as the centre and with confrontations between the faculty association and the governing body over the dismissal of tenured faculty staff, embarked upon to demonstrate the 'tougher' approach which the new situation demanded. McGill and Carleton represented the collegial approach. In the former, global budgets were devolved to departments leaving the deans, who formed a cohesive group, playing a middle management role from an institutional perspective. In the latter, although decisions were highly centralized, the deans played a part in the process and operated as senior managers of the university, not just as CEOs of their faculties. It would be easy to find examples of bureaucratic and technocratic approaches in the way UK universities approached the cuts in the UK in the 1980s and subsequently. None of the top ranked universities opted for anything but the collegial style in the 1980s as also did Salford, the most heavily cut university; this was certainly one of the most important reasons why it survived. However, under the continuing pressure of financial stringency universities have become much less collegial and, in many post-1992 universities, much more 'technocratic' in handling staff reductions: a vice-chancellor recruited from Australia may be typical of the school of thought which argues that 'committees cannot be held accountable, only managers' (Schwarz 2003). Hardy's evidence points in a different direction: although the demands for making do with less and for greater accountability push universities towards detailed planning mechanisms and controls, collegiality 'remains an important mechanism in managing the competing pressures' and 'is more conducive to meeting the challenges facing higher education . . . Moreover it is much more likely to encourage creativity and innovation' (Hardy 1996: 183).

Even if we look at the private sector we find that modern, particularly science-based companies, operate with a high degree of collegiality, quite unlike the top-down management style that is the characteristic, for example, of the manufacturing sector. A report from the Centre for Tomorrow's Company points up the positive relationship that exists between employee ownership, participation in wider policy decisions and the company's level of performance: a participative style of management in employee owned companies appears to produce increases in productivity, quality innovation, sales turnover and profitability. Companies in the US where employees owned more than 10 per cent of the stock, outperformed all the leading indices over an eight year span with a £100 investment in 1992 being worth £370 in 2000 compared to £186 in all companies in the FTSE share index (Claverly and Goyder 2001) suggesting that participation or collegiality can be justified as offering greater effectiveness in a business sense rather than simply being viewed as a means of incentivizing employees by demonstrating that they have a stake in the company's success. De Vries argues that evidence from some of the most successful companies is that they know how to select, develop and retain people who make a difference. Trust is an important element in leadership and 'with trust comes candour, the willingness of people to speak their minds. When people are reluctant to discuss their ideas and thoughts openly, realism disappears and the quality of decision making deteriorates' (Kets de Vries 2002). Such companies empower their staff, exploit team work and encourage group decision making.

The main argument for a collegial style of management in universities is quite simply that it is the most effective method of achieving success in the core business. Unless the academic community, which is responsible for the direct expenditure of about 70 per cent of a university's budget, is given a substantial stake in how the budget is to be constructed and allocated, it is unrealistic to expect it to be committed to the budget strategy that emerges. Unless academics who run departments which have turnovers that equate to that of a medium sized company are regarded as having the standing and competence to contribute to a discussion on university financial policy then they will feel less committed to the institution and be much less reconciled to the financial policies it adopts. Unless academics who are involved in the public life of the country – advising government and corporations, making significant advances in research, or organizing teaching in innovative and cost effective ways – are incorporated into the central decision making processes about institutional policy, the policies that emerge will not focus on the issues that they, who are the main contributors to a university's performance, will regard as the most important for achieving institutional success. This is not an argument that universities, particularly in hard times, should be run on the basis of a consensus, but that universities work best when difficult decisions, especially those about budget reductions, are exposed to comment and are seen to be based on rational argument. This will ensure a trust in the process even if it cannot eliminate disagreement with the policies to be pursued. The contrast between a managerial and a collegial approach to running a university could be taken to imply that academic failure may be more tolerated under the collegial approach. Nothing could be further from the truth. In many ways the decisions of a properly constructed community of scholars operating in a competitive market are likely to be tougher than a managerialist regime because, as RAE or research council panels have demonstrated, on academic matters the academic community is likely to draw lines and make judgements more confidently than non-academic leaders. A promotions committee operating in an academically successful university reviewing recommendations for promotion from lecturer to senior lecturer or reader, or from reader to professor may take more time than a single chief executive would do over the details of each case and how it matches with the prescribed criteria for promotion but will generally be more decisive in its outcome because making judgements about academic quality whether in respect to student examinations, or in assessing research proposals or in refereeing articles for publication lies at the heart of academic life. Academics at successful universities do not shrink from making hard choices because they make them almost daily on issues of academic performance. The evidence of the league tables seems to point to the fact that the managerialist style where a significant academic voice is excluded from strategic decision making and where academic opinion is distanced from day-to-day institutional management significantly disadvantages an institution. Other factors are, of course, involved but if we look only at the pre-1992 universities, with their greater entrenchment of academic participation in governance and management it is nevertheless possible to identify institutions where a more managerialist approach to the running of the university may have contributed adversely to their position in the tables.

This does not mean that collegial institutions do not require leadership and management but only that their leadership and management needs to be tailored to their communities. It is obvious, for example, that a department, however distinguished its members, needs to be well led to ensure that its performance matches its potential. Methods of choosing heads of departments vary. Jarratt recommended a direct appointment by the governing body, on the recommendation of the vice-chancellor, but did not discuss what criteria a vice-chancellor should employ. Some universities follow a consultation process coordinated by the vice-chancellor, others a straight election with some restriction as to the levels of seniority of the staff eligible to stand. Neither process is altogether satisfactory: an imposed appointment will get less out of the staff than a head they have selected and may be less effective in sorting out disagreements, but an elected post may throw up single issue candidates whose competence and judgement in managing colleagues and representing the department in bids for resources may be limited. In research intensive universities the most appropriate staff to lead a department will have to be persuaded to take the job because the weight of administration involved means reducing their research commitments or slowing down their publication rates.

Schwarz has argued an extreme view:

> academics are not going to vote for a manager who advocates cutting their programmes. The result is that only those people with no plans or those who promise everyone whatever they wish to hear are elected. University managers, including deans and heads of departments should not be elected but should be selected for their management ability. This will give them dignity and authority. Also managers who are hired can be fired – a key element of accountability.
>
> (Schwarz 2003)

Such a crudely managerial statement would not accord with the experience of research intensive universities. This assertion of the effectiveness of the process of appointment over election was coincident with a well publicized election at McKinsey, one of the world's most successful management consulting firms, to fill its top post from amongst its partners. The truth is that there is little evidence to support Schwarz's view amongst professional groups and in many such fields, for example, in legal and accounting firms, elections appear to work well.

If we accept that the performance of academic departments is key to a university's success a university must have a close regard to their leadership, and the bottom-up processes of election necessary to demonstrate support and confidence amongst the departmental staff and the top-down appointment from a higher authority, need to be brought together in a process that offers proper safeguards to both departmental and university interests, but leaves the university with the right to make an appointment by external advertisement and recruitment if internal procedures fail. Similar considerations apply to appointments at the levels of dean and pro-vice-chancellor but different solutions may be required. Unless the dean is in medicine, dentistry, veterinary science or agriculture, or is the holder of a substantial devolved budget, election by a faculty board seems to be the most desirable process because the board is seeking an appointment which will best represent its interests at higher levels. Confidence in the dean at faculty level may be a crucial element in persuading colleagues to accept difficult decisions when they have to be taken, such as to reduce course offerings, close a department, or expand student numbers without the promise of matching resources. Where the dean is a devolved budget holder an appointment from within the faculty but by a university committee represents the most desirable approach (assuming there is an appropriate candidate) although as we have seen appointments from outside are increasingly common. Such appointments, however, are unlikely to command the kind of support that might be accorded to an internal candidate when unpopular decisions have to be taken. For a pro-vice-chancellor, since the post holder acts for the vice-chancellor, while widespread consultation is necessary, the appointment must ultimately be nominated to the governing body by the vice-chancellor after endorsement by the senate. Again, external appointments have become more frequent but Smith *et al.*, who provide a useful account of how pro-vice-chancellors are appointed, confirm that the great majority of research intensive universities continue to make internal appointments rather than opting for external candidates (Smith *et al.* 2007).

In each such case, therefore, the senior academic managerial posts are best filled only after extensive academic involvement even though the university retains the final right of appointment. This degree of collegial involvement is not, as Schwarz might argue, a gesture to a pre-Jarrett tradition but a reflection first of the need to take great care over the most important academic managerial appointments, second of the need to make sure that the appointees are acceptable to the professionals whom they will be 'managing' and third of the need to identify the academic community with the process.

To sustain success, universities will always have to take decisions or make choices between alternatives which are contested because they affect colleagues adversely. Mostly these decisions involve money: whether to close a department or reinvest in it with the rider that it must have new leadership and shed some staff; whether to back project X with matching funds and not project Y; whether to make a new building for one department a priority over all other capital proposals; whether to increase the maintenance budget at the expense of new academic posts. But sometimes they involve just people or academic principles. What is to be done about a professor the quality of whose work is in steep decline? Should bright young fast trackers be promoted over more senior colleagues who have contributed a great deal to the institution? When should the university actively oppose an external initiative that might affect its future and when should it resist submitting a damaging response in order to fight another day? Collegial universities are actually much more effective at taking these kinds of decisions than top-down institutions especially if they have a cabinet form of governance which is well suited to discuss them. A university which is geared to success will have developed mechanisms for taking such decisions, in a way that enables relevant consultation and due process to occur. Top-down non-participative institutions are much more likely to take such decisions in isolation, without the benefit of close academic scrutiny and discussion; as a result they may be less good decisions and they may alienate sections of the academic community they are most dependent on for success.

Leadership

Leadership constitutes an ambiguous quality in universities and a considerable amount of recent research sponsored by the Leadership Foundation has served only to confirm this. As we have seen the culture of different disciplines inclines them to different perceptions of leadership: an individual leadership style at the vice-chancellor level which would be effective in a university dominated by science and technology might be controversial in a university dominated by humanities and social sciences; faculty based structures that require powerful deans to operate them may work successfully in science, technology and medicine but may be much less successful when applied in the same university to non-scientific faculties. Different institutional missions – research intensive, primarily teaching orientated, internationalist or primarily regional – demand different kinds of vice-chancellors. Goodall argues from an extensive statistical and bibliometric study that top research universities must inevitably be led by leading researchers (Goodall 2009) while the evidence provided by vice-chancellor appointments at primarily teaching orientated universities suggest that managerial qualities are often more looked for. Universities in crisis can be greatly assisted by charismatic leadership styles – Salford at the time of its 1981 budget cut being a good example – but some other universities facing similar budget reductions where there were explicitly strong vice-chancellors were not so successful; very successful universities have sometimes had the self-confidence to accommodate dominant vice-chancellors who have taken them to further success. But more usually the vice-chancellor who tries publicly to exercise a high profile managerialist style is doomed to failure either because even in a middle ranking university there are a sufficient number of academics with strong external reputations to mount a resistance to the exercise of personal power or because in a low ranking university the approach deepens rather than raises the morale of the academic community. Similar problems occur in business. Bankers are said to have created a 'tycoon index' as an aid to assessing lending risks because so many companies run by high profile executives, which have grown rapidly through acquisitions, have subsequently defaulted (Harris 2002). Collins, examining a group of companies which radically improved their performance, found that their chief executives were almost all appointed internally and had no public profile at all (Collins 2001). Strong leaders in universities are for the most part successful because they build robust structures and strong teams and work with them to seek institutional success not because they are always out in front leading the charge. What they also have 'is an understanding of how academics work and an ability to enter into their world' (Ramsden 1998: 126–7).

Midgley and MacLeod examined the attitudes to leadership from selected vice-chancellors of leading universities and all expressed in different ways the need to listen, to persuade, to create an environment for effective decision making and to shape a university vision in partnership with the academic community and lay governors. Consensual rather than charismatic or visionary leadership seems more to match the demands of the most successful universities, or as one person put it: 'It's about listening, then deciding and then leading forward, and not about managerial direction and confrontation' (Midgley and MacLeod 2003). Bolden *et al.* in a well researched report to the Leadership Foundation confirm that 'effective university leadership requires a combination of both individual and collective leadership – what Collinson and Collinson (2006) label "blended leadership" ', although in a carefully nuanced paragraph Bolden suggests that 'despite overwhelming support for a collective leadership approach' staff expressed the need for 'inspirational or visionary individuals, particularly in times of change or transition' (Bolden *et al.* 2008):

> The VC/Principal, in particular, was looked to as setting the overall direction of the organisation, consulting with others but taking the final decision on strategy himself/herself; with a similar perspective often being afforded to Deans and Heads. To this extent it could be argued that the designated leader needs to be given the authority to act on behalf of the group, in effect to be seen as 'doing it for us' (Haslem *et al.* 2001) or acting as a 'socialised charismatic leader' (Howell and Shamir 2005). It may be that if an inspirational leader (not necessarily in a formal management role) embodies shared values they can act as a formal point for collective endeavour and facilitate the engagement of others in the leadership process.
>
> (Bolden *et al.* 2008: 72)

Another more pragmatic approach might be summarized in the Bain (a very successful vice-chancellor of Queen's University, Belfast) principles: 'Lead more and manage less; appoint the best people [to manage]; delegate extensively; focus your efforts [on a limited number of activities]; be visible; don't procrastinate; don't expect gratitude; don't hold grudges; don't believe your rhetoric; don't stay too long' (Bain 2003).

Leadership, however, cannot be restricted to a single post or even to a team or subset of colleagues in the centre. Leadership must be dispersed around a university, in departments, in research groups, amongst administrators and academic support staff, as well as in central decision making. No central leadership group can deliver university success unless there is leadership elsewhere in the institution, particularly at departmental level and within departments, which can, on occasion, confront the centre with alternative strategies. Leadership at the department end of the centre:department matrix is just as necessary to university success as leadership at the centre and one of the key tasks of the centre must be to build up and support leadership in departments. Ramsden (2000) presents a series of principles of academic leadership at the dean/departmental level:

- Leadership is a dynamic process which involves creatively managing tensions between for example tradition and change, having clear goals but giving people the independence to pursue them, executive action and supporting colleagues, endorsing academic values but coping with external forces, adopting both short term objectives and long term issues.
- Leadership is focused on outcomes, that is 'to create conditions that enable high quality research and teaching, and to raise the awareness of staff so that they can welcome change' (pp. 126–7).
- Leadership needs to accept that its operation is multi-level, both institutional and in regard to individual staff.
- Leadership is relational; it occurs in situations and it must be colleagues who determine whether you are a leader.
- Leaders must also be learners about how to do the job.
- Academic leadership must be transformative; it is about 'helping ordinary people to do extraordinary things', helping academics to embrace change, and as a leader, 'transforming ones' own performance' (pp. 126–7).

Ramsden argues that dispersed leadership is essential if universities are to pursue 'active strategies', but 'the more leadership is distributed, the more necessary it is to have clear objectives and high level vision at the centre to which local leaders are committed' (Ramsden 2000: 256). And at a time of potentially negative change for some staff his approach to academic leadership 'calls for a stronger focus on the "softer", human side of leadership as enabling and supporting people, and in aligning their goals to the future of the institution in an innovative way' (p. 256) rather than a top-down, bureaucratic style more concerned to exemplify authority and to impose change.

University structures must then encourage leadership not to try to stifle or circumvent it. These structures must give leaders at all levels an opportunity to contribute to university policy as well as to react to policies developed through the normal processes. This means finding ways and machinery to enable them to do so without necessarily erecting a top heavy committee system. It is especially important that structured face to face dialogues take place with the resource allocation authorities so that a department's needs can be examined, discussed and judged strategically not just addressed formulaicly. If academic leaders, wherever they are situated in an institution, are to be guided by a compass rather than a road map it is important that they are persuaded that the directions the compass gives are the right ones. The task of leadership, whether at the most senior level of the vice-chancellor or at lower levels, is to persuade other leaders of this so that they can persuade their colleagues. The organized anarchy interpretation of university management espoused by Cohen and March (1974) may have had force in the conditions of the 1960s and 1970s but in successful universities at least it has given way to new forms of collegiality where academic and other staff are more willing to adjust their contributions to institutional goals providing they have been convinced by them. Harnessing these contributions is the true task of leadership.

The university and the student body

One of the least convincing metaphors of the higher education market is the student as 'customer'. Look around any university campus as students flow between classes or sit in seminar groups and it will be observed that they exhibit none of the characteristics of the penny wise customer in a retail outlet. Perhaps the analogy is rather stronger at the crucial 'point of sale' when a student is a candidate for a university place, but in successful universities the fact that whether the candidate's own qualifications are sufficient to secure entry are as important an element in the equation as the university's own wish to attract students casts doubt on whether the customer/producer analogy is helpful. Even the National Student Satisfaction Survey while influential in league table rankings seems to have had little formal impact on student behaviour. Certainly for an organization that is very much in partnership with its 'customers' in a teaching and learning process, once they have become university students, the normal university tends to treat them in a formal sense very much as a monopoly contractor. With the introduction of high tuition fees it was argued that this relationship would change but the evidence does not suggest it except in regard to a greater resort to legal action over matters to do with examination results. At the high point of student radicalism in the 1970s it appeared as if student membership of university committees was likely to revolutionize students' contribution to university governance. The revolution faded as student activism declined into more generally consumerist attitudes, but even consumerism has lost its force, as students concentrate more on their finances and on their prospects for future employment. If we think about universities as organizations it is hard to see clearly where the student role in institutional governance has disappeared to. Students may remain members of senates/academic boards and of governing bodies where their views are politely listened to but they are rarely the members who produce new ideas or force through reforms. Indeed the one aspect of student life where the 'customer' analogy may have something of the ring of truth is in relation to students' own organizations: students unions, once the spearhead of aspirations for a larger role in university governance, have become much more active as service organizations catering to a demanding group of consumers.

Yet universities ignore the student voice, difficult as it is to identify, at their peril. From a position of distrust, if not fear, of students unions universities have come to accept them as professional organizations that assist the university in the provision of necessary services. The president of the union, once the spokesman from the barricades, has become a partner in the management of the university and in at least one of the most successful universities is a member of the central steering committee of the university. However, much more important than this sort of positioning, especially in the much less politicized atmosphere of the current period, is the close involvement of students in their academic departments and the formalized methods of consultation about courses, teaching methods and examination systems. This is where the most searching dialogue should take place.

Successful universities stay abreast of changing interests and fashions in regard to educational matters by talking to their students, by seeking out formally and informally their views, and making the adjustments necessary to ensure that the process of education remains attuned to student needs. At the same time they provide routes for quick and effective consultation on immediate campus wide issues so that there is a ready made safety valve if the dynamics of student politics, or some particular grievance, needs urgent attention. The more the president of the students' union can be shown to be a partner in the management of the university the more the student role in making the university work effectively can be realized. Successful universities do not emphasize the student role in governance, although it exists, but the more informal equalities of student relations with academic and administrative staff, with the running of university services and the student contribution to the intellectual life of the university through societies and departmental groups. It is the departmental relationships which count for most, not the grand policy issues that a small number of students participate in the discussion of at major university committees.

Transparency and the availability of data

It is curious that universities, devoted as their staff are to the collection and analysis of information, are often amongst the least professional of organizations in investing in the machinery that will provide data on which good decisions can be made. In a competitive climate it is necessary to make comparisons with one's competitors and to analyse where one's institutional strengths and weaknesses lie: how strong is the undergraduate intake, programme by programme, and where do we stand in comparison with our strongest competitors? What is our research income, department by department, our publication rates and how do our departments compare with our competitors? What are our student retention and completion rates, our value added rates, and our student employment rates? Are departments slipping down or moving up the tables? What are the costs of our central administrative and academic services and how do they compare with similar universities? Do we spend more or less on support staff? Have we more or fewer professors or senior staff than universities of similar size and mission, or more of fewer cleaners (per square metre)? Data of this kind are widely available and can be assembled in useful and thought provoking ways, but many universities only assemble them in isolation and *ad hoc* to answer a particular question and, even when they have done so, fail to distribute it for the academic community to see. Good decision making is dependent on good data and in universities where key policies on, for example, GCE A level intake requirements can initially be formulated at a departmental meeting well away from central data sources, it is essential that such data is made widely available in a comprehensible form. Nothing will cause a departmental meeting more concern than to find that not only is the department just along the corridor doing better but that it is itself slipping down a table of comparator departments in other universities. When the central resource allocation committee is interviewing a head of department about next year's budget allocations the committee and the head of department should both have by them not just comparative data about student/ staff ratios within the university but how the department rates on a range of scores with its competitors. Not only will good data stimulate performance in departments but it strengthens the institution's grip on strategy. Ensuring that it is widely available, discussing it at departmental meetings, committees, senates and governing bodies, and seeking to draw the necessary conclusions represents an essential background to sustaining university success.

Transparency of data needs to be extended to transparency in decision making. This is not just a matter of writing good minutes and communicating decisions quickly. Heads of departments, who we might describe as the battalion commanders of the system, need to understand how central university decisions are made, when items are coming up on agendas, what other decisions may affect them and how they can make an input to a meeting even though they are not a member. The transmission of information electronically makes it possible for agendas and minutes to be made available automatically to all heads of departments and to other interested parties. This, it might be argued, can increase lobbying and slow down decision making but experience suggests that the advantages of improving the flow of information and reducing levels of suspicion outweigh the disadvantages. It also acts as a salutary curb on the committees themselves. University politics can seem to be tortuous and conspiratorial; the more they can be opened up and made internally accountable the better universities will be served and the more effectively they can be managed.

5

Managing the core business

Managing the core business is less a matter of trying to manage teaching and research as distinct elements in a university's work programme and much more about providing the conditions in which excellence will flourish. The chapter reviews the impact of the quality assurance movement and the RAE together with the much more important steps which an institution itself can take to improve performance in a competitive institutional environment. It concludes that such improvements are more the product of a particular kind of organizational culture which drives incremental change than specific, one off, policy decisions, optimistic vision statements or process driven external monitoring.

Creating the conditions for good academic work

Teaching and research are individual activities even when they are conducted in teams and their conduct in a university setting is the product of the professionalism, scholarship and quality of intellectual inquiry, married to appropriate technical skills, which the academic staff bring to the activities. To some extent, therefore, one might argue that if the best staff are appointed and in sufficient numbers, if the infrastructural support for teaching and research is appropriate, if entry to the university is sufficiently competitive to require good levels of pre-university academic level of performance, and if the internal social fabric of the institution encourages intellectual and social exchange amongst students, the concept of seeking to 'manage' the delivery of teaching and research is both unnecessary and undesirable. That would certainly have been the view of universities up to the 1960s and 1970s. Nevertheless the Reynolds Committee (the first body set up by the then Committee of Vice-Chancellors and Principals (CVCP) to look critically at the management of academic processes, and the first RAE, both of which reported in the early 1980s, found worrying divergences from good academic practice and very sharp differences in the quality of research in the then university sector.

The twin pressures of accountability for increased state resources and of competition between institutions encouraged a new acceptance that the institution had a legitimate and corporate responsibility for performance in these fields and a need to see how it could be enhanced. Prestige, funding and the dynamics of student recruitment, combined with new accountability processes, convinced universities that this called for the exercise of a central management role; the creation of the Quality Assurance Agency (QAA) and the continuance of the RAE reinforced this. Nevertheless the extent of central institutional involvement, the level at which it is undertaken (central, faculty, departmental), and the degree of academic self regulation remain critical issues which may vary between research and primarily teaching based universities and on the organizational culture of the institution.

The picture is further confused by the interventionism of external authority which in the case of the QAA can make significant bureaucratic impositions on the conduct of teaching. The QAA concentrates its monitoring on the processes of teaching – the mechanisms, the procedures, the codification of aims and objectives, the lines of authority. It does not engage in any concern over content, what is actually taught or the academic strength of a programme and has abandoned taking any evidence on performance in face to face teaching. Docherty argues that this reflects 'an ideology that is not interested in freedom but rather in constraint' and that the QAA is part of a wider culture of 'managerialist surveillance' (Docherty 2008: 144). Whether this last statement overstates the issue there can be no doubt that the QAA methodology demands compliance in an area of academic life where creativity, imagination and inspiration for learning should be at their most intense; it represents the negation of the excitement of intellectual enquiry or the sense of a learning partnership between teachers and students. The QAA is after all an audit service, and like all audit services, has the power to make public criticisms which can wreak long term damage on institutions: its reports are intended to serve as evidence to be drawn on by potential applicants for university admission and are key components in league tables. (It is alleged that in one case where the QAA recorded a verdict of 'limited confidence' even the university's financial credit rating was affected.) It is not surprising, therefore, that institutions feel compelled to engage in 'gold plating' their quality assurance, an activity defined by the QAA itself as 'employing unnecessary bureaucratic procedures in an attempt to guarantee a good audit outcome' (QAA 2008) and 'preparing large volumes of module boxes, dry runs, road shows and mocks, involving all departments in briefings' (JM Consulting 2005), nor that an industry of quality managers and committees has grown up in universities to ensure compliance.

Birnbaum has described the quality movement, and particularly TQM (total quality management), as a 'management fad' (Birnbaum 2000) but unlike other management fads in higher education, accountability through quality audit has taken firm root in the culture of state–university relations. Universities are right to seek to protect their reputations by achieving favourable QAA audit outcomes – it would be managerially irresponsible not to do so because of the damage to the academic community if a bad report was to be made – but wrong if they then fall into the habit of believing the rhetoric that goes with it. (In too many university central offices there is a tendency to take a jehadist view of QAA principles and seek to enforce them unquestioningly on academic colleagues.) Universities must keep in the forefront of their policies the importance of teaching that is original, imaginative and constantly refreshed with new ideas and new insights from ongoing research and scholarship and not allow themselves to be pressured into permitting process to drive out creativity.

A somewhat similar situation exists with the RAE/REF, although here the academic objectives carry more respect within the academic community. The policy of concentrating research in research active departments is of long standing and has been greatly reinforced by the results of successive RAEs (the concentration of funding in the top rated departments increased from 82 per cent to 86 per cent between 2001 and 2007 (Evidence Ltd. 2009); the attraction of the best departments to the best potential new appointees has always been present. Research activity is spread widely in UK higher education but one quarter of research articles published in 2007 contained at least one author from four of the top rated universities: Oxford, Cambridge, Imperial College and UCL (Evidence Ltd. 2009), institutions which also received 25 per cent of the 2008 RAE research funding. Although 75 per cent of the funds went to only 26 institutions, the distribution of institutions qualifying to receive RAE support is in fact not narrowing and in 2009, 25 institutions were awarded research funding for the first time. Despite this the RAE has its serious operational downsides: the pressure to publish to fit RAE timescales, the exclusion of colleagues from RAE lists in order to achieve a higher rating, the delegation of teaching and examining to part time staff in order to preserve full time staff's time for research, the tactical game playing that enters the construction of the institutional submissions. Like a QAA audit RAE results can spell lasting success or a blow to ambition for institutions and can inevitably generate internal tensions which encourages authoritarian decision making, communication breakdowns and a loss of collegiality. In combination the QAA process and the RAE can be viewed as the kind of intrusions into the core business of universities which might lend some justification to accusations such as Docherty's above. Docherty offers an interesting response to these kinds of pressures. He suggests there are two universities within each institution:

the 'official university', beloved of government agencies and newspapers and that new constituency called 'customers' or 'stakeholders' . . . that describes itself in terms of mission statements, research reports, more or less colourful prospectuses and websites, excellence in teaching standards . . . and so on.

(Docherty 2008: 138–9)

and:

the 'clandestine university' . . . that is occluded behind the journalistic ease and flash of prospectus and league tables . . . that knows itself to be operating somewhat in a subversive fashion . . . [that] is interested in the pursuit of the 'unknown' and in a search for the limits of our knowledge . . . and is identified precisely with *unknowability*, with teaching and research as a combined *search* for knowledge.

(Docherty 2008: 138–9)

In responding, as they must for public policy, self advantage and reputational reasons to these external pressures on teaching and research, successful universities must not forget the 'clandestine university', but must seek to protect it because this is the ultimate source of the vibrancy of their intellectual life and scholarly endeavour. Universities need to respond effectively to these pressures in order to preserve 'clandestinely' their inherent values and ambitions as institutions. And because they are sceptical about New Public Management thinking does not mean that they do not have the responsibility and the incentive in a competitive university world to exercise their own management powers in their own way to monitor and improve performance in their core business.

Teaching

A comparison of the league tables (see pp. 11 and 14) shows that the most research intensive universities generally perform best in teaching, a conclusion that seems to be born out by the satisfaction levels recorded in the National Student Satisfaction Survey, which also records that some of the lowest satisfaction levels appear in the lowest ranked institutions. (This may also reflect that universities doing well in research will have more staff and more resources to draw on.) Their student completion rates are also higher, which may also reflect that they attract academically better qualified students. There are no examples of a primarily teaching university being rated higher for teaching than any of the top 26 research intensive universities nor any which had more favourable student completion rates.

One element in any university's monitoring of teaching must be the maintenance of appropriate data published in useable and comparative form (see pp. 105–106). This should measure academic programme by academic programme, entrance levels, completion rates, final degree classifications, and subsequent employment rates, and the results need to be scrutinized by a central body with powers to enquire into deviations or items of potential concern. Personal tutoring, counselling services and appeals systems require regular review to ensure they remain fit for purpose. These represent bedrock professional tasks to safeguard the institution's effectiveness. Questions of programme content, however, should be matters for academic peers within a faculty or school structure. Not only should new programmes be submitted for critical scrutiny and discussion but regular faculty reviews of programmes should be undertaken to ensure continuing intellectual relevance and coherence, supported by the kind of data referred to above. Staff student liaison committees and departmental meetings should keep ongoing issues under close review.

Maintaining and incentivizing teaching effectiveness is much more a matter of human resource management. There is no doubt that many ambitious departments anxious to improve their research ratings at a time when they have had to accept more students have given way to the temptation to delegate teaching and examining responsibilities to part time staff and research students (following the near universal precedent of the US research university system). In 2009 the Higher Education Academy issued a report which suggested that while 92 per cent of the respondents to their survey thought teaching should be an important factor in promotions only 43 per cent actually thought it was, a figure which fell to 32 per cent in the most research intensive universities. By comparison 84 per cent of respondents thought research was an important factor (HEA 2009). Research progress lends itself to assessment by a staffing committee in a way that teaching does not and until staff are prepared to submit themselves to automatic student assessment reporting and to peer observation, it will continue to remain so.

In spite of the presence of staff development units or centres of academic practice and the provision of institution-wide programmes in teaching skills and approaches the management of teaching remains primarily the responsibility of academic departments or of peer groups sharing and comparing expertise. Departments need to talk about teaching, and with their students; less experienced staff need to be monitored and to sit in on classes given by more experienced colleagues; ideas about teaching methods need to be shared; teaching strategies appropriate to the discipline need to be devised. Good departments produce good teaching as much by peer pressure as by formal methods. It can easily be forgotten that a further component of good teaching is the intellectually curious student. One argument put forward in the 1960s for students studying at universities away from home was the social and intellectual benefits of sharing accommodation and taking part in campus life. Arts centres, student orchestras and theatre groups, subject based societies, political clubs, student union activities and student journalism create an intellectual climate which may mould educational development in students much more than their teachers will do. Universities have a direct interest in sustaining the non-academic intellectual life of the institution because it creates precisely the kind of engaged students, intelligent citizens and innovative graduates that the institution and the national economy needs.

Universities will generally appoint a central committee with a title like the 'academic quality committee' or the 'teaching and learning committee' chaired by a pro-vice-chancellor to oversee general educational issues. Of course, such a committee can do little or anything actually to improve academic quality or teaching and learning because the reality of academic life takes place in the classroom and in departmental decision making but it may exercise an important facilitative and even stimulative role. It may also play an important role in monitoring the external examiner system in terms of the quality of the external examiners appointed and in ensuring that external examiners' criticisms and recommendations are reflected upon and implemented; in this context it must occasionally act as an enforcer. Such committees, however, rarely 'rock the boat' by demanding better staff / student ratios, more expenditure on the library or more up to date IT facilities. The committee will derive its real importance from its interpretation of QAA rule changes in quality assessment or audit practice and the steps that have to be taken within the university to prepare for QAA audit visitations. Since the quality movement's chief concern is about process the committee must ensure that the university's processes are impeccable, that the appropriate boxes can be ticked, and that consistency of practice can be assured. The committee's role must therefore be essentially protective and bureaucratic; it is the 'official' university's front line in delivering a clean audit but if it is to be truly effective it must also provide a rampart behind which the 'clandestine' university can flourish. What the committee's role should not be is to set itself up either as an agent of the QAA or as a body which can impose its academic judgements on the academic programme as a whole unless so requested by the senate/academic board.

Research

Unlike teaching, where comparative performance can only be measured by the dubious statistics of degree classifications and retention rates, research suffers from a surfeit of performance measures, bibliometric and in relation to research grant income, patents, licences and consultancies. Indeed the quantification of citations of published work lies at the heart of most world league tables and of institutional or publication rankings. More immediately the assessment for UK universities of research performance in the RAE/REF is a determinant of institutional national and international standing and a key driver of funding. It is not surprising, therefore, that almost all universities will have a pro-vice-chancellor with a special responsibility for research and that research is seen as somehow 'manageable' in a way that teaching is not. The journal, *Perspectives*, carried a special issue on research management and administration which emphasizes that research management represents a growing profession in itself within universities (Vol 13, no 2, 2009). Green *et al.* (2009) provide a detailed account of how Imperial College uses 'business intelligence' to determine research strategy. The extent to which research is 'manageable' is, however, very much open to debate: academics do not do research to order or choose areas of research specialisms to fit institutional strategies, but they do require time, space, facilities and incentives and can be assisted by management support and by having a research climate to work in, all of which can be provided in institutions which are managed with research priorities in mind. A human resources policy which lays emphasis on research promise in the appointment process, which gives young newly appointed staff low teaching loads in their first two or three years to enable them to initiate their research programmes, which gives generous study leave opportunities and which is known to reward highly research active staff with early promotion is laying the foundations for institutional research success. Institutions demonstrate their priorities by being flexible in the provision of research accommodation, equipment, technical support and library facilities, or support for scholarships for doctoral students; they establish powerful research support offices to assist with research grant and contract applications, and research exploitation, they establish graduate schools which are active in postgraduate recruitment and graduate support which help to create a research climate; they offer specialist fundraising support to build up research centres, institutes and consortia.

This is no more than managing the university so as to create the conditions in which research might be expected to flourish. It emphasizes the prime characteristics of the good research environment, that it stimulates research activity, creativity and innovation within the academic community. Without this individual research may survive but institutional research intensity will not. But managing research goes much further than this and becomes a key area of institutional strategy. Any university faced with a department which, for whatever reason – internal discord, ageing staff, poor leadership, ineffective internal research management, failure to keep pace with changes in the external research environment – is failing in research will know that only active management can redeem the situation. But before action comes analysis (the 'business intelligence' referred to in Green *et al.*'s account at Imperial) – are there pockets of excellence, what is the distribution of external research income and of publications within the department, is the crisis at the senior or the junior staff levels (or both), how strong is student recruitment (undergraduate as well as postgraduate), is the department working in growing or declining nationally identified priority research areas?

Such analysis depends on the provision of effective data and probably on external advice from within the discipline. But in the end decisions will need to be taken – close the department, seek the departures of non-research active staff, recruit new research active staff in given research areas, reinvest heavily in research accommodation and facilities, head hunt for new research leadership. Managing such a process, creating a strategy and implementing it, demands skills of a high order, abundant support within the academic community, the recognition by the department itself that it has been judged by its peers to be failing (rather than by a non-expert management team) and the availability of the financial resources to carry it through. These are not, therefore, decisions that can be made from the office of a pro-vice-chancellor (research) or a dean alone but become intrinsic to institutional strategy and resource management. They may also involve hard choices between different options where academic, financial and even physical planning considerations all come into play.

Reviewing the future of a department with these serious options in mind should be exceptional if the management of a university's research is handled effectively. A university research strategic plan might be expected to require annual reviews of departmental research performance, backed up by detailed data on every individual and comparing performance on a discipline by discipline basis with other institutions. Such reviews provide the opportunity for dialogue with departments about resource requirements, the research environment and potential opportunities for and impediments to progress, and for agreeing targets for future performance. Research strategic plans are much more valuable as a process for thinking about research support needs than for any kind of planning of how research itself will progress. In particular it can rarely predict the external opportunities that may arise from national or international initiatives for which competitive (and often collaborative) bids are sought and which may or may not require some measure of matching financial support, or the possibility of capturing some external research group or facility looking for a new home. It is in these situations that the quality of research management is also evident – in the ability to respond quickly, assemble the human, financial and physical resources that may need to be committed mount a major bid, and to resolve the strategic and other issues that may be involved.

Good research management of this kind requires team work, the coordination of inputs from a number of elements of a university's central management and ready support from its central management committee. Unlike teaching, research is essentially a competitive game both at an individual and at an institutional level; a university that wishes to be a major player must set its processes up accordingly. Research support services must grow with specialist research support professionals participating in the process of research grant applications. In parallel, technology transfer offices have grown in strength and expertise with some universities generating plausible income streams from intellectual property. A recent study, however, confirms that universities that achieve high incomes from this source see such income as a spin-off from their investment in fundamental research rather than as an end in itself (Shattock 2009). A pro-vice-chancellor or dean given responsibility for research must be quick on his/her feet, must have academic judgement that is trusted by colleagues, must be relentlessly positive and collegial in style and must have leadership skills to win support for innovative but essentially risky proposals. Research is inevitably dependent on resources and a pro-vice-chancellor, dean, head of department or project leader must be expert in mobilizing them to produce results.

Improving performance in the core business

Successful universities, operating in a competitive environment, will always seek to improve their performance in teaching and research. However, such improvements are made much less through specific approaches such as 'quality enhancement', in the jargon of the quality industry, but in the generic aim of sustaining the concept of being a good university. The components of this begin with appointing excellent staff, encouraging and incentivizing them and being willing to act when performance is unsatisfactory; but includes providing the right infrastructure for academic work, creating a climate of collegiality where staff are able, as professionals, to participate in critical decisions about the measurement of performance in teaching and research, generating sufficient income to provide staff with time to research, to think and to teach, and students with the facilities to study. But above all it involves maintaining the excitement of intellectual enquiry and the sense of a learning partnership between teachers and students. Sustaining these principles demands a self reliant management style which is able to be at once inclusive and decisive, and supportive and competitive. Continuous improvements in performance are more the product of a particular kind of organizational culture which drives incremental change than specific, one off, policy decisions, optimistic vision statements or process driven external monitoring. There seem to be no short cuts to generating a climate where academic talent and ambition will thrive.

6

Good governance

This chapter argues that good governance is not a guarantee of university success but that effective governance that is congruent with an institution's aims, objectives and culture can make a significant contribution to it. It notes that in the modern period governance is regarded as synonymous with the activities of the governing body but for academics, governance at the level of faculty boards and departments is likely to have a more immediate impact. Efficiency and effectiveness at these levels encourages greater academic participation in governance and management issues. Senates/academic boards vary in size and effectiveness, and even small elected senates find that the pressure of business demands that they set up standing or steering committees to act for them. The chapter argues for close working relations and partnership between senate/academic boards and governing bodies; situations where governing bodies become over dominant in the structure discourage innovation, academic opportunism and quick decision making. Governing bodies remain a crucial element in institutional governance and the chapter lists seven areas where lay members make key contributions, but successful universities try to ensure that governance is kept in balance between an active lay contribution, strong corporate leadership, an effective central steering core and an involved and participative senate/academic board and academic community. Where any element is weak the institution is disadvantaged.

Effectiveness in governance

It is a characteristic of the modern period that when we talk about university governance it is assumed that we are referring to the activities of the governing body. This is partly because in the post-1992 universities the role of the lay dominated governing body is formally much greater than in the post-1992 institutions and partly because national attention has been particularly directed towards the performance of governing bodies both because of a succession of well publicized scandals and because they have been seen as the front line for delivering accountability for institutional performance. The recommendations of the Dearing Committee (NCIHE 1997) and of the Lambert Report (Lambert 2003) and the pressures exerted by the Committee of University Chairmen (CUC) through the medium of its *Guides on University Governance* (CUC 1995, 1998, 2000, 2006) together with the complementary impact of reforms in corporate governance from Cadbury (1994) through to Higgs (2003) have concentrated government and HEFCE's interest on the top layer of university governance. As we have seen in the previous chapter, reforms in the governance and structure of how teaching and research are managed have proceeded apace quite separately (although it has been convincingly argued that the two sets of reforms spring from common New Public Management intellectual roots; Deem *et al.* 2006). Most reports on governance whether in the private sector or in universities are a reaction to something going wrong: the Cadbury Report (1994) reflected shareholders' concern that some Stock Exchange listed companies were corruptly managed and that the way to produce an improvement was to reform company governance structure at board level; the first CUC Guide was a reaction to a succession of incidents of misgovernance in post-1992 universities and colleges. (However, observance of Cadbury rules did not avert a banking crisis any more than the CUC Guides did not prevent a new series of governance crises in universities in 2008–9.) The Hampel Committee, established to update Cadbury, rightly de-emphasized the technical aspects of governance when it said in its report:

> People, team work, leadership, enterprise and skills are what really produce prosperity. There is no single formulae to weld these together and it is dangerous to encourage the belief that rules and regulations about structure will deliver success.
>
> (Hampel Report 1998: 7)

Cambridge, whose governance structure was heavily criticized from inside and outside the University, nevertheless topped every conventional university league table at the time. Did Cambridge succeed academically in spite of its governance shortcomings or because some parts of its governance process were strong and others weak?

The truth is that successful universities are not successful because they have effective governing bodies (although an over dominant governing body might act as a serious obstacle to success), but a significant contribution to their success can be made by effective governance structures which are congruent to their aims, objectives and culture. Governance is not just about what happens at the governing body; a strong senate or academic board may contribute much more to institutional success through its role in governing the academic community in respect to academic process, academic strategy and policy discussion, as well as in reviews of research performance or teaching quality, than ever a governing body can. It is, therefore, just as important to be concerned about the senate's effectiveness as the governing body's;

there are certainly senates and academic boards which have seriously handicapped universities, either because they are ineffective or because they have blocked change. Governance at lower levels is almost equally important in ensuring that processes are applied fairly, judgements made without prejudice and duties and responsibilities distributed in the best interests of the institution as well as the staff's.

A key element in the satisfaction of academic staff in the way a university is run is not whether the governing body is effective but whether their department is appropriately represented on higher bodies and whether these bodies are open to grass roots academic opinion. This requires academic staff to be active in seeking representative roles and willing to commit themselves to the expenditure of time and energy in playing a role in governance. They are more likely to be so if governance is perceived to be conducted effectively. Agendas, papers and minutes need to be produced in a timely and business-like manner to assist rational discussion and to help conclusions to be reached. As Lord Franks wrote in his Committee's Report on Oxford: 'an efficient civil service is the best guarantee of academic democracy' (University of Oxford 1964). Essential elements in the successful operation of good governance at this level are the calibre of the chair and of the secretary of the meeting: both should be given training in the crisp but considerate prosecution of university business. Committees should be about action and decisions, not about discussions that fail to reach conclusions; routine business should be delegated to the secretary or chair so that meetings can concentrate on substantive items. Efficiency and effectiveness are as important at these lower levels of university decision making as they are at the most senior because these bodies represent the building blocks of a governance structure which, if it is to be trusted by its participants, must conduct the necessary business (which is usually in the heartland of the academic process) sensitively but with the maximum of speed and the minimum of fuss. There is no reason why academic business cannot be processed as effectively as any other kind of business providing the climate of the institution lends itself to doing so. The essence of good governance in the modern age is that it delivers strategic decisions quickly and effectively with a maximum of degree of participation by the university community.

The senate or academic board

Any discussion of the role of senates and academic boards must recognize the difference in the powers accorded to them in the pre-1992 university constitutions and the post-1992 (Shattock 2006). In the former we see a bicameral system of governance where the senate has 'supreme' powers in academic matters, with the governing body responsible for finance, building and general management of the institution, while in the latter a unicameral system exists with academic affairs clearly subordinate to the authority of the governing body. In practice a post-1992 academic board can exercise as much influence as a pre-1992 senate in determining academic policy and creating academic strategy, and many do, but the legal position remains and may colour how decisions are made and on what sorts of issues. Senates and academic boards vary in their composition between those that are drawn in specified numbers from designated constituencies (e.g. faculty boards) and therefore have a defined membership, and those that are largely representational, including perhaps the ex-officio membership of all heads of departments or even of all professors. This latter composition, which only occurs in some pre-1992 universities, can, by its nature, be open ended in size and can involve theoretical numbers of over 200. Inevitably this leads to absenteeism and a reliance on some form of executive committee. There is little that can be said in favour of this kind of unreformed body – it does not involve its membership effectively in decisions, it is wasteful of resources, and critical decisions tend to move away from it to the executive committee or some group like a 'Monday morning meeting' or a Senior Management Team (SMT) because the senate is too big to discuss major decisions effectively. The business becomes increasingly formal except when discontent arises on some sectional issue; when this occurs it is difficult to ensure that a rational decision is reached. It is difficult even for a smaller elected senate to keep pace with the day-to-day pressures placed on a university in modern times but the larger, representational senate has no chance of doing so and this has further contributed to it becoming sidelined. Most seriously, the inevitable takeover of decision making powers by a smaller group whether an SMT or some more representational body can prevent the academic community from being forced to confront managerial issues that have to be solved effectively if the institution is to be successful; it marginalizes them and turns them into spectators of the way the university is run rather than being active participants.

Modern conditions do not allow even the smaller, elected senate to play as full a part in decision making as in the past because it would be necessary to call it into session too frequently, so delegation to a standing or steering committee which incorporates a 'Monday morning meeting' agenda, but discards the trivia, becomes essential. Such a body needs to incorporate both key academic and administrative officers – pro-vice-chancellors and deans as well as senior administrators and should be appropriately serviced as a formal university committee which reports on its activities to each senate meeting. Chaired by the vice-chancellor this body, operating within appropriately delegated powers, should, as we have seen from Chapter 3, act as the 'strengthened steering core', and the university 'cabinet' steering the weekly business of the university to those bodies best qualified to deal with it and tackling some of the most difficult and sensitive itself. Not only should its agendas and minutes be available to heads of departments but its reports should form a main item of a senate meeting. There will be other senate committees for resource allocation, for academic policy and for undergraduate and graduate matters. Lambert, by implication, criticized 'participatory' university governance and called for 'dynamic management in an environment where decisions cannot wait for the next committee meeting' (Lambert 2003: para. 7.6) ignoring the fact that it has often been in those universities where dynamic management was most exercised that scandals and disasters have taken place. Of course ossified committee structures can act as a serious obstacle to good decision making but an effective committee structure represents a strength not a weakness to an institution. Quite apart from the need to draw on a broad spread of critical judgements in academic matters, it binds the conduct of university business together, it tangibly involves the academic community in managing the university's affairs and it incorporates into the governance process a range of interests and expertise that few, if any, other organizations can offer.

The essential characteristic of the successful standing/steering or executive committee is that it acts as the hub of the committee structure and is in close touch with other major committees. It must be able to act speedily and decisively on behalf of the university, it must coordinate business going to the senate and offer recommendations as to how to settle contentious issues and it must also monitor the implementation of decisions so as to ensure that the university does not lose momentum. However, it should not be allowed to become a closed community – a rotation of members and office holders is desirable not just to bring in new ideas but to involve more individuals in the key tasks of running the university. It must be dynamic, resilient and intellectually active – members cannot be passive participants but must actively confront issues and want to solve them. The meetings should also be fun; members should look forward to them, enjoy them and find them sometimes exhilarating and challenging. Chairing such a body is a significant task; unless the vice-chancellor knows what the options are on the issues before the committee and can see the priorities for decision he or she will rapidly become overwhelmed by the scale and complexity of the business. There simply is not time to know all the facts on any issue. To make a success of chairing such a committee the vice-chancellor must work extremely closely with the registrar and his or her staff, who, because they are producing most of the papers for decision, need to be active contributors to the discussion.

The relationship between this body and the senate and the council and other bodies within the university is important to the way the operations of the university are perceived internally. To the council it must be seen to deliver a coherent, strategic set of messages on the university's development showing clear evidence that the university's management is meeting the targets it has set itself, but to the senate it needs to show itself capable of producing solutions to problems and to be able to invite solutions or approaches to issues that have to be decided by the institution. It needs to involve senate in policy discussions, educate members on the way issues relate to one another and engage them in helping to resolve them in a way which fits the institution's aspirations. If it dictates to senate it loses its confidence; if it presents indecisive advice to council it risks losing its ability to steer the university's policy framework.

The relationship between senates and academic boards and the governing body

The relationship between an active senate/academic board and a governing body can raise issues of various kinds. In the pre-1992 universities the statutory position of senates makes their relationship with their governing bodies necessarily more of an equal partnership in a bicameral system of governance. Even so it is not any longer possible to accept the statement by Moodie and Eustace that: 'The supreme authority, providing that it is exercised in ways responsible to others, must therefore continue to rest with academics for no one else seems sufficiently qualified to regulate the public affairs of scholars' (1974: 233). Very substantial changes have occurred since 1974 when this was written: universities are no longer fully funded by the UGC and derive their funding from more diversified sources much of it from the private sector, they have taken on a much wider range of public responsibilities, and the state, on behalf of the public, demands much greater accountability for the funds it has allocated not just in respect to expenditure but also for performance. These changes, reinforced by a Financial Memorandum which sets out the terms under which the funding councils make funds available to universities, have required a significant shift of governance back to the governing body, thus reversing the trend in direction during the period between 1945 and the early 1980s. The governing body is accountable both for the stewardship of funds, solvency and internal controls, and for the ultimate determination of institutional strategy. In the post-1992 institutions it is also responsible for the determination of the educational character and mission of the university. A significant question which arises, therefore, is how to construct a governing body structure which is 'sufficiently qualified to regulate the public affairs of scholars' without seeming to reduce the appropriate (and in the case of the pre-1992 universities) the legitimate influence of the senate. The Jarratt Report suggested in 1985 that:

> The relative decline in the influence exercised by Councils has increased the potential to resist change and to exercise a national conservatism. Vice-chancellors and university administrators have in the past been trained to believe that harmony between the two bodies should have a high priority in a university. It may well be, however, that a degree of tension between them is necessary in the circumstances now facing universities, and can be creative and beneficial in the long term. That can only happen if Councils assert themselves.
>
> (Committee of Vice-Chancellors and Principals 1985: 24)

The Jarratt Report was published at a time when universities were struggling with the consequences of the 1981–4 budget cuts and reflected as much the short term problems of establishing priorities, as the longer term relations between senate and governing bodies. Certainly, 25 years later, there would be few supporters of the view that there should be a 'degree of tension' between senates and governing bodies; indeed the more closely they can work together especially in strategic planning and financial management the more effective the university will be. It is true that in the 1980s many senates were unwilling to accept the new realities of financial stringency but there is no evidence that governing bodies were any more adaptable to the new realities than senates. In Cardiff, for example, the governing body was supine in the face of budget cuts and it was only external intervention that prevented bankruptcy (Shattock 1994).

One could argue that nothing could be more likely to be disruptive in a pre-1992 university than a rift between senate and the governing body where a senate espoused academic policies which the governing body rejected, either because it thought them not affordable or because it disagreed with the strategies that lay behind them. This could only lead to stalemate: the governing body would not have the power to create and implement an alternative academic strategy without the consent of the senate. But such a rift would not occur in the same way in a post-1992 university because the power to determine the educational strategy of the institution is ultimately vested in the governing body. An academic board may propose policies but is not in a position legally to block a new policy imposed by a governing body. Indeed there is plenty of evidence of governing bodies imposing strategies on unwilling academic boards. Even as one discusses such possibilities, however, it becomes clear that such divisions severely inhibit the progress of an institution, are likely to discourage staff from seeking to launch new initiatives or acting opportunistically in respect to new academic ventures and to hobble an institution that wants to take decisions quickly. Just as tensions between an academic department and the senate may inhibit academic progress in a particular disciplinary area, so tension between a governing body and a senate is likely to be destructive of academic progress over much wider areas. The atmosphere generated will certainly prompt key academic staff to begin to look elsewhere and will be a deterrent to attracting good people to new appointments. Even in a period of severe financial retrenchment a governing body would be unwise to seek to impose a financial restructuring of a university without consultation with the senate as to the academic and other implications.

In the new universities where tension between governing bodies and academic boards can be institutionalized by the intervention of strongly, managerial vice-chancellors under pressure from their governing bodies to keep their institutions out of deficit, the conditions of financial stringency have made it difficult for academic boards to exercise a distinctive role except in relation to a narrow interpretation of academic policy. The necessarily dominant role exercised by governing bodies in 1988 when polytechnics were transferred from local authority to national control has been an impediment to the development of the close collaboration which characterizes the relations between most pre-1992 governing bodies and their senates. This, together with financial stringency itself, has certainly inhibited innovation and the kind of entrepreneurial academic activity which can be common-place in the most successful of the pre-1992 universities.

Yet partnerships between governing bodies and senates and academic boards are particularly important in periods of financial stringency or actual retrenchment to ensure that the financial/managerial policies and the academic policies are properly aligned. One of the most disturbing findings in a Leadership Foundation report on elements that make up an effective governing body is that 'Just under half of governors and just over a third of senior managers reported that they "don't know" or that there were "not at all" or "rarely" or only "sometimes" constructive working relationships between the two bodies' (Schofield 2009: 57). In a situation where governing bodies meet only four or five times a year and where, in post-1992 universities, governing bodies have minimal academic representation and so are heavily dependent on the advice of the vice-chancellor one would have thought regular and frequent contact with the academic community was a necessity. In universities where such relationships are close they are maintained by a substantial academic membership of the governing body and governing body committees, by joint committees between the two bodies (for example on strategic planning) and by frequent informal social engagement. To carry out their necessary responsibilities effectively governing bodies must under-stand the context of the core business of the university; there is plenty of evidence that dependence on the interpretation of this delivered by a dominant CEO alone can be dangerous and misleading and can lead to the kind of academic mistrust and disillusionment which gives rise to precisely those conditions which prejudice institutional success.

The governing body

If governing bodies have become more important as a control mecha-nism they remain, for universities that use the strengths they can bring, an extremely important component in the management of the university. From the nineteenth century to the present, the involvement of lay members in the governance of universities (outside Oxbridge) has distinguished UK universities from universities in the rest of Europe. In the period up to the Second World War a prime consideration in the appointment of lay mem-bers of governing bodies was their ability to assist in the process of raising non-state income. This need fell away in the post-war period when univer-sities became fully funded by the state and when the economic conditions in which local companies were willing to make capital grants in response to university appeals changed. But it has always been the case, and never more so than in modern conditions, that the close involvement of expert lay people who can bring high level experience of management in other fields into play in the resolution of university problems, in financial forecasting and in making strategic choices, is of great value. Their individual contribution can be summarized under seven headings:

- *Technical and professional advice*
  However professionally well supported a university may be on the financial, legal or property side of its affairs the availability of senior and experienced lay members with a professional background in these fields can be invaluable whether in assessing external advice in respect to decisions on investment policy, legal actions or site purchases or disposals, or in considering financial targets or strategy in relation to building programmes; either may bear heavily on the academic choices a university must make. Discussion at a finance committee where members can bring this kind of expertise to the table can give an institution the confidence to go ahead with a project or can encourage legitimate doubts about the risks involved. Lay members can give the kind of dispassionate advice which must be listened to even by the most committed of academic advocates.

- *Taking the long view*
  University staff, especially those dealing with the daily, weekly and monthly task of keeping pace with external competition can all too easily become reactive rather than pro-active about certain issues. Lay members of governing bodies, like non-executive directors, are able to reflect more on longer term priorities and on immediate needs which their university colleagues may choose to ignore. Lay members may, for example, be concerned about the inadequacy of the financial information the university is generating and may therefore throw their weight behind a capital intensive upgrading of the IT system when internal staff would be willing to risk continuing with the existing system, however unsatisfactory, and spend available funds on academic development. Lay members may give greater priority to avoiding breakdowns, modernizing the system or correcting critical shortfalls of information than staff who have day-to-day responsibilities for keeping the system going. Lay members may take a more ambitious view of site planning because they are thinking on a 25 or 50 year horizon rather than just for the next decade. They will almost certainly take a more positive view of the importance of investment in long term maintenance than a vice-chancellor concerned to maximize the next RAE return. Laymen can sometimes be the chief spokesmen for a university's long term future over the short term interests pursued by their academic or administrative colleagues.

- *Acting as the referee for internal arguments*
  Universities like any other organization can become locked into issues where different sides of an argument become deeply entrenched. These arguments are often best settled by replaying them in front of an informed, but not necessarily expert, committee of lay members empowered to ask the innocent question which opens up the issue in a way that an increasingly 'internal' argument has failed to do. Not only can replaying the argument to a lay audience expose flaws in one side or the other's case but it invites the commonsense impartial solution. The well informed lay member is especially valuable for being a dispassionate observer of the

institution, sensitive to its ambitions but willing to incur its displeasure by pointing out its weaknesses, praising its success but serving as a construct-ive critic when it has failures. The lay member who is only a critic on such occasions is, however, much less valuable than a member who is prepared to serve on a group established to find out what has gone wrong or put the matter right. Lay groups can also be valuable in assessing projects for which entrepreneurial business plans have been drawn up by influential staff both because they can ask questions which the internals may have missed (or occasionally not dared to ask) and because if they pronounce themselves satisfied they engender confidence in the project amongst more cautious colleagues.

- *The layman as critical friend*
  Internal staff rarely recognize a potential drop in performance until it has happened and is drawn to their attention by external authority. A lay member may spot the signs well before the internals and call for an evaluation which identifies a trend to which the internal community had been oblivious.

- *The technical aspects of governance*
  Lay members, like non-executive company directors, play important roles on audit and remuneration committees. However, the non-executive director analogy quickly breaks down at the governing body level itself because no company would seek to run its affairs through a board whose membership contained only one executive director, namely the vice-chancellor. Even in the post-1992 universities where some governing bodies are actually established as company boards, it is anomalous to regard lay members as analogous to company directors because their actual involvement in the day-to-day management of the company is slight and there is no share value or profit level by which a measure of the contribution of the management can be arrived at. Lay members also sit in the capacity of being quasi-representatives of the public interest; in recent years this has been enhanced by the identification of the governing body's responsibilities in legislation, the Financial Memorandum and the CUC *Guide*.

- *Reading the environment*
  The Dearing Report stressed the contribution lay boards can make in identifying changes in the external environment which may bear on internal university discussions. At the most obvious level it would be a short-sighted institution which set up an investment committee without external members knowledgeable in the investment business. But at a wider and more fundamental level one of the most important contribu-tions that lay members can make is to act as the eyes and ears of the institution in business, government and professional circles that university staff would not normally penetrate. Whether at the macro level in respect to the national economy or in respect to new threats or opportunities at

the regional and even the local level the layman can bring an external dimension to university discussion about strategy which is of immense value. Dearing underestimated the extent to which university staff themselves, as advisers to government, consultants to industry or as public figures in their own right, are sensitized to environmental change but was right to stress the unique experience that lay members can bring to internal university debates about strategic planning and long range forecasting about the future.

- *Appointing a vice-chancellor*
Perhaps the most important task a governing body has is the appointment of the person to lead the institution. In post-1992 universities this is the task of a lay dominated governing body alone; in pre-1992 institutions it is a responsibility shared with the senate, normally through the agency of a joint committee. Evidence suggests that these exercises are not always carried out well partly because of the time demands they can make on busy lay members, partly because such events only take place relatively infrequently (on average once every five to seven years, so that the carry over of members from one exercise to the next is small) and partly because the chair, while perhaps experienced in making senior appointments in other walks of life, may not always be so familiar with the messages to be drawn from the curriculum vitae of would-be vice-chancellors. Over reliance on headhunters, while a convenience in some aspects of the exercise, is no substitute for the good judgement of the selection committee. Universities may also make it harder for themselves by almost always making an external appointment. There may be good reasons for this, including the need to bring in new blood and new ideas, but it is worth noting that in industry nearly 75 per cent of appointments to chief executive posts are made from the inside emphasizing the priority given to succession planning, continuity and 'knowing the business'. While this may be prompted by some considerations that do not apply in universities it has the particular advantage that the selection panel is better placed to make an assessment on which to judge future performance and the institution does not suffer the hiatus in policy making which often accompanies the period when an external appointment is settling in to the new post and assessing the strengths and weaknesses of the institution he or she is going to lead. Universities tend to underrate the ability of competent people to rise above the associations they have developed within their own institution and to overrate the concept of appointing a vice-chancellor from outside as a necessary protection against complacency. In continental Europe the election or appointment of rectors from within institutions, which is even more invariable than the UK tradition of appointing from outside, does not seem, in leading universities, to have produced any greater or lesser tendency to initiate reform. Certainly in the UK it is not possible from the rare cases of internal appointments to establish a lower success rate or a higher failure

rate than for external appointments suggesting that selection committees should make a more balanced assessment of the comparative advantages in their own situation than they may sometimes do.

Keeping governance powers in balance

In the modern period we have seen a mixture of a greater belief in market forces and political ideas about the potential effectiveness of governing bodies acting as change agents thus driving the balance of university governance away from what has been described as 'the English ideal' (Knight 2002). This has led to a downgrading of respect for the academic contribution to effective governance in spite of the evidence provided by institutional performance which strongly suggests that those universities that encourage a considerable academic participation in governance are the most successful in the league tables and that those that discourage it the most are amongst the least successful. The Capsa difficulty at Cambridge, on the other hand, suggests that governance that is solely academically driven can suffer from other weaknesses, most notably a 'cosiness' which weakens accountability and results in a serious loss of authority in carrying out the essential legal requirements of corporate governance (Shattock 2001b). However, there is also a question as to whether the almost exclusively lay boards of the post-1992 universities are anything like as effective as it was argued they would be. Bennett's (2002: 298) findings indicate that the boards in his sample:

> could be said to be very efficient but passive bodies, in that they deal with a large number of items at board meetings but mostly without discussion or debate. They could also be said to be rather ineffective bodies, not appearing to have any major impact on the strategic plans and major governance matters of their institutions or overly involved with the monitoring of executive performance.

By contrast, in some institutions we are beginning to see the emergence of over dominant boards, and dominant chairs, laying down performance targets and holding their senior officers to account in ways which would be regarded as crude in any FTSE company (Hodges 2009). The growing interest in very small boards dominated by lay interests represents a step towards an almost complete loss of the academic voice in a university's development.

Governing bodies, whether in pre- or post-1992 universities, need to do a lot better than this. Unfortunately the picture painted by Bennett of a weak or passive governing body will not necessarily be balanced by a strong senate or academic board – indeed, rather the contrary is often the case. More often it encourages the emergence of an over dominant vice-chancellor or chief executive. Successful universities will want to have strong governing bodies working effectively with strong senates and academic boards. But the concept of a strong governing body without a strong senate or academic board is likely, over time, to erode institutional initiative and dynamism. There is a need to rebalance university governance both to retain a strong lay voice in the running of university affairs and to ensure that there is adequate machinery by which the academic community can play a substantive role. 'Shared governance' works both ways – it encourages governing bodies to engage in dialogue between themselves and the academic community and to refer questions to the senate/academic board for a view rather than accepting automatically the chief executive's interpretation of the academic community's views, but it requires the senate/academic board to respond promptly, as partners in governance, and not necessarily as defenders of the *status quo* (Shattock 2002). It needs to be remembered that in all the major incidents of misgovernance in the UK since the 1980s, whether involving the governing body or the executive or both, it has been the academic community which has blown the whistle. Until recently the most serious threat to good university governance has come from over dominant or occasionally ineffective executive teams, whose performance was not sufficiently monitored by governing bodies, rather than from over ambitious governing bodies themselves or from dissident academic communities. In 2009, for the first time, we saw the damage that can be caused by overbearing governing bodies previously only found in the Further Education college sector. The support for so called 'Carver' boards, named after a prominent advocate of small boards in US community colleges, is an indication of a new and dangerous trend in UK higher education.

As Tierney found in his study of US universities and colleges:

> A successful governance process is one in which multiple constituencies have been involved in the main problems that confront the college or university. An unsuccessful campus is one where structures exist but because of angst or alienation no one participates and the dialogue focuses on the structures rather than the issues and the problems.
>
> (Tierney 2008: 171)

Successful universities try to keep the powers of governance in balance – they appoint able and forthright laymen because they value the contribution they can bring, they develop strong corporate leadership where the vice-chancellor leads an effective central steering core which is accountable to but maintains a close dialogue with a senate or academic board that reflects the views of a vibrant academic community. They encourage academic leadership at all levels and a full participation by the academic community, or a representative part of it, in the decision making process. If any of these key components, the lay element, the executive or the academic community start to make negative contributions the institution will find itself disadvantaged. If they work positively together, however, good governance makes a significant contribution to university success.

7

Extending the boundaries

This chapter describes the way the boundaries of what in the past were thought to be the legitimate business of a university are being extended. It reviews how new approaches to the exploitation of knowledge and knowledge transfer, the increasing assumption of a regional role and the management of internal income generating activities are changing the nature of university management. It argues that these activities need to be integrated into the central policy and management framework of the university and that this places new demands on the effectiveness of decision making processes and on the professionalism of those involved.

The broadening focus of university operations

A number of forces have come together since the early 1990s to extend the boundaries of what was once thought of as legitimate university business into a variety of new areas. The first of these is bound up with theories of how 'innovation', much of it the product of university based research, contributes to a knowledge economy, that is an economy fuelled by new mostly scientific and technological ideas rather than by improvements in manufacturing methods and production. In the late 1990s MIT estimated that if the companies founded by MIT graduates and faculty formed an independent national economy it would be the 24th largest in the world. The 4,000 companies employed 1.1 million people and had an annual world sales of $232bn, roughly equal to the GDP of South Africa (Bank Boston 1997). This analysis certainly influenced Gordon Brown, then UK Chancellor of the Exchequer, both in the UK Government's heavy investment in so-called STEM disciplines (science, technology, engineering and medicine) and in the MIT-Cambridge Institute whose purpose was to transfer entrepreneurial attitudes from the US to the UK. Cambridge was, however, already a seed bed of entrepreneurial activity. In 1969, a senate committee in Cambridge under the Nobel Prize winner Sir Neville Mott recommended setting up a 'science park'. This was followed up, not by the University which had set up the committee (whose primary task was to review a report which recommended that to preserve the university city's character new industry should be discouraged from locating near it), but by Trinity College, which used its private monies to found the Cambridge Science Park (Castells and Hall 1994). Less than 30 years later the chairman of the Cambridge Network, an organization comprising more than 1,000 companies, could demand the restoration of the fast train 'venture capital line' from Cambridge to London, disrupted by the Hatfield rail crash, arguing that Cambridge contributed nearly £9bn to the national gross domestic product and that the service was essential to maintaining face to face contact with London financial institutions. The University Director of Research Services backing him up claimed that this link was 'vital to the efficient working of the University' (Kelly 2002).

If one driver has been the prospect of direct economic advantage to be secured by the interaction between university research and industry and commerce, another has been the impact of universities on the 'creativity' of urban or regional environments. Florida (2001) has argued, using US data, that 'the presence of a major research university is a basic infrastructure component of the Creative Economy' (p. 292) because its research encourages direct economic activity through spin out companies and industrial collaboration, because it attracts talent from outside the area and because it contributes to the creation of an open, progressive and tolerant society which itself encourages 'creativity' to flourish. Manifestation of this thinking in the UK can be found in the 'science city' projects which have been adopted notably in Newcastle, but also in York and in Birmingham, as well as in the encouragement for the establishment of higher education centres and even full universities in towns and regions previously untouched by higher education.

A third and related driver is the recognition of the regional role – economic, educational/training and cultural – that universities should now be playing. In one sense this is not new: in England the civic universities were founded in large part to meet local needs and the polytechnics were strongly local institutions with a predominantly local catchment; in Scotland and Wales there was always a strong sense of regionality. But increasingly universities were drawn to focus on national issues, especially in England. The devolution of higher education to separate funding councils in Scotland and Wales solved part of this problem but in England from 1999 the English funding council instituted a modest 'third stream' of funding to stimulate institutions to undertake knowledge transfer programmes essentially concentrating on regional outcomes. Internationally the interest in higher education and its regional impact has grown to the extent that it not only encompasses policies to found 'regional' universities but has also given rise to a significant academic literature (c.f. Chatterton and Goddard 2000; Charles 2003; Lawton Smith 2003; Porter 2003; Gunaseka 2006; Goddard and Puuka 2008; Drabenstott 2008; Benneworth and Sanderson 2009).

A fourth and final driver has been universities' own need to generate income from private sources to diversify their income base. This has taken them into the conference business, retailing, marketing themselves to fee paying international students, and fund raising and commercial ventures of various kinds, activities which may be peripheral to the core business of the university but whose surpluses provide the income from which the core business is increasingly financed.

These new activities have profoundly changed the task of managing universities, and have greatly extended the boundaries of university strategy and the scope of university operations. Every university is affected by these changes but the more successful the university, the more its activities in these areas increases and the greater the complexity that is imposed on its operations. Not only have these activities led to the creation of a range of specialist professional posts – science park directors, technology transfer directors, heads of research offices, directors of short course programmes or of continuing education, directors of arts centres, theatres, conference organizations, of retailing, or of international offices – but to the need to coordinate the activities, manage them and their operations to best institutional advantage, and keep under review their interactions with the core business of teaching and research. These wide ranging activities have thrust considerable new executive responsibilities on the shoulders of university management and widened the spectrum of activities over which judgement has to be exercised. The requirement that universities should be 'useful' (Shattock 1997) has imposed a transformation of the demands placed on central university management and a considerable re-education of managers.

The exploitation of knowledge

From the 1980s there has been a transformation in the way universities have collaborated with external bodies in research: the traditional description of industrial research contracts with universities, where the company identified the piece of research which the university laboratory was to undertake, has been increasingly overlaid by longer term partnerships often brokered by government intervention. Etzkowitz and Leydesdorff have written extensively about a 'triple helix' of university-industry-government relations which require the creation of boundary spanning mechanisms to link together universities and firms in order to develop the shared interest in knowledge based economic and social products (Etzkowitz and Leydesdorff 1998). They suggest that 'a common interest in a "third mission" for the university in addition to teaching and research, has emerged world wide' (Etzkowitz and Leydesdorff 1998: 203) and that networks in innovation and technological development are transforming the 'matrix of disciplinary and institutional organisation among and within the sciences' (p. 203). Universities and firms are assuming tasks in which they previously complemented one another:

The boundaries between public and private science and technology, university and industry are in flux. As the university crosses traditional boundaries in developing new linkages with industry, it devises formats to make research, teaching and economic development compatible.

(Etzkowitz and Leydesdorff 1998: 203)

They go on to argue that:

Fundamental changes occurring at organisational and institutional levels within and between university, industry and government, constitute a new environment of innovation replacing the linear model. Bilateral government-industry and university-industry ties have expanded into trilateral relationships at the regional, national and multi-national levels. Encouraged by government universities have become a key element in innovation policies throughout the world.

(Etzkowitz and Leydesdorff 1998: 204)

However, these organizational issues are overlaid by more fundamental issues relating to what has become known as 'entrepreneurial science' (Etzkowitz and Webster 1998). The linear model of pure research leading to applied research and then development has been overtaken by a more time-sensitive pressure for the commercialization of research ideas. Thus Gibbons *et al.* (1994) define Mode 2 research as 'where discovery and application are more closely integrated'. Commercialization, Gibbons *et al.* suggest 'is organised less around the translation of discoveries into new products than in searching for design configurations with the potential for development' (p. 3).

Increasingly it is not a question of generating new discoveries but of making use of the knowledge base that is already available. So single company to university laboratory relationships are being overtaken by pre-competitive consortia or clubs of companies, and sometimes by governments who commit resources and manpower to work with one or more universities on R and D issues, pooling equipment and research expertise. This can involve industrial and university teams working together in the same laboratory with a much greater urgency and 'near market' sense of mission than in the past, and in conditions which are much more commercially sensitive than previous industry sponsored research. Under such arrangements

knowledge production is characterised by a closer interaction between scientific, technological and industrial modes of knowledge production, by the weakening of disciplinary and institutional boundaries, by the emergence of more or less transient clusters of experts, often grouped around large projects of various kinds, and by the broadening of the criteria of quality control and by enhanced social accountability.

(Gibbons *et al.* 1994: 7)

These external demands have had an impact on academic organization. Where once the academic department, based on a single discipline, reigned supreme, cross departmental research units and centres are being created to serve as vehicles for research. These centres are formed outside the department because the research leader needs a degree of autonomy, not available inside a department, to coordinate activities and deliver research products to time to the sponsors. Etzkowitz and Kemelgor have written about 'the collectivisation of academic science' in the US (Etzkowitz and Kemelgor 1998) and have described how a university research centre can develop much closer links with external contractors, even to the extent of forming its own company, than research groups operating within traditional departments. Such centres are created by research 'leaders' – academic entrepreneurs – and depend for their success on generating continued financial support from industrial partners. They do not necessarily operate like a research group in a department but can simulate some aspects of industrial research laboratories buying in skills that are needed on a short term basis sharing valuable equipment between external customers and providing a 'neutral ground' in which company collaborators can work with university personnel. Relational rather than contractual interactions between university and company staff are often a key to the prosecution of a successful project (Abreu *et al.* 2008). Geiger and Creso (2008) have described how leading US universities (Harvard, Stanford, MIT, Duke, Arizona, etc.) have created interdisciplinary groupings of exactly this kind; in the UK the Warwick Manufacturing Group which combines research, consultancy and training funded by industry, government and tuition fee income provides a comparable example.

These changes have revolutionized the organizational structures that universities formerly had in place to interface with industry, and demand a new range of skills and policy mechanisms. On the skills side, instead of the traditional requirement for universities to have someone on their staff to 'liaise' with industry, they now need staff who have the ability to build networks, who have a capacity for brokerage, and who can offer strategic skills in identifying and matching market niches with university research strengths, skills in company formation, in understanding industrial training requirements and in taking a wider vision about the university and the economy. Where there are powerful research centres addressing industrial problems it is likely that their own specialist expertise will far outweigh the more generalized expertise to be found centrally in the university, and their policy imperatives may be much more orientated towards the needs of a defined market than the university's. The situation, therefore, becomes much less tidy and controlled; tension can be created between academic entrepreneurs in academic departments and those in research centres, and between both and the centre of a university especially where a division of income arising from intellectual property is concerned; questions of coordination, authority and the interpretation of university regulations can involve senior university committees in sensitive arbitration and negotiation, and sometimes legal support.

Not only does this new world demand technical coordination and managerial decision making at the centre but it raises profound questions as to whether the policy issues that they throw up should be considered through some separate 'commercial' decision making process or should be integrated into the normal mechanisms. At the academic department level questions arise as to departmental research policy and as to the relationship of a department to an independently resourced research centre, especially when the director of the centre's success in generating income and staff posts challenges the status of the head of department, as can easily become the case. At the centre of the university, policy issues in regard to resources, funding, space, overhead levels, income share and intellectual property, together with issues about employment, salary levels and special arrangements in regard to staff in the centre and the department can create precedents that other parts of the institution may be keen to capitalize on, or can demand hard choices about priorities. In all such choices the pressures that can be brought by industrial partners, the existence of national institutional performance indicators for income derived from industry or the chance of losing the research leader to another institution, may also become factors in the debate.

Two levels of decision making are apparent; one relates to core university issues and the other is in the broadest sense 'commercial'. Decisions about the level of overheads to be charged, whether a patent is to be applied for or a licence given, how the intellectual property rights are to be distributed, whether a spin-off company is to be created, and/or whether the university is to take equity in it, are technical or commercial and should be taken by a body set up for the purpose, perhaps itself operating as a company. Its decisions can then be judged on the basis of commercial or technical criteria – they will be 'business' decisions appropriate to the 'business' world in which the university is operating. Decisions, however, which touch on matters of academic organization or on potential conflicts in regard to the use of university resources or to substantial departures from university practice should be taken through the normal mechanisms.

Setting up a special body for 'commercial' decisions provides a commercial discipline and a set of commercial criteria which ensures that its decisions are 'business-like' and not distorted by academic and other internal issues. It also distances bodies that have a representational element in their constitution from decisions which can only be effective if they are taken on strategic commercial criteria and to commercially inspired deadlines. But decisions which affect the academic heartland should not be devolved to such a body but should be referred to those bodies that are responsible for central decision making. If the university is to enter and perform confidently in this new world of research and development then its central bodies have to be integrated with it and understand its pressures, not be protected from it. They have to recognize that the external environment demands a flexibility and a tolerance of diversity which might not apply in purely academic matters and that market pressures must sometimes hold sway over issues of equity and a desire to hold to established practice. When the director of an industrially driven university research centre makes outrageous demands about the remuneration of his or her staff, or conflicts of interest arise between departments and individuals over time spent in spin-off companies, or between a head of department and the director of a research centre over questions of accountability, it is important that they are settled on the basis of sound university judgement and in the best long term interests of the university rather than on commercial criteria. In this way the university will become used to making the adjustments necessary to adapt to the new environment and its senior members will remain fully responsible for the shift of attitude involved. If, on the other hand, all such decisions are hived off to another specially constructed body the university can begin to move to a form of institutional schizophrenia where all matters that fall, as it were, outside the traditional boundaries, are the responsibility of some external body, and the university becomes insulated from the process of adaptability required.

It is certainly not easy to draw a clear line between what counts as policy and what can be described as technical or commercial good practice. One difficulty is that there are few models to draw on because, as we have seen in Chapter 1, these complexities are concentrated in the most successful research intensive universities and these universities also tend to have idiosyncratic structures. The diversity of such activities in a major research intensive university defies simple categorization, but broadly they may be said to cover intellectual property issues, the exploitation of research findings in spin-off companies where the institution takes equity in the company in return for its investment in the original research, licensing to external companies, or setting up incubator facilities or whole science parks where academic entrepreneurs may base themselves. The scale of these activities can be immense. In the US, Geiger and Creso (2008) report that by 2005 the Association of University Technology Managers claimed that universities were responsible for nearly 10,000 active licences and almost 3,000 start up companies. In the UK the Annual HEB/CI Survey for 2007–8 reported 219 new spin-off companies based on university owned intellectual property and over 900 spin-off companies passing the three-year-old marker. Professional rules of thumb suggest that a university might expect to generate an exploitable innovation at the rate of one per year per 30 academics in STEM subjects and that one in five patents may be expected to result. Most of the leading group of universities have now set up university companies or separate internal organizations to take the 'commercial' decisions required having previously tried unsuccessfully to handle them in house. Thus Oxford has ISIS; Cambridge, Cambridge Enterprises; UCL, UCL Ventures; and Warwick, Warwick Ventures. Most universities which have a substantial commitment to STEM subjects are beginning to generate significant income streams: Nottingham for example generates some £3m a year from exploitation of its intellectual property; UCL floated one of its spin-off companies on the London Stock Exchange and sold its 15 per cent holding for £7m; in 2008–9 ISIS covenanted £2.9m profit back to the University. But to do so demands a professional expertise which was simply not available until the

1990s. Then, the belief was that a small research office which combined responsibility for passively processing research grant and contract applications with overseeing a university's intellectual property rights provided the necessary central support for research. Now it would be the normal expectation that there would be a pro-vice-chancellor with designated responsibility for research together with a professional support staff, which in Nottingham's case totals 45, that will contain expertise in grant writing (for major collaborative applications), finance, intellectual property and company formation. At the top of these organizations one might expect to find highly paid professionals operating with considerable freedom and authority who are able to take a strategic view of the exploitation process as well as the technical skills which the academic community normally lacks. Exploitation may not yet be 'big business' but over time a university which invests wisely and maintains its portfolio of patents, licences, partnerships and companies may reap substantial benefits in reputation as well as in income.

Another set of considerations come into play in investing in an incubator building or a full science park. In Cambridge, for example, science parks have been investments by colleges on land acquired some 500 years ago, and college finances have benefited from their profitability. At Surrey, the University was able to devote its own land to the venture and retain the profits. At Warwick the science park is a joint venture with local authorities and its incubator building a joint venture with a bank, with the profits from the park being reinvested back into the science park company. At other universities contracts have been entered into with commercial developers. But in many cases the use of the university name, and the reputation which the university can develop for successfully developing a science park, outweighs the commercial payback that it might produce. The essence of a well run university science park is not that it makes direct profits for its founder, though this has certainly been the case at Cambridge and Surrey, but that it attracts companies who want to work with the university and provides a home for academics who want to start their own companies: its focus is much more towards extending the boundaries of university activity into the external world of exploitation and innovation than to generating new resources. There needs, therefore, to be a synergy between science park tenants and the research and training activities of the host university which offers opportunities for research collaboration, joint bidding for resources, and a source of student employment. Science parks can add a dimension to university life in significant ways, through student vacation employment schemes, student project schemes, joint bidding under the many research council and government schemes that require industrial/university partnerships, together with the indefinable advantages that a university can gain from the close proximity of a collection of science-based companies linked in various ways to the university. In some the science parks have become quasi-industrial development agencies, launching initiatives with 'business angels' and other investors to support local companies, creating satellite incubator facilities on sites round the region, and establishing mechanisms to fund research that links university departments with science park companies.

Thus the demand for the application of science has taken universities into activities which were hardly conceived of some 30 years ago when patents were only rarely sought and the end product of most science was publication in a journal. Such activities are not now limited to science, and social scientists, economists, sociologists, geographers, psychologists, and above all staff from business schools, have also found opportunities for technology transfer (Abreu *et al.* 2008). Organizationally, the creation of large multi-disciplinary, externally sponsored research centres have set internal problems, but their impact in terms of attracting graduate students, generating income and funding buildings have shaped universities in ways that could not have been foreseen. Exploitation can only take place on the back of long term investment in fundamental research. In a large scale study of entrepreneurialism and knowledge transfer across Europe the three most research intensive universities – Lund, Nottingham and the London School of Hygiene and Tropical Medicine (LSHTM), all three of which had extensive exploitation portfolios of companies, licences, science parks, or, in the case of LSHTM, international health care programmes – all emphasized that fundamental research remained the key driver behind success in exploitation: at Lund 'The leaders of the most renowned research groups are key personalities with charisma, knowledge and dedication as well as entrepreneurial spirit' (quoted in Shattock 2009: 36). The study concluded that: 'Entrepreneurialism in research grows out of fundamental research; it is therefore natural that large concentrations of research expertise . . . if supported by appropriate knowledge transfer machinery will usually produce the most commercial and other outcomes' (Shattock 2009: 203).

The regional agenda

Locational factors encourage the development of industrial partnerships but all universities are being drawn in to contributing to regional agendas. There is a growing literature now that demonstrates that regions have become important players in the global economy and that regions, rather than national governments, have the key role in tapping into global corporate networks and capturing and embedding 'foot loose investment'. 'World class places', writes Kantor, 'can help grow these assets by offering innovative capabilities, production capabilities, quality skill, learning networking and collaboration' (Kantor 1995: 35). According to Goddard (1999: 39):

> Regional success has been characterised by a range of different models but with a common agreement as to the factors underpinning success: agglomeration economies, economies of scope, trust, networks of small firms and supportive institutions. Central to successful innovation are the structures, modes of interaction between knowledge producers,

disseminators and users. Since technologies embody both people and ideas as well as physical artifacts, transactions involving extensive inter-action and iterative communication are widely believed to be necessary as a means of facilitating exploitation.

Other writers have identified the concept of the learning economy emphasizing the importance of interactive learning as the basis for innov-ation and change in the modern developed economies (Lundvall and Johnson 1994) and Goddard has extended this to the idea of 'the learning region' and has demonstrated that attention has been widened away from 'a rather narrow focus on high technology and manufacturing industry and the private sector ... To include social and organisational and business, consumer and public services' (Goddard and Puuka 2008). On the one hand, investment in research intensive universities by regional authorities, as described by Douglas (2007) in the US (or by the North West Development Agency in the merger of the University of Manchester and the University of Manchester Institute of Science and Technology in the UK) in the right local economic conditions can aim to transform their regional economy by acting as a hub for the development of new industries, while, on the other, university based networks can form the hub of a wider learning region.

The increasing recognition of the economic importance of regional initia-tive, through the creation of development agencies means that universities ignore their newly acquired regional responsibilities at their peril. A regional agenda may also help to define a university mission more clearly. A university located in a relatively impoverished or low technology area may be unable to develop innovation and large scale industrial partnerships because such partners do not exist locally or regionally but may still become a successful regional university by utilizing its expertise to relate more effectively than might be the case for major research intensive with SMEs. Such universities are natural agents to develop the regional skills base. Of the regions in the UK, 10 had a retention rate of graduates from universities in the region of above 50 per cent. Regional universities linked to community colleges offer a particular source of re-economic progress. The case study of Plymouth University described by Temple (2009) shows how a university can make a major regional contribution by exploiting its teaching strengths. However, as the comprehensive review of the Higher Education Innovation Fund (HEIF) – the 'third stream' of HEFCE funding – makes clear, there are attitudinal problems which a successful regional university must overcome. Although HEFCE has allocated more than £200m for additional staffing in the knowledge transfer area, 57 per cent of universities responding to the survey indicated a lack of academic engagement in their staff, and 50 per cent a lack of capacity to match up to regional needs, while 40 per cent noted a lack of demand from industry (PACEC 2008). For regional engagement to be successful universities must find ways to enthuse or incentivize their staff for the purpose.

Organizationally the relationships that playing a successful regional role seem to throw up are difficult to assimilate into a conventional university management structure. On the one hand, a university may have a science park entering into collaboration with regional partners and with European neighbours, or on the other, a research centre serving as a prototype for using interactive Mode 2 research with major local companies as a base for a global research, development and training portfolio. Simultaneously the local chamber of commerce may be seeking to persuade the university to enter a partnership with SMEs and the major city in the region may be making a joint proposal involving the university for lottery support for some capital scheme designed to enhance the city's status, and the university may need the city's support in respect to planning regulations to bring a major scientific facility, of great interest to the university, to the region. Such projects quickly become major strategic issues where financial risk, city pride, employment opportunities and academic prestige offer competing disincentives and incentives. Reconciling institutional risk, self interest and local and regional aspirations can place considerable demands on central university policy makers and emphasizes why many universities have found difficulty in identifying decision making machinery that can operate at the necessary speed to make an effective contribution to resolving such issues.

It is almost axiomatic that any collaboration with a local or regional authority will be more time consuming, more frustrating and more complicated than dealing with a research council or a large company, because local and regional politics will play a part in the final decision. Vice-chancellors have to make hard choices as to whether they personally should be the key negotiators but hours spent pushing this kind of project forward are ones which cannot be spent on the university's core business or on representing the university in the wider educational world. But it may not be easy to delegate the task: relationships and 'the deal' may depend on mutual knowledge and trust, the commitment of the university may be required at any given stage, an understanding of the financial and managerial risks cannot perhaps be shared. In such circumstances universities need to know where their own critical decisions should be taken; they need to protect their vice-chancellor from being the deal maker in case new factors emerge later and they should draw heavily on the experience of their senior lay members who may have close links with external decision makers.

Managing the extended portfolio

As universities increasingly diversify their funding base they take on responsibilities and management tasks which are very distinct from their core business. Some management theory would suggest that this is a clear sign that a university should outsource the tasks but this will limit the income and profit they may generate and may leave the university dependent on external organizations for key services (see Chapter 3). Universities have always found ways of managing non-core business activities: the record of Oxbridge managing very successfully the two largest of the world's academic publishers or a school examination board, again, very successfully, suggests that universities have long experience of operating as conglomerates on a large scale. Universities run conference businesses, bookshops, gift shops and supermarkets; they let out sports facilities and teaching rooms; they run arts centres; and they manage offshore recruiting offices or pay agencies to help them recruit overseas students. The income deriving from these activities is rising. But all of them in their several ways raise policy issues for an autonomous institution. Does the conference trade crowd out students in the vacation? Does it contribute to lower student rents? Does the bookshop provide a better service than an externally owned bookshop chain or internet suppliers? Is it responsive to academic departments' needs? Does it compete unfairly with a students' union secondhand store? Are the supermarket and the gift shop environmentally friendly? Are the opening hours geared to social need or commercial profitability? Where do the profits go? Are the sports facilities overused by external paying customers? And so on. They also raise important management issues. Are the staff professionals in the field of activity and are they paid accordingly? Should they have less secure contracts than comparable non-academic staff working in traditional university activities? How is their performance monitored? Who do they report to? What further opportunities for income generation are there to be developed? How should universities fund capital investment in 'commercial buildings'?

Fund-raising and generating international student numbers raise similar issues. Fund-raising whether via the alumni or via a more general appeal requires professional expertise and a significant investment not just in staffing but in the time and energy of the vice-chancellor. Princeton, the most successful fund-raising university in the US, expects to spend the equivalent of 10 per cent of what it raises to resource the activity. In the UK context this means facing up to the allocation of scarce resources, away from the academic line, to what must inevitably be a speculative venture with a pay back time extending probably well beyond the vice-chancellor's expected term of office. It is little wonder that most development offices are under resourced. International offices, on the other hand, can see an immediate return in fee income and, since 1990, have operated in a boom market where international student numbers have been growing year on year. There has been less resistance to these offices growing, therefore, but too often the market is seen as a 'cash cow' which has not required an integration with overall strategy except in terms of counting the income. A few universities have pursued creating long term strategic partnerships with other institutions round the world but for many the globalization agenda has been interpreted as income for tomorrow rather than as a positioning mechanism. They do not have a 'foreign policy' and their professionals in the field are too anxious for quick wins to suggest one.

A university needs to think through where these issues are settled and by whom. Taking commercial, or business-type decisions in a university context cannot be divorced from the university's activities as a whole. However strong and effective an earned income board or a business decision making process may be it cannot act outside the university and many of its most important projects will need to be approved through the university's normal machinery. Not only does this introduce a new dimension into university decision making itself but the university members involved need to learn how to understand the implications of the decisions they are charged to take and to balance long term goals against short term difficulties. It also requires consideration of sophisticated policy arguments prepared by well qualified staff. These are not decisions which can be taken on the run between one committee meeting and another by people who have not read their papers. Increasingly these decisions require a near professional understanding of the issues and a clear sense of what the university strategic needs are and how these issues fit with the core business; this places greater demands on university committees and, necessarily, a grasp of university management/ financial issues needs to become more widely dispersed. University management has, as a result, become more complex, multi-layered and multi focused than in the past.

Universities as conglomerates

Pushed by Governments (innovation policy, regional development) and pulled by the need to diversify their income base universities have become conglomerates with some of the characteristics of city states. Not only are they taking on a much wider remit and a more corporate set of 'business' issues, but they are having to depend on a much wider range of qualified staff. And success is often dependent on the level of investment a university is willing or able to make in the necessary professional support staff in areas like exploitation, fund raising or internationalization, breeding whole phalanxes of additional staff who operate executively outside the day-to-day control of the academic community. In all these areas policy issues are enmeshed with the practical day-to-day and universities have to recruit professionals not simply to run them but to develop policies and strategies for them. These professionals like the senior university officers will not be happy to operate on the basis that their advice in their area of expertise, once given, can be set aside by a group of amateurs who form the responsible committees. As, therefore, the university's agenda broadens, so it must let in to its counsels professionals who are not themselves teaching and researching members of the institution. As university business becomes more complex the academic community becomes more dependent on professionals from outside its ranks. Ensuring that these groups work in harmony and with mutual respect must be a key aspect of university management in modern times.

More and more the most successful universities are becoming independent academic corporations: their agendas are broadening from the core business of teaching and research, they are developing financial turnovers that identify them as significant economic entities in their own right and their income is diversifying rapidly away from dependence on the state. But as they are drawn into regional affairs, commercial enterprises or foreign markets they can lose sight of what made them successful, namely their academic success. Somehow in the modern era universities have to incorporate this extension of the range of their activities into a holistic policy framework; the most successful universities will continue to preserve teaching and research as the primary elements of their core business because the evidence suggests that the more effective they are in that the more effectively they contribute to this broadening agenda. For this reason deciding how the policy framework can be integrated and where decision making is best devolved to professional or commercial bodies represents a significant organizational and political challenge which goes to the heart of deciding not only how effective an institution is to be in these activities, but how they will change its essential character.

8

Building an image, establishing a reputation

This chapter draws parallels between corporate branding and reputation and building and sustaining a university image, and the advantages which a high brand image can give an institution. It explores the variety of markets that universities are engaged with and the benefits conferred by location and buildings, but concludes that in the long run university reputations are also strongly linked to performance. It describes steps that can be taken to build a university corporate image and illustrates how reputation can impact on student applications (and thus on financial security), on relations with industry, commerce and employment, and on fund-raising. It emphasizes that in a more marketized higher education system, institutional reputation, and achieving and maintaining it, will be of increasing importance.

A university 'brand'

In the corporate world brand equity is an important determinant of corporate value. A company's good reputation enables it to:

- command premium prices for its products,
- pay lower prices for purchases,
- entice top recruits to apply for positions,
- experience greater loyalty from consumers and employees,
- have more stable revenues,
- face fewer risks of crisis, and
- be given greater latitude to act by their constituents.

(Fombrun 1996: 73)

A university's reputation can have broadly similar effects. As with companies, a strong reputation creates a strategic advantage (Fombrun 1996) while a loss of reputation represents a business risk second only to business interruption (Maitland 2003); a deterioration in reputation or image may also be a trigger for action (Dutton and Dukerich 1991). According to Doyle (1998) the average UK or American company will be valued by the stock market at about twice their net balance sheet assets but companies that have a strong brand image or that have products which have distinctive brands may be valued at four times their net assets. He quotes Nestlé as paying six times its net assets for Rowntree to obtain the Rowntree brand. Some companies receive royalties for renting or licensing their brand name to other companies, just as some universities franchise their programmes to colleges overseas. Successful brands create wealth because they retain customers and attract new ones, enable companies to require and maintain market share, generate high prices and create a strong cash flow which can be used for investment in new products and future growth. There is plenty of evidence that when customers are asked to sample products and have been told in advance their names, they invariably choose those products with high brands over others: the branding helps you to choose the product even if the product itself is not greatly distinguishable from several others. A student would, on this basis, be more likely to choose a university with a high brand image over a university with a much lower image even if the degree programmes offered in the particular field were very similar. Brands tend to position companies – Rolls-Royce or Mercedes-Benz offer status and prestige, Volvo responsibility and safety, The Body Shop environmental friendliness, Marks and Spencer value for money, and so forth; it would not be too difficult for university analogues to be identified. Rhoades, commenting on the US says that:

> The reputation race is fuelled by an insatiable need for funding. Richer institutions are much more able to increase their reputation than poorer institutions. And this process is self reinforcing: as the race goes on, the wealth inequalities and differences in reputation tend to increase. The result is the establishment and strengthening of hierarchies.
>
> (Rhoades 1990)

Russell Group universities attract large numbers of highly qualified candidates, almost irrespective of the quality of individual degree programmes while Million+ universities are heavily dependent on the clearing scheme to fill their places. The name, the Russell Group, defines the UK's most senior research intensive universities, even though the position of some of its institutional members is exceeded in research league tables by institutions that belong to the less prestigious 94 Group. 'The Russell Group' represents a powerful brand, as does the 'Ivy League' in the US and the Sandstone group of universities in Australia.

'Brand' comes from the Norse word 'brandr' meaning literally to burn (hence branding of sheep or cattle), that is to identify or differentiate. In a mass higher education system, or in a globalized higher education market, creating a brand is more about creating name recognition than the all-encompassing branding suggested by the statement attributed to David Ogilvy 'the brand . . . gives a set of principles to an entire enterprise' (Brymer 2003 quoted in Temple and Shattock 2007). Perhaps the best example of branding and its financial importance to universities can be seen in the fees charged for MBA programmes where the leading UK institution (the London Business School) is able to charge more than five times as much as lower ranked institutions which teach a fundamentally similar curriculum. It is literally true that the association of high fee levels and quality in potential applicants' minds has led some universities in the MBA market to find that every time they raised the fees they attracted more applicants. What you are buying at the London Business School is high calibre staff, a very competitive group of MBA colleagues and the School's reputation. When this high fee regime is extended, with variations, across a full range of graduate programmes the differences in income between highly and less highly rated institutions can be considerable. A university with 40 per cent of its total student population on high cost graduate programmes will have a very different financial profile to one which has only 15 per cent of its students on low cost graduate programmes. When the international tuition fee component is added the finance available for investment in future development is multiplied yet further.

The foregoing is intended to emphasize such similarities as may be found between companies and universities in terms of the value of a strong brand or image. But there are also important differences. One is that although it is probably possible to identify companies which have the 10 or so most valuable brands – according to *Business Week*: Coca-Cola, Microsoft, IBM, GE, Intel, Nokia, Disney, McDonald's, Marlboro and Mercedes (Tomkins 2002), as compared, perhaps, with Harvard, Yale, Princeton, Stanford, MIT, Cal Tech, Cambridge, Oxford, Imperial College and ETH Zurich – many of the universities date at least from the seventeenth and eighteenth centuries and some from earlier while, although some of the commercial brands may be 50 years old (Coca-Cola, IBM, Disney), most date from the last 25. Indeed if a university can command (in Europe) mediaeval buildings and courtyards or (in America) eighteenth-century buildings and ivy covered walls or (in Australia) sandstone blocks, it is likely that its image will be greatly enhanced. As Gueno has shown (see Chapter 1) the age of universities in Europe can statistically be associated with research excellence suggesting that 'the Merton effect' may also be influenced by a branding that is linked to age of institution and style of buildings, which themselves provide a metaphor for a long scholarly tradition.

Another significant difference between companies and universities is that universities face in many more directions than companies. Fundamentally companies direct their activities towards satisfying their shareholders and achieving profits while universities have no such clearly defined parameters of activity. This is well illustrated in building an image. Universities are highly dependent on attracting undergraduates because this provides the basis for the majority of their state funding but they must also attract research support from research councils, government departments and agencies, and from industry and charities. Because they are dependent on state funding they have a strong incentive to emphasize those aspects of their work which coincide with government policies; because they play a significant role in their local and regional community they need to take account of local interests; because they have alumni and other potential donors they need to cultivate these interests; and because they are dependent on funds from international student fees they must emphasize activities which attract publicity in areas overseas from which they attract those students. Although companies as conglomerates may be in many different businesses, universities have academic departments/faculties which themselves have very different markets. Universities will also have different priorities in maintaining or achieving an excellent performance, which may appear to external markets to be in conflict with one another: thus a university might have more to lose if it did not maintain the standing of its engineering or medical school even if giving them resourcing priority could affect the much higher academic reputation of, for example, its history or mathematics departments. These markets can also overlap: academic departments in the same institution will attract students from the same schools and colleges but the reputation of weaker departments may sufficiently damage the reputation of the university to be a deterrent to candidates for other departments. At the research level different academic departments may have relationships and receive research contracts from the same company or with the company's closest competitor.

A further significant difference is the effect of location. Where companies may be spread over many regions, universities (other than the Open University) are primarily located in one place and take much of their colouring from that location. Many universities draw strongly on the positive image of the city in which they are situated: thus, Bristol, Leeds, Manchester, Nottingham and Sheffield all benefit from the image that these cities have established in the eyes of potential applicants living in the south. Liverpool has not so benefited, although in the 1950s the situation was rather the reverse. Warwick would not have been so successful if it had been identified with Coventry within whose city boundary 50 per cent of its campus actually sits. St Andrews, though relatively inaccessible to the south, derives benefit from the media image of the town generated by its golf club and of course from the 'William' effect. Of the 1960s universities, Sussex and York benefited from the attractive image of Brighton and York, while their predecessor, Keele, derived no such advantage from the Potteries. Bath and Surrey Universities, both former colleges of advanced technology which chose to move from their original sites in Bristol and Battersea, derived a great deal from their new locations, while Bradford and Salford, universities with the same origins, but which chose to remain on their existing sites, have had to overcome a much less favourable national image. (In the early 1960s, the Salford senate voted not to accept an invitation to move to Chester, a move which might have had a transforming effect.) In more recent times the Polytechnic of Central London changed its name with great benefit to its corporate image to the University of Westminster, while the University of Luton has transformed its fortunes by becoming the University of Bedfordshire (Temple and Shattock 2007). Kirp describes how in the US,

Beaver College, a long established liberal arts college, rescued itself by changing its name to Arcadia University (Kirp 2003).

University reputations and image, while they may be heavily influenced by age and location, are not determined by them. As with companies, reputation cannot be achieved simply by applying public relations techniques or by one-off achievements but is linked to long term performance. The LSE, not located in an especially attractive part of London, or in very interesting buildings, has an image and reputation based on academic merit and the intellectual contributions it has made to social and political thought. Sussex, which had a glittering reputation in the 1960s and was endowed by Basil Spence with some distinguished and memorable architecture, has not sustained its early promise and has been outpaced in reputation by Warwick, located in the much less fashionable Midlands and by York, which has with more justification than Warwick drawn benefit from its association with its parent city. LSE and Warwick have put considerable investment into public relations in its broadest sense to enhance their reputation and image but a number of universities have spent far more significant sums in self promotion without noticeable success: De Montfort, for example, the boldest in this respect of the post-1992 universities, undertook expensive changes in logos and extensive cinema advertising which did not deliver the kind of steady rate of expansion that they were intended to achieve. With well over a hundred higher education institutions competing for national attention, applicants and resources, it is obvious that only a few can consistently stand out from the pack and claim a distinctive identity; it is not surprising that in some institutions the marketing director has been made a member of the senior management team and given a pro-vice-chancellor title. The following quotation from an interview with a new vice-chancellor exemplifies the importance which most institutional heads place on the need to improve their institution's image in a marketized and competitive university environment:

> The University of Reading is probably the best kept secret in the Thames Valley . . . [the interview then lists the University's strengths] . . . But not all of this is quite as visible as perhaps we should be. We're good – really good – but I have a strong sense we have to make a much better job of selling ourselves. How many people in the region know that Reading is one of the top twenty research universities in the country? . . . Institutions are becoming much more diverse – and more aggressive – in an attempt to secure a larger share of the limited available resources to attract the brightest students, and recruit and retain the best staff.
>
> (Burn 2003: (33) p2)

Building the corporate image

Although it is self-evident that a university has to show many different aspects of itself to the different interests it has to address, every university will seek to underpin the reputation of an individual success story with an over-arching image of its own reputation. Huisman (2007) in an analysis of 44 website welcome addresses from UK vice-chancellors notes that a high proportion emphasize their institution's age. A few academic units such as the Molecular Biology Laboratory or the Cavendish at Cambridge, and perhaps one or two business schools can claim name recognition in a public sense distinct from that of their universities, just as some Oxford and Cambridge colleges certainly can. In many universities corporate images feed off particularly distinguished academic units rather than vice versa. Manchester's post-war reputation was based first on its famous Physics Department and later on Jodrell Bank, Hull's reputation revolved around chemistry, Southampton's around engineering and naval engineering, Reading's around agriculture. In spite of much excellence in terms of campus, location and the existence of the Sainsbury Centre, East Anglia is perhaps best known and its image defined by its research into the environment. Strategically this may be sensible for research purposes but a corporate image needs a wider appeal.

If we believe that reputation is a key institutional asset, then it requires positive steps to be taken to manage it and a strategy for maintaining and enhancing it needs to be created. No university can afford the kind of sums large companies are prepared to devote to market research and identity formation but successful universities will certainly have an office devoted to public relations or public affairs. Bearing in mind the many markets a university must compete in, separate strategies will be necessary for the local and regional press, the national and the international press, with a special concentration internationally on countries which send significant numbers of international students to the UK and to the particular UK university. Separate strategies are also necessary to interest particular sections of the press. But the press is relatively less important than television, radio and the web in projecting a university to a wider audience. Oxford and Cambridge have always benefited from their relative proximity to London, while colleges of the University of London, most obviously LSE, have been keen to exploit their ready availability to radio and TV reporters. Universities away from London – unless like Edinburgh, they are sited in a city where major media resources are located – are inevitably at a disadvantage, especially when TV interviews or visits by film crews are being competed for. To overcome its dependence on the availability of TV studios in Birmingham, Warwick built a TV studio on its own campus giving its academics ready access to comment directly on events around the world, without the delays and opportunity costs of travelling off campus to do so. (But like a small number of other 'out of town' universities it has also acquired a London centre so that it can compete for media attention on their own territory with the London institutions.) More than ever successful universities need a reputation, and recognition, not only in the UK but internationally. Overcoming the disadvantages of ready access to the media and of not having a reputation which is certified by age requires investment and commitment, and neither are easy to maintain when the pay back is essentially indirect and cannot be quantified. What would be second nature to an ambitious company may be the subject of much heart searching in a university where the strategic importance of competing for media attention is less understood.

But content is important. If a university wishes to be taken seriously for its research then frequent references to undergraduate exploits in the popular press will do little to reinforce its reputation. Picking the stories that generate media interest and the personalities that are media friendly makes an important contribution to defining an institutional image. A university that has a large building programme can enhance its image for innovation by inviting appropriate personalities to open them and by ensuring that the opening is well covered by the media; a university that attracts distinguished visitors should be alert to exploiting the media value of interviews, visits to laboratories, etc. Such events emphasize the need for the university itself to be media friendly, with senior figures being willing to comment on events and with an alert central office which maintains close daily contact with the press and media, has access to a well ordered archive of photographs and pictures and the skill to persuade academics that they are helping the institution by making themselves available to give interviews at inconvenient times. Associating the university with other high profile organizations, for example, with top companies or charities in research, with leading banks, law firms or accountancy firms for training or joint research activities, or with other public or private sector bodies or government departments, all contribute to positioning it in the public eye. A well developed public affairs function needs to go beyond the media to opinion and reputation forming in a wider sense. In what sectors does the university need to enhance its image? What are the university's internal strengths and weaknesses in content and presentability? How can a public affairs strategy be aligned to support the university's strategic objectives? How can the impact be monitored? What is its internet strategy? Universities have an extraordinary variety of ways to generate media interest, through research, through events and through student activities, but such advantages need to be employed strategically. Too much concentration on a few headline pulling areas may be counter productive and offer too narrow a focus. More important to the strategy may be opinion forming events designed to reinforce and broaden its academic image which bring prominent personalities to the university to address public issues before an invited audience. Social events in desirable locations, when reinforced by some relevant presentation, may emphasize the university's commitment to a particular activity and may provide the opportunity to attract partners and collaborate. Such events will be located in London, New York or Hong Kong, or wherever the target audience is to be found but they should be part of a programme which prioritizes particular themes or audiences, not one-off and easily forgotten occasions. Above all they call for a high degree of professionalism because in embarking on such a programme the university is entering a field where deficiencies in performance will be very noticeable to audiences well used to the significant resources customarily employed by private sector organizations.

Universities can and do overemphasize to themselves the importance which external authorities attach to the traditional functions of teaching and research; research advances, especially, can be so obscure to the public that they have little impact unless they can be linked to some practical outcome well in the future. Universities should, therefore, utilize their adjunct organizations – arts centres, theatres, science parks, conference centres, etc. – for 'horizontal branding' that is to associate the institution strongly with non-academic but worthy activities. The Boat Race does much to reinforce Oxbridge's continued high status in the eyes of the public. A successful science park, or an arts centre attracting good reviews, can contribute immensely to a university's reputation in the sciences or the humanities, even though their actual connection with academic science or humanities degrees is tenuous. Any activities which bring large numbers of people on to the campus – artistic performances, conferences or sports facilities are the most obvious – should be used to emphasize the unique characteristics of the university because, even though the message may be quickly overlaid by the particular activity, they represent a level of contact that may be renewed in the future either as the parent of a student, an attendee of graduate or short course programmes, or as an unconscious advocate of the institution's merits at some other event.

What this emphasizes is the need to pay attention to the university's external appearance. In times of financial stringency the first reduction in many institutions is to the maintenance budget. This is a short term economy in any case, but failing to refurbish buildings, to keep them well decorated, to invest in the landscape, to erase graffiti as soon as it appears, to remove litter or to maintain up-to-date directional signs, to be committed to re-planting, daily cleaning, external decoration and all the other steps necessary to provide an attractive visual image for the university, is to ignore a vital aspect of the way people think about institutions. A handsome, well maintained campus and well presented, well equipped buildings are not only good for the external image and for an institution's credit rating amongst likely lending banks, but is good for morale amongst staff and students. Nothing is more depressing than showing a visitor around a down-at-heel campus, where maintenance has not been carried out and where institutional inefficiencies demand constant apologies. Support staff in particular – porters, cleaners and groundsmen – like to take pride in their work and regard a university's commitments to a high quality environment as being a contribution to academic success. An attractive, well maintained campus is an important selling point to potential new staff, to student applicants and their parents and to potential funders: it gives confidence that the university is well managed and it demonstrates pride in good performance; unattractive, poorly maintained campuses tell another story.

A characteristic of the successful institution is the high morale of its support staff: an essential principle of successful marketing is that 'front line staff determine how customers perceive an organisation' (Doyle 1998: 47). Universities may not direct sell in the way that many commercial organizations do but they relate to the public in very similar ways. They direct visitors, they advise parents on the location of academic departments, they organize car parking, they handle lost property, they serve in catering outlets or on the fees desk or in campus shops, they make the institution work on the ground. Helpful, positive, friendly staff represent the best face a university can present to the world; the driver who extols the virtues of the institution to the visitor he has picked up from the railway station is in some ways the best advertisement the university can have. Indeed universities should recognize that their external image has a significant impact on staff at all levels. Thus Gioia and Thomas (1996) argue that a strong institutional identity, especially if it is linked with a competitive, rather than a defensive approach, can provide staff with the confidence to be proactive. They found that top university management teams that were able to link strategic change to an improved institutional image fostered substantive improvement in performance, and that progression could be achieved from substantive improvement through improved image to further substantive improvement (Gioia and Thomas 1996). What this suggests is that establishing a strong external reputation or brand brings significant internal benefits: it raises confidence, generates high morale, encourages staff to be proactive and reinforces institutional momentum. Costly attempts to establish a reputation or brand image without the substance to support it are likely to be ineffective externally in the long term and will provoke scepticism and lack of confidence internally, but successful universities that invest in public reputation building are likely to find that it strengthens their position in both.

Branding, reputation and performance

The most striking change in the public image of universities since 2000 has been the increasing reference to league table positioning. The claim to be a 'top 20' or even a 'top 10' or a 'top 50' university (in the Shanghai Jiao Tong league table) is made in job advertisements and in student recruitment literature. It is evident that league tables are widely used by both home and international applicants as a key method of positioning an institution. An important new element in the league table data is provided by the National Student Survey which can produce departmental as well as institutional material. This data provides a useful check on the attempt to develop nationally or internationally recognizable institutional brands, an enormously difficult task in a market where there are so many institutions doing very similar things. If we accept that only a very few universities can claim to have acquired a brand which differentiates them significantly from others (an institutional brand may in fact be much more relevant at a local and regional level, especially if a university is dependent on a largely regional catchment of students) it is nevertheless the case that reputation is of critical importance for all institutions. Eighty per cent of employers asked about criteria for graduate recruitment said that the overall institutional reputation was the most important for judging the quality of an HEI (Morley and Aynesley 2007). League tables do not necessarily supplement but certainly underpin institutional reputation for mobile (as distinct from prospectively home-based) students, for potential new staff recruits, for institutional partners and for possible donors. Good reputations take time to acquire but are difficult to lose: they are associated with age, with the company they keep (Russell Group, 94 Group) their buildings and campus, and the presence of key departments and individuals. Some universities possess an established 'reputation capital' (or 'brand equity') which is sufficiently strong to survive temporary downturns in their performance which would destroy commercial companies dependent much more immediately on instant customer responses. Reputation is therefore a key asset which has to be earned more transparently now than in the past. It is of little use to claim to be a 'top 20' university when the league tables show you to be averaging around thirtieth place. Alternatively if your mission is primarily regional and teaching orientated it is not sensible to claim to be exceptionally caring about students if the National Students Survey tells a different story. Huisman sees the images of the 44 institutions welcome statements he surveyed as being: 'some bold, some pretentious, some modest' (Huisman 2007). It is worth recalling Docherty's distinction between the 'official' and the 'clandestine' university (Docherty 2008) and question how far Oxford's number one position in the 2009 rankings or another university's 'top 10' or 'top 20' influences the most discerning candidate, the person whom a university might most want to attract as a student, colleague or donor. And we might salute a university which advertises in the *Financial Times* as follows:

> No one ever said it would be easy.
>
> We believe that a university should be a safe place to get it wrong. Because it's only when we experiment, when we really push ourselves, that we actually learn. And what is a university if it's not a place dedicated to the pursuit of knowledge? That means expanding human understanding through innovative research. But it also means passing it on through passionate dedicated teaching. Now that's easier said than done. We've learned that by treating every student as an individual, giving our academics space to flourish, and by embracing the fact that we're all coming at it from a slightly different place, we can achieve remarkable results.
>
> Find out how we're competing with the best whilst opening up the competition for everyone at le.ac.uk/this-is-Leicester.

A calculated soft sell, it may be, but it marks Leicester out as espousing a set of values that do not rely exclusively on the exploitation of league table positioning. Managing reputation is, therefore, not simply the responsibility of the marketing director but of those responsible for the institution as a whole.

Image and reputation

It is astonishing how little most universities invest in creating and maintaining an effective image and reputation when so many of their operations are dependent on it. If we return to the quotation from Fombrun at the beginning of the chapter it is clear that universities which acquired high reputations can command many of the same kinds of advantages that companies do: they can attract better fields of students and can capitalize on their reputations, if they wish, to charge higher fees for graduate programmes and to international students; they will generate more interest in their students from employers; they will have a more secure income base, and a more effective underpinning for fund-raising; they will recruit better staff and will retain the loyalty of their existing staff who will take pride in the reputation that they have shared in achieving. Reputation brings intangible benefits; it creates strategic advantage. Most universities regard the media reactively, responding vigorously to criticism, real or implied, rather than taking a proactive approach. Few universities give media training to their senior staff and even fewer have a public relations strategy which is approved by their more senior committees and have mechanisms for monitoring whether it is working effectively. Most universities confuse marketing with public relations and are inclined to believe that attractive prospectuses and websites are an adequate approach to raising their institutional image in schools or in international markets. Some universities have history or location on their side, but in a world dominated by branding and images this is not enough. Universities have unquestionably become more subject to market forces and those that wish to prosper in this environment will need to adapt, at least in part, to their disciplines – one of which is that, in a competitive world, name recognition and reputation give important advantages, generate resources, increase the security of the business and enable investment that would otherwise have to be made in 'keeping up' to be directed towards product enhancement and innovation and new ventures, all essential features of the operations of successful institutions. We cannot ignore the fact that the arrival of university league tables in the UK is changing the way universities are ranked in the public mind. Fombrun (1996) describes how the creation of published league tables for business schools in the US both challenged the reputations of established schools – Harvard could no longer be regarded as the leading school – and provoked a sharp increase in competition with schools being forced to modernize, upgrade their buildings or commission entirely new ones, amend their curricula and embark on ambitious profile raising campaigns. The impact was profound. Universities are less near-market than business schools but they will nevertheless find it impossible to ignore the reputational effects of not being in the top 10 or of slipping down the tables. Successful universities will ensure not only that they protect their position in these tables but that the reputation it establishes is used effectively.

9

Ambition

Ambition fuels success in universities as in other organizations. This chapter describes how ambition is generated by competition and how this manifests itself in making academic appointments. Appointing staff is not only a key area of competition between universities but the internal processes of appointment and selection make an important contribution to longer term institutional success. Ambitious university communities stimulate younger staff to higher levels of performance, to innovate more and to take more scholarly risks. They also engage all their staff in a wish to succeed. The chapter emphasizes the importance of a human resource strategy which encourages appointing the best staff at all levels. It concludes by showing how institutional ambition benefits students both within the university and afterwards, and encourages links between them as alumni with their former institution.

Institutional ambition and corporate commitment

No organization can achieve success without being ambitious and competitive; success does not just happen, it is achieved. Doyle writes:

> Like an athlete competing for success at the top level, there is no chance of success unless an organisation is totally dedicated to winning, and willing to make almost any sacrifice to get the prize.
>
> (Doyle 1998: 24)

Universities would not want to subscribe publicly to such an extreme statement but anyone who has been a close witness to the atmosphere of a research intensive university in the 12 months before an RAE return was to be submitted, would recognize its force. The truth is that the best universities have always been ambitious and competitive; this is not new: Manchester paid higher professorial salaries than other civic universities before the First World War so that they could attract the best professors and they lost

Rutherford to Cambridge partly because Cambridge was able to offer him a better package (Annan 1999). Oxford and Cambridge watch one another's progress obsessively (like Harvard and Yale) but have only since the mid-1990s had to consider the prospect of rivalry from elsewhere: Imperial, LSE and UCL have had a common ambition to supplement Oxbridge. York's and Warwick's ambition has always been to overtake the civic universities and to challenge the system leaders, as was Sussex's in its early years. There is no doubt that a league table culture now grips much of higher education. Hazelkorn (2007) on the basis of a substantial international survey of university leaders and senior administrators found that 'there was a new obsession with the status and trajectory of the top hundred' universities internationally; 92.8 per cent and 82 per cent of institutions want to improve their national or international ranking; 70 per cent of all respondents want to be in the top 10 nationally and 71 per cent want to be in the top 25 internationally. Ambition is latent in the system. It is not limited to aspirants to the 'top 10': a post-1992 vice-chancellor was not too proud in 2002 to circularize his heads of departments with pleasure that *The Daily Telegraph* had promoted his university to the Second Division of its league table (out of four).

There is, however, a world of difference between institutional ambition and ambition for the university voiced by a vice-chancellor, who may not yet have engaged the enthusiasm of a sceptical academic community. What distinguishes the most successful universities is that institutional ambition is general within the institution, that the university's competitive position, and the need to protect it, is widely understood and that its successes are greeted with enthusiasm, just as its failures are met with concern that they should not be repeated. Institutional ambition of this kind makes actions, both positive and negative, possible which would otherwise be impossible or possible only at a much slower pace and in a much more constrained manner, in universities where it does not exist. Suggestions, for example, in Oxford or Cambridge that they are slipping out of the world class (whatever that is) or in Imperial College that it is not overtaking Oxbridge as it believes itself to be, or in LSE that its world position in the social sciences is under threat, will immediately stimulate calls for greater activity, new fund-raising campaigns and action to eliminate weaknesses. When only 40 professors signed a round robin about the state of affairs at UCL the Provost resigned. If York or Warwick were to slip out of the 'top 10' there would be similar calls for change. It is often argued that instruments like the RAE encourage a degree of atomization in universities, where staff are more concerned about their own and their department's successes than their institution's, but this seems much less to be the case in these institutions. Cynicism is often voiced inside universities about the media claims for institutional success advanced by their central authorities. While this emphasizes that there is need for image and performance to cohere if the image is to survive for long, it also illustrates a serious gap in perception between the centre and academic staff. But in the most successful universities, where there is considerable pride in performance, the benefits of success and the need to maintain it are much more appreciated. The value of this corporate commitment to institutional success can be manifested in a number of crucial areas of a university's management.

Making academic appointments

If there was one single component in creating a successful university it would be in the making of academic staff appointments. A key to Stanford's rise to eminence in the period 1955–75 was the recruitment of 150 new professors (Keller 1983). Around 50 per cent of the average university's expenditure is made on academic salaries and it is these academic staff who are responsible for success in the core business of teaching and research. If every appointment represents a strategic decision by the university (see Chapter 2), choosing the field for the appointment, making the selection from amongst a group of well qualified applicants, and ensuring, once they have taken up the post, that the appointees' potential can be realized, each represent critical steps in institution building. When more junior members of academic staff are being appointed the institution is creating its academic feedstock for the future, the staff on whose success in teaching and research the institution will be basing its own hopes of future success; when senior appointments are being made the institution is picking its academic leaders, the people who have been chosen to release the potential of their colleagues and launch or help to launch the kind of academic initiatives which will maintain the institution's future. In spite of the obvious importance of selecting the best people it is extraordinary how universities vary in the degree of seriousness with which they approach this task. There are many universities that impose artificial financial ceilings on advertising posts or limit calling candidates from overseas for interview, ignoring the fact that attracting a strong field of candidates is the essential first step to making an outstanding appointment. There are universities that impose restrictions on how many candidates should have their references taken up, or on whether the selection of a short list for interviews should be made before references are taken up (all in the cause of not imposing too great a burden on a human resources office) thus limiting the ability of the institution to assemble as much information as can be made available to help the selection process. There are universities that make appointments without reading at least some of the publications of candidates or of having heard them give a seminar or presentation. There are universities that leave the appointments entirely to the departments or faculties with no central involvement, such as the appointing committee being chaired by a pro-vice-chancellor, or in the case of a professor, by the vice-chancellor, and there are universities that offer little opportunity to their own academics in the field to play a part in the selection.

Ambitious universities leave no stone unturned to appoint the best people: they headhunt the best graduate groupings in departments in the field, they search internationally, they spend an inordinate amount of time in deciding who should appear on the short list and they involve many members of staff in the process, and they eventually select only the best, and if the best are not in the field, they readvertise and start again. If there is a possibility of losing the best candidates to other universities they speed up the process, bring the interview date forward or try to offer a package of support facilities that they believe the competing institution may not be able to rival. Because they are a successful and ambitious institution they will attract good fields of good candidates whom they will treat like colleagues whether or not they are appointed if only on the pragmatic assumption that they will be appointed elsewhere and will continue to be colleagues in the discipline. At the level of reader or professor, they will ensure that they appoint high quality external assessors and they will headhunt ferociously (themselves and not through professional headhunters) in order to ensure a strong interview list; they will not make appointments unless they are sure the appointments are good ones.

One of the most striking differences between universities is the extent to which they attract staff from outside their own country. Mahroum created league tables of what he called 'magnet' institutions in different disciplines which attracted staff from overseas. These showed that (in 1999) UCL led in clinical medicine with Oxford not far behind but in biosciences Oxford led, with Cambridge second and Imperial College third; in science, technology and clinical medicine combined Cambridge dominated with 840 international staff, Oxford was second with 705, and Imperial, UCL and Edinburgh, third, fourth and fifth respectively. One needs to be careful about interpreting such figures since the cost of living, political stability and even climate as well as the particular disciplines within the institution may all affect the results (high employment figures for international staff could reflect an inability to recruit national staff as with the 1990s crisis in nursing appointments). Mahroum concluded that reputation and location constituted the main factors which served to reinforce historic league table positions. Over half the turnover of staff in these fields in Cambridge and Imperial was of staff from overseas, and 40 per cent at Oxford (Mahroum 1999).

The advantage of having strong departments in the first place is that they attract ambitious candidates for posts who want to work in them – the Matthew effect referred to in Chapter 1. Such departments are confident of their standards and will not accept appointments that do not match them. Moreover they know the competitive strengths of rival departments in other universities and can make appointments either to compete with them or to complement their own. At the professorial level the best departments will not bring forward a proposal to advertise a post unless they are reasonably assured by comprehensive enquiries that they will generate a strong field: they may have already identified the two or three best candidates who are available. They will know their research and teaching skills from extensive consultation around the university system and they will take the trouble to obtain a full picture because they know that an unsatisfactory appointment will be with them for a long time and may fatally affect the future of the department. For the university likewise, and for the professors from other disciplines involved in the appointment, it will be recognized that appointments at this level must add something, must bring some quality or technique or skill that the department lacks. Thus each appointment should aim to improve the department rather than simply allow it to maintain its position. Each appointment will also be celebrated in the department and more formally in the university; when it is a professor the appointment will be accompanied by a press release, and, ultimately, by an inaugural lecture; when it is a more junior member of staff his or her more senior colleagues will look forward to the arrival of a new research stimulus. There is a sense of mutual privilege: the university feels that it has attracted a high quality member of staff and the new member of staff feels that he or she is joining a high quality set of colleagues.

Re-structuring

A university that is geared to success is reluctant to contemplate failure and when it does it can be ruthless in dealing with it: a department that has slipped in the rankings cannot expect much sympathy. Staff in an ambitious university will expect the university to take some action to restore the department's reputation. Re-structuring programmes in less successful universities often cause deep concern, loss of morale, and excite claims that the centre is taking the opportunity to achieve a reorganization that it had wanted to do for a long time. This contrasts sharply with restructuring in an ambitious university where re-structuring will be thought the natural result of a falling off in academic performance. Indeed such is the power of peer review that the staff who may be responsible for the poor performance are much more likely to offer themselves for departure, providing appropriate severance packages can be made available, than would be the case in other universities. In other words a successful university which is ambitious to improve will not only be more able, and have less opposition, to move quickly to put things right, but the staff themselves will be more willing to take the consequences of poor performance; peer pressure will be more effective than central management in making the necessary changes.

Innovation and new development

Ambitious universities want to do new things; they set up innovation funds, they invest in new developments, they encourage staff to bring forward new proposals, they give 'above the call of duty' support to staff applying for external funds because each such step helps them to compete more effectively. If as is sometimes said 'the price of success is constant paranoia' then most successful universities are driven by a fear that they are being outpaced by competitor universities. Thus ambition and competitiveness lead to more risk taking but also to more success. The atmosphere emboldens ambitious staff to propose new developments which they would never have proposed elsewhere; young staff take risks with their research plans because institutional ambition transmits itself to individual ambition. Even when new ideas fail there is a general feeling that it is better to have tried them than not to have done so. By contrast in unambitious universities staff can be defensive, cautious about new ideas and anxious to find fault with them, unwilling to take risks and critical of those that do, and grudging in celebrating success. Such attitudes act as a damper on performance: young staff entering an ambitious university may flourish, win promotion and garner academic esteem; the same young staff entering an unambitious university may make progress much more slowly and may even fail altogether.

The ambitious university community

Ambition may begin in academic matters but in some universities it extends right through the university community. Older institutions may take international excellence for granted but in newer universities the university's ambition may be seen to stretch right through the staff: the estates staff may see it as a challenge to ensure that the grounds match up to the university's ambitions in academic areas, and the catering staff, the porters, the cleaning staff, the librarians and the sports staff try to emulate them. The seeds of institutional ambition once sown can be nurtured to extend to all aspects of institutional life: a university conference business that wins the award for the best conference venue feels that in its own field it is matching the performance of its academic colleagues, the campus supermarket that attracts more business and makes better profits each year can feel a justified pride in performance. And since these activities are run to generate resources to invest into academic activities they can see their success as contributing to academic success. The university porter who, while showing a visitor to an academic building, talks about the new building about to be erected next door, may offer a more convincing demonstration of institutional ambition and enthusiasm than the professional interchange with academic colleagues inside. The ambitious university community worries about getting the small details right, about making the campus work well, about providing a good service, ensuring that buildings look smart, that the grass is cut, the flower beds weeded and that the university is something they can be proud of. They want to point to the success recorded in the local newspaper or the evening news in just the same way as academic colleagues note references in the educational press or on the radio or TV.

The human resources strategy

A besetting weakness in many universities is to regard non-academic appointments not simply as secondary to academic appointments but as of having no material significance to the success of the institution: what is required, they say, are simply pairs of hands to provide the necessary support to the academic community. The emphasis is on 'support' or providing a service or even, to quote the most pejorative description, an 'ancillary service', not on the need for powers of initiative and organizational skills, the assumption being that these attributes are the preserve of the academic community. This, however, reflects a profound failure to understand the nature of university organization and the integrated relationship between good academic performance and good academic support or between a sound institutional strategy and effective analytical and policy formulation skills or between decision making at all levels and effective implementation. Taking time and trouble in the appointment of secretaries or technicians or finance clerks may not be as obviously significant to university success as the appointment of professors but the cumulative effect of appointing, developing and retaining good staff at all levels who have high morale and work well together can be of critical importance both in departmental performance and overall in the institution maintaining an edge over its competitors, moving more quickly and being publicly regarded as being more effective.

Many universities take little or no interest in the quality of the appointments in the category (in the pre-1992 universities) of academic-related staff (that is the administrative or professional staff appointed on salaries comparable to academic salaries, in central, faculty or departmental administration or in libraries, IT services or other professional academic support functions) yet these appointees may provide the key elements in translating good academic performance and effective exploitation of local assets into institutional success. If at the most senior levels of institutional decision making a combination of academic and administrative skills are required to deliver effective institutional management then it is essential that administrators should be selected with as much care as their academic colleagues and that they have a career structure which prepares them for responsibility. Ambitious universities will expect to draw their young administrators from the same cadre of highly qualified postgraduates as their young academic colleagues but they will also look for qualities of managerial potential. Effective university management is demanding and complex and calls for first class intellectual skills as well as the ability to manage in an academic environment. Young administrators need to be selected not simply to fill a given position but on their longer term potential as senior university administrators. They should be encouraged from an early point in their careers to contribute ideas and solutions to institutional problems, they should have quite frequent changes of duties to broaden their professional experience, and they should be stimulated by participation in policy discussion. If they have the time and the inclination they should be encouraged to do some university teaching as a way of widening their understanding of academic life. The career formation of these administrators tells us a great deal about universities' own understanding of the complexity of their needs at the highest levels of policy. Where some universities pay little regard to the aspirations and interests of their able young administrators until the administrators themselves make career moves to other institutions, others consciously seek to develop their potential with a view to deploying them into ever more complex, sensitive or taxing tasks. A university that has a core of ambitious and able administrators to call on to tackle managerial problems is much more likely to create innovative and cost-effective solutions. Ambitious universities recognize that they thrive on talent and that they have to develop talent wherever it is to be found and use it to their best advantage. Sluggish, conservative administrators, librarians or IT staff constrain universities and limit their opportunities, as well as contributing breakdowns and creating internal dislocations, while lively, energetic and forward looking staff in these areas can help drive universities forward and fuel their competitive urge.

The student body

No one benefits more from institutional ambition than the student body. Good institutional morale is communicated to students through staff–student relations, through the quality of the university estate, through the academic support services and through the number of events that take place in the university. Students are given self confidence by their university appearing high up in the league tables. But another influence is the students' union which is often unconsciously influenced by attitudes in the centre of the university: successful universities usually have successful students' unions which sponsor large numbers of student societies and social activities. Large vacation conference trades and other examples of an active university business life provide opportunities for student labour. But the ambitious university also attracts the attention of employers. In an age when no employer can fully comprehend the strengths and weaknesses of every university, nor can afford to conduct 'milk round' visits to more than a select few, those universities which stand out from the rest receive the most attention. A reputation for institutional dynamism becomes translated into a self-fulfilling prophecy of a student reputation for energy and ambition. Universities that are positive, outgoing and are seen to be successful capture their students' long term support in a way that more sluggish and defensive institutions fail to do; they build strong links with their alumni, and alumni-university relationships are maintained for mutual advantage. Former students are some of a university's best ambassadors and publicists; but their continued support is conditional on the picture they have of their course and the institution as a whole.

Good universities have always been competitive and ambitious: institutional histories bear testimony to the extent to which fund-raising, attracting key professors or starting new activities have been integral to individual universities' development. The effect of the changes in the 1980s and the impact of new public management reforms has sharpened the competition not fundamentally changed it. The publication of league tables in the media has dramatized for university staff information about their university's positioning of which they were perhaps not so aware in the past and has had a further incentivizing effect but most staff were already aware of the competitive pressures of university life both internally and externally. However, as Keller argues, while you need to know where you stand in the competition, if your strategy is simply to defend your position you will be overtaken; attack is the best form of defence (Keller 1983). What is new is that the RAE/REF, in particular, has put universities into actual competition for research status and therefore for resources. This has certainly raised the competitive stakes, because precise comparisons can now be made between institutions. One important result of this has been to show how previous assumptions in regard to categories of institution and their relative standing within the system have been overturned by the differential progress of particular institutions. It is possible to identify universities whose positions have fallen relative to others as well as universities which have improved. This has acted as a considerable spur to institutional ambition; it has also excited some institutional envy. Competition has at times, particularly in relation to the RAE, prompted actions which would probably not have occurred in the past. Managing institutional ambition may in the future be almost as much about restraining institutional exuberance in some institutions as about encouraging it.

10

Inhibitions to becoming entrepreneurial

This chapter explores the factors which prevent universities becoming entrepreneurial in spite of the environmental pressures to do so. It reviews the concept of the 'Entrepreneurial University' and suggests that the state itself and its funding mechanisms may be a major inhibiting factor; it draws a distinction between 'derived' autonomy and 'self directed' autonomy. Three university case studies are described to draw out internal inhibiting factors. It then identifies four intrinsic inhibiting elements: the state, organizational culture and tradition, the existence of too many layers of authority and the absence a 'strengthened steering core', that prevent these universities from taking advantage of the more entrepreneurial climate that has been stimulated by increased market forces and institutional competition.

The Entrepreneurial University

The modern period, where market forces and institutional competition play so much greater a part in shaping the higher education system than in the past, favours institutions which can chart a distinctive course, which are less reliant on the state, flexible in seizing opportunities and ambitious for institutional advancement.

These characteristics have often been summed up in the phase 'the entrepreneurial university' which was first introduced in Clark's *Creating the Entrepreneurial University* (1998). The claim to be an 'entrepreneurial' institution is, a decade or so later, widely used in higher education to an extent that one could reasonably assume that a revolution in the management of universities was underway. One of the difficulties lies in the definition of the word 'entrepreneurial' in a higher education context.

The Oxford English Dictionary traces its origin to the eighteenth-century French 'entreprenour', used to describe people who hired premises in which musical performances were given against an expectation of box office income: they were, therefore, risk takers. Clark's concept, however, is much broader: a diversified budget is indeed one of the most significant elements but how that budget is deployed is at least as important as how diversified it is. The word 'entrepreneur' can have disparagingly commercial overtones but alternatives such as 'innovative' or another Clark word, 'focused' do not capture what the concept is trying to describe, which is much more about a drive to identify and sustain a distinctive institutional agenda which is institutionally determined, not one effectively a product of state funding formulae. Definitions of entrepreneurialism in the strictly economic sense are also hard to come by. Audretsch (2002) in a comprehensive literature survey for the EU Commission, for example, concludes that there is little consensus about what actually constitutes entrepreneurial activity. Clark in the case studies in his 1998 book describes a group of universities which are breaking out of the constraints imposed by restrictive funding systems or the bureaucratic conventions of state run higher education (in continental Europe) by encouraging innovative academic behaviour, engaging in wide ranging partnerships with external bodies, generating non-state funding that can cross subsidize activities and be used to incentivize further entrepreneurial academic activity. In his second book on this theme *Sustaining Change in Universities* (2004) he enlarges the concept in phrases like 'the adaptive university', the 'proactive university' and 'the self reliant university'.

For his 1998 study Clark chose the University of Warwick, as it then was, as his exemplar of the entrepreneurial university concept with its central management committee, 'the Steering Committee', as the prime example of 'the strengthened steering core', emphasizing a flat decision making structure; its science park, the Warwick Manufacturing Group and other innovative centres as 'the expanded developmental periphery'; the University's earned income activity as providing 'the diversified funding base'; the use of non-state funding to support academic departments, as providing 'the enhanced academic heartland' and the overall culture of the institution, flat structures, good communication, opportunism and competitiveness as creating 'the integrated entrepreneurial culture'. Since 1998, however, with the intensification of marketization with the introduction in 2006 of variable tuition fees for home students and an increase in the recruitment of high fee paying international students, every UK university has seen a shift in attitude towards entrepreneurialism in its commercial sense.

Following on from Clark's study the EUEREK research project (Shattock 2009: 4) took the definition of entrepreneurialism in a university context rather further. In summary it reads as follows:

> Entrepreneurialism in a university setting is not simply about generating resources, although that represents an important element, but is also about generating activities that may be funded in innovative ways, and may involve financial or reputation risk. These activities may either be in response to anticipated and/or particular market needs, or are driven by the energy and imagination of individuals; in combination, they create a distinctive entrepreneurial profile.

This definition picks out a number of themes. The first is that entrepreneurialism is characterized by a range of activities which may involve risk, though the risk may be of reputation as well as financial. They may be driven by external markets of different kinds or by the creativity or innovative flair of individual academics leading to research centres, collaborations with external bodies, new self financing programmes or spin out companies. And it is where a profusion of these activities occur which can change the shape of an institution, that we can say that a university has become entrepreneurial. A university can thus be entrepreneurial in an academic as well as a managerial sense; to a considerable extent a reputation for entrepreneurialism rests on the activities of entrepreneurial academics, academic 'intrapreneurs' who build new academic enterprises around (most frequently) their research – generating research grants and industrial collaborations, recruiting research students and post-docs, creating innovative Master's degrees and short course programmes, offering consultancy, attracting colleagues to join them, creating a unit or enterprise which gains national and international recognition. Such developments will be funded by a mixture of 'soft' and institutional money, and may involve at times financial and reputation risk. It is the encouragement that university managements give to such activities that helps determine how entrepreneurial a university may be; it is very much in this sense that entrepreneurialism is deeply embedded in the most successful universities. A university under this definition which was simply good at generating non-state resources, could not be described as entrepreneurial unless it used those resources to stimulate and incentivize academic entrepreneurialism, investing in innovative academic ventures, and promoting activities which diversified the academic profile away from what would otherwise have been the characteristic product of a state funding formulae model.

There are many inhibitors to universities becoming entrepreneurial but it is clear that not the least of them is the state itself. The state may want to see institutional diversity but the allocation of its resources is via formulae which are designed to influence the higher education system to move in directions which the state believes to be appropriate. The transparency of the funding methodology combined with the competitive nature of the funding system puts universities under pressure to allocate resources in line with the formulae so that in practice their internal resource allocation decisions and therefore the shape of the institution is substantially dictated by technical decisions taken by the funding councils. Institutional strategies, however dressed up with the rhetoric of mission statements, become determined by the accidents of student demand and the consequences of remotely determined and mechanically applied funding formulae. Universities may appear to be autonomous but over dependency on state funding constrains them to follow an externally determined agenda. They may be described as having only a 'derived' autonomy rather than the 'self directed' autonomy implied by the phrase the 'self reliant' university. The entrepreneurial university will have psychologically broken free from the tramlines of state policy to chart its own individual strategy.

To try to analyse why or under what circumstances some universities are inhibited from taking up the challenges of the new entrepreneurial climate three case studies are discussed and compared with two institutions which can rightly be described as entrepreneurial, if in different ways.

University A

This university, although located in close proximity to a wealthy environment, attracted less than 10 per cent of its income from non-state sources and was, in consequence, almost entirely dependent on formula-based state funding. Since it was not research active it attracted only trivial amounts of research funding from the RAE and therefore received a teaching (T) income based entirely on its student numbers. But because it ranked low in student choices (it took two thirds of its numbers through the UCAS Clearing Scheme) and because it was primarily an 'access' university with low retention rates it was constantly at risk of not meeting its student number targets and of suffering a clawback of funding by its funding council. An improvement in its financial position by diversifying its income base was therefore an obvious priority in order to improve the teaching base, to make the university more attractive, and to enable it to follow a less reactive strategy. The university, however, showed itself to be constitutionally resistant to the entrepreneurial agenda: senior members of the University were given access to the successful approach to generating earned income at another university but declared that the financial literacy required by the process was outside their present competence; advised that one of its university companies in serious deficit was unlikely to be turned round it preferred not to face the difficult decisions that this entailed and the company continued to fail; student debt to the University had risen to a high level but remedies which involved organizational changes and examining good practice at other universities were not implemented, and annual write-offs continued to exercise the audit committee so that the University financial base was further weakened, placing an obvious pressure on the University's strategy.

Strategy itself remained exclusively in the hands of the senior management team which had become locked into a defensive mode of thinking so that it was unable to accept external advice which involved opening up any of the processes. Suggestions that a wider academic involvement in strategy would be advantageous were sidelined. While the senior management team paid lip service to ideas about entrepreneurialism, it was unable to realize them because they demanded changes in the way the University was managed. An impartial observer would conclude that the University could only improve its position if its inadequate state funding was prevented from further haemorrhaging through failure to meet recruit targets, if it collected student fees more effectively and if it increased its funding from non-state sources. But this was a university where a sense of hierarchy between the senior management team and the rest was endemic, where there was a resistance to bottom up ideas and where it was only feasible to launch entre-preneurial policies successfully from the centre (that is from the senior man-agement team) except that its bureaucratic culture prohibited such policies from being considered. At University A there was a gulf between the senior management team, made up almost solely of full-time non-academic man-agers, and a disempowered academic community starved of resources and bereft of any influence over policy. University A knew the entrepreneurial script but its structure frustrated its practical application.

The university took the route of a merger with another fairly similar insti-tution to escape facing up to the pressures of self directed change. The merger was a failure and has resulted in a larger but similarly dysfunctional institution.

University B

University B is a major university which had failed to punch its weight in research and which for the previous decade had been headed by a vice-chancellor who was more concerned to maintain the *status quo* than to com-pete with other institutions. As a result the university slipped down the tables; its decision making style was administrative, giving primacy to process rather than to the actual decisions it produced. It built up a large central bureau-cracy and central support services which consumed a very high proportion of a budget which was itself not reinforced by any substantial external earnings so that the university was starved of funds for investment in new academic ventures. The university had developed an over elaborate sense of hierarchy with strongly delineated status divisions between academics on the one hand and administrators on the other (precisely the opposite delineations to those that applied in University A). Resources were allocated to faculties and departments exclusively by formula with a fixed proportion reserved for the centre, and no incentives offered to reward innovation. There was no ration-alization of an overlarge departmental structure in spite of the warnings provided by poor performances in the RAE.

The university council recognized the fact of the university's decline and appointed an energetic vice-chancellor with a remit to push the university up into the top 10. The new vice-chancellor reduced the number of faculties, merged the prolixity of departments into a reduced number of schools, set up a 'strengthened steering core' which contained the deans of the new enlarged faculties so that they became part of central management and not just the spokesmen for their faculties, and established a joint council and senate strategy committee. The central bureaucracy, both administrative and support services, was radically cut back and a unitary (rather than the previ-ous 'tertiary') administration was established under a new registrar. The effect was to change radically the top structure of the university with the aim of providing conditions appropriate to the development of academic initiative lower down. All this was positive, as was the decision to abolish the previous cumbersome resource allocation system, but its replacement was not a judgemental system which encouraged competition for resources but one which remained rooted in formulae derived from the funding council. A shadow earned income machinery made little progress because administrators, inured to their previous support staff status, were unable to challenge departments effectively on their plans to generate income and no one was willing to insist that a significant element of resources earned should come to the centre for investment in new ventures. The new super faculties, to which extensive powers were devolved, proceeded to begin to build up again the administrative structures and costs that had been cut out of the centre. What seemed to be happening was that a dynamic new vice-chancellor was able to make immediate structural changes designed to create the conditions to encourage academic initiative but when each new structure was introduced the institution unconsciously set about subverting it by recreating the bureaucracy that it was supposed to replace. Eight years later the vice-chancellor retired. Much had been achieved in the refurbishment of the campus and the development of an 'expanded developmental periphery' but the 'academic heartland' remained un-enhanced and the university remained anchored in the twenties in the league tables.

This suggests that a long period of bureaucratic management can undermine the wish to create an entrepreneurial structure. Cultural change at the faculty/departmental level is extraordinarily difficult to achieve even when initiative is deliberately passed down from the top. Moreover, long established hierarchies of academics over administrators make administrators uncomfortable at challenging academic conservatism; a lifetime of service does not prepare people for partnership with the academic community. A university may admire the entrepreneurial model, and even concede its success, but may not necessarily be convinced it can work in its own institution. University B had previously benchmarked itself against its traditional comparators, other civic universities, against whom it performed moderately well. But when compared with the published league tables in which many newer institutions had passed it, the university was shown to have performed much less well. Nevertheless the instinct deep down remained that these new institutions were somehow not fair comparators – their achievements were somehow exaggerated by the league tables, and the University should continue to compare itself with its 'family' even though such comparisons would not provide the incentive to match its ambition. Core rigidities were resistant to top down change.

University C

University C like University A came from a local authority background but had recruited students well so that it had expanded rapidly. It was much less hierarchical, in that academics and administrators operated in comparative harmony, but like University A it had a heavy administrative bureaucratic centre which ran the institution. Also like University A, its non-state funding line was weak and its state funding was derived from the T not the R line. All three universities devolved budgets from the centre, A to departments, B and C to faculties. In B's case where the research culture encouraged differential departmental funding based on the funding council's allocation of R money, departments also attracted research support of their own through research grants and contracts. But in University C allocations were made solely to the deans, who were permanent appointments, whose success in the job was seen primarily in financial terms, that is, staying within budget. Departments, even those that were research active, were solely dependent on their dean for their funding, and could not rely on receiving what R funding they were entitled to under the formula. Income from non-state sources such as international student fees, overheads on research or short course income were retained centrally by the dean and could be allocated to cover financial shortfalls in other departments. On the one hand, the university adopted a strategy which strongly encouraged the development of research and entrepreneurial activity, but on the other, its concentration on balancing the books at faculty level, making each dean financially accountable and giving departments no financial autonomy, deprived departments of the ability to build up funds to pump prime new initiatives or to provide an adequate research infrastructure. Research success in one department was treated as a cash cow to pay the debts incurred by shortfalls in student numbers or other unexpected costs in another. Since departments were at the bottom of a long chain of command through deans, to a deputy vice-chancellor to a senior management group in which financial rather than academic priorities represented the dominant concern, it was not surprising that the drive to improve the university's research standing had stalled and that innovation and new initiatives were frustrated. At the top level of the institution the intention was to grow research and make the university entrepreneurial but the structures that had been designed to keep the university out of deficit in the difficult post-1992 years combined to stifle the initiative that was required at the bottom to bring this about.

Cambridge

If we apply Clark's taxonomy to Cambridge one can identify very clearly 'the developmental periphery', 'the enhanced academic heartland', 'the diversified funding base' and 'the integrated entrepreneurial culture', but in 2001 one looked in vain for 'the strengthened steering core'. One of the main criticisms of the Report on the governance and management of Cambridge (Shattock 2001b) was the absence of a clear focus for decision making and an effective machinery of management and governance; worse still, what was identified was a convoluted system of governance which maximized the opportunity for stopping central University initiatives (so that the centre devoted much of its time devising strategies to avoid the road blocks) while offering little encouragement for the development of University initiatives from outside the centre. In spite of its wealth the University was unable to move funds around flexibly and on its operating budget was forecasting a deficit of some £10m. Yet what Cambridge had was highly independent, dynamic academic departments which, with minimal administrative underpinning, maintained an extraordinarily entrepreneurial culture.

Cambridge was *par excellence* an academically run university where departments and colleges resented and resisted interference from the centre, where professional management costs were alarmingly low, where there were few effective rules for intellectual property rights, where overhead charges on externally funded research took no cognizance of the University's market position, where the individual academic was bound only minimally by regulatory constraint, and where relationships between academics and administrators at the formal level of university management were as bad as they could be found anywhere.

How was it then that Cambridge was so undeniably successful? First, it represented an extreme example of 'self-directed' autonomy; indeed a visit to Cambridge was (and is) almost like a visit to an independent state, not just to an autonomous university. Second, in spite of the rigidities in its financial structures it had significant reserves and had the self confidence that goes with that. It was at the opposite end of the spectrum to University C, which was in danger of crushing the life out of entrepreneurial behaviour by the imposition of corporate financial controls: for Cambridge the bottom line was primarily intellectual and academic not financial. Finally, Cambridge had a long history of achievement; its organizational culture was long established and its respect for academic excellence was of very long standing. Cambridge was the living embodiment of the Matthew effect where high calibre academics attract other high calibre academics and where, in addition, the quality of the academic environment added a further dimension to its attractiveness to scholars. In the end these characteristics outweighed or counteracted the University's weakness in developing an effective central steering core. In Cambridge, in place of a central steering core, there was a dispersed understanding of what Cambridge is about, a unifying culture which in some ways pulled the University together. This was sufficient to keep the University in business as one of the top ranked universities in the world.

Eight years later Cambridge had largely remedied its weakness. It had established a central decision making machinery, made changes in the make up of the senior cadre of academic and administrative officers and taken steps to restore trust within the academic and administrative community. This had served to re-unite the University's sense of purpose. But Cambridge's strength lies in the vibrancy of its academic culture, the vigour of its academic 'intrapreneurs' and the shared understanding of the University's essential values. Cambridge represents a supreme example of how a positive organizational culture could compensate for weaknesses in central governance and management.

The London School of Hygiene and Tropical Medicine (LSHTM)

The LSHTM represents an unusual example of academic entrepreneurialism. As a postgraduate only institution concerned with research on a global scale on health in a worldwide community it rejects the usual processes of seeking to exploit its research for financial benefit; it takes an entirely altruistic view of its research outcomes. However, less than 20 per cent of its funding comes directly from the funding council and 63 per cent from research grants and contracts and it runs a distance learning Master's programme initially set up entirely for entrepreneurial reasons to generate additional core income, over and above the income it derives from international student fees. It has a well developed 'strengthened steering core' with an SMT that meets weekly, which is closely linked and responsive to its academic community, but it also has a hard nosed policy of giving only a restricted number of the senior academic staff permanent appointments leaving the remainder of the staff dependent on their ability to generate their salary through research contracts (although the impact is reduced by the availability of bridging support to carry staff over between different projects); there is a strong emphasis on performance management. The School is intensely globally competitive to achieve major research objectives but remains highly collegial in its governance arrangements. A feature of the School's development is how it has adapted its management structures in two major reorganizations to enable it better to address its various research markets so that over a period it has moved from 15 departments to only three to facilitate greater collaboration in deploying research expertise in order to improve the success rate in major research grant applications. Another feature is the way it interacts internationally with major grant giving agencies to maximize its positioning to benefit from new global initiatives in the health field. But what sets it apart from Universities A, B and C is the compelling nature of its organizational culture, the way it combines a commitment to competition with a commitment to professional and institutional values, its shared approach to future institutional development and its acceptance of the need to maintain financial stability in a situation where the survival of the institution depends on its ability to continue to attract grant income (Shattock and Becker 2006).

Inhibitions to becoming entrepreneurial

This chapter argues that there are some intrinsic inhibitions which prevent some universities becoming entrepreneurial:

- First, we must identify the state. While on the one hand we should not criticize *per se* the transparency by which the components of total funding are laid bare for each university because this offers accountability, the effect can be to dominate the way funding is distributed at the institutional level to faculties and departments. It is also evident that the climate of financial stringency and of institutions operating at the limit of their resources has sapped the will of many universities to reach their own judgements on differentials within institutional resource allocation. Equally serious are the levels of external regulation, quality mechanisms and accountability which only the most successful and self confident institutions seem able to keep in perspective. Too much micro management by funding agencies can further whittle away 'self-directed' autonomy.

- Second, there is organizational culture and tradition. Universities that have operated historically in a bureaucratic or essentially defensive mode do not find it easy to change: it is not enough to make a change in top management; it will need a consistent approach to change management over many years. Universities are bottom heavy organizations and the entrepreneurial message from the top will take a long time to percolate down to the levels where it needs to be understood and acted upon. Moreover much of the bureaucratic framework is locked in at the technical levels of decision making – whether recurrent resources are distributed on a formulaic basis which mirrors the funding council; whether departments' earnings are locked away in the departments that generate them or are shared on an agreed basis with the centre so that some element can be invested back by the centre in new initiatives; whether budgets are devolved to colleges or faculties and are then shared out equitably with no room left for investment in new projects; or whether academic structures encourage break-outs by talented individuals, or impose constraints which stifle initiatives. Universities will not become entrepreneurial if they do not impose their own criteria on internal resource allocations, or if a diversified income base is not used creatively, or if an institutional climate becomes risk averse through an over concentration on the financial bottom line. Many organizational cultures seem almost designed to discourage the academic 'intrapreneur', and impose disincentives and impediments on any academic who threatens to create some new initiative, which might turn into a new programme or even a new centre or institute. Academic 'intrapreneurs' need to be encouraged, incentivized and celebrated because it is likely that over time it is from the fruit of their activities that the university will earn a reputation for distinctiveness. If budgets are devolved to deans or college heads they must be required to retain a sum to support innovation and new ideas.

- A third inhibition lies in structures which impose layers of authority between the operating units, the academic departments, and the strategic centre. These layers are often defence mechanisms designed to transfer detailed control from the centre to an intermediate level closer to the activities. Too often, they distance the centre from the action points, and, because they are accountable upwards, they impose bureaucracy and concepts of common treatment where incentives and differentiation is required. In some institutions as in University C the powers of the dean reduced those of the heads of department so that just where leadership was most needed it was fatally weakened.

- Finally, universities tend to lack an effective 'strengthened steering core'. Either they have a senior management team which, as its name implies, manages the institution in a hierarchical manner and is sometimes only made up of managers (either non-academic or academics who have been converted into managers) or they have an institutional head who uses the central team essentially as an agent for the implementation of policy. The incorporation of deans into this structure as members of key decision making bodies can ameliorate the position but if they are line managers of their faculties they are in danger of being turned into the agents of top management for policy implementation, rather than serving as representatives of the operating units and feeding ideas into the centre. Universities need a 'strengthened steering core' because personal direction by a chief executive is not effective except for short periods of crisis. The central decision making machinery, however, needs to be mixed, comprising both academics and administrators, which can mediate and reconcile external environmental pressures and internally driven initiatives whether bottom-up or top-down, and who can maintain close communication with departments in a way which both shapes departmental policies and transmits them upwards to become elements of institutional strategy. The lack of such a mechanism in Universities A and C is symptomatic of a wider separation of management from the academic community. Its existence at LSHTM provides the integration of academic and managerial elements of institutional leadership and its inter-permeation with the operating units. Cambridge was bound together by a culture which was intensely internally competitive, and was buttressed by resources and reputation. If the Cambridge structure could be exported and applied in any of Universities A, B or C it would result in institutional failure or at least in a decline in institutional performance. At Universities A and C the academic community would lack the research excellence to utilize the departmental freedom which the Cambridge structure offered; at University B the bureaucratic culture would prevent its exploitation.

What Cambridge and LSHTM teach us is that building a positive organizational culture takes time and nurturing. A strengthened steering core on its own, as in University B, may not be enough to change a culture but, whereas at LSHTM or at Warwick in Clark's study, it becomes integral to the formulation of policy, receptive to initiating and coordinating new ideas, it can be a transforming agent of institutional advance.

While the word 'entrepreneurial' has entered the higher education lexicon its institutional achievement is thus by no means so common. 'Derived' autonomy is much more common than 'self directed' autonomy. Within the

UK system, to become genuinely entrepreneurial, institutions need strong academic participation in management; an institutional culture which is created by a management team will not extend much beyond that team. Institutions need close working relationships and trust between the academic and administrative communities so that the administrators have the self confidence to work with the academic community as equal partners and can challenge it on policy issues without appearing to seek to become a dominant partner. To be successful as an entrepreneurial university academic staff of high quality are required; there is little evidence that entrepreneurial activity flourishes on a sustainable basis in second or third tier institutions. Being entrepreneurial means first, being entrepreneurial in academic matters not in finance alone; financial success follows academic success, and reinforces it, but cannot create it. Being entrepreneurial means managing the university holistically where it is recognized that all activities are interrelated and where getting each activity right develops an institutional forward momentum building self confidence to take risks and to invest in success. Entrepreneurial universities compete vigorously in the national and international academic markets for excellent staff, for students and for major grants, and they are ruthless at analysing their failures; they will not be satisfied with a modest performance which can be dressed up to look as if it meets the targets set by the state because they will want to succeed in every forum in which they compete. 'Entrepreneurial', 'stand up' universities are not necessarily comfortable institutions to work in but their vigour and dynamism maintains high morale which itself offers a more effective platform for progress than the defensive, over administered and over controlled approach to university management to be found in some contemporary higher education institutions.

11

Turning round failure, arresting decline, managing retrenchment

This chapter reviews institutional failures in higher education and compares the strategies for reversing them with turning round corporate failures. It applies Dunlap's four principles (1996) to university situations and identifies how far they apply. It argues that university or departmental failure must be viewed in the round rather than as the product of a particular activity and that any strategy for recovery must address the full range of its work. It reviews arresting departmental decline from the perspective of a departmental head and concludes that a centre:departmental dialogue represents an essential ingredient to departmental turn rounds. It emphasizes in all such cases the need to achieve academic consent. The chapter looks at mergers as a strategy for arresting institutional decline, and using data from the private sector, concludes that there are dangers in assuming that corporate mergers have strengthened companies; indeed the evidence points the other way. It concludes that university mergers from strength may prove to be successful but not from weakness, and it argues that arresting institutional decline must continue to rest in an institution's own hands. Finally, the chapter considers the issue of managing institutional retrenchment and identifies a series of basic principles which can be applied.

What constitutes university failure or decline?

Institutional or departmental failures in academic life do not generally occur quickly like an Enron, a Marconi or a Northern Rock, but represent the slow working through of a number of factors, most obviously the changing preferences of students, the ageing of key staff, the failure to adapt to external pressures or the falling off of grant income. Unlike companies where rising costs, falling order books or unwise acquisitions tend to make potential failure manifest over quite a short timescale, both university and departmental decline is often not identified until some external event brings it to light, such as a poor performance in the RAE, a failure to win a research grant competition or a sudden fall in student applicants. Universities are not good at maintaining long run data series which indicate where a department or institution is slipping down league tables (see Chapter 4), and are too prone to criticize the league table rather than face up to the indications that these sources of data provide evidence that changes must be made. Prior to the RAE/REF, institutional and departmental research reputations were protected by image not substance because comparative data, unless mined from research council grant records, was not available. Even now there are universities which do not monitor their student applications on a rolling five year basis to determine trends. Another category of decline, and indeed failure, is financial and can arise out of mismanagement. In the modern period academic decline in terms of research or in the student market precedes financial decline by a year or two only because of the linkage of RAE ratings or the achievement of student number targets with recurrent grant levels, but there have also been cases (Cardiff and Lancaster being examples) where financial mismanagement alone has provoked severe institutional crises; in Lancaster's case the institution survived without long term damage, in Cardiff's it survived only because it was taken over by the University of Wales Institute of Science and Technology (UWIST) in a merger which brought in new management. Other financial crises have arisen because of incautious investment in expensive capital programmes, the collapse of a major department in a heavily devolved structure or the revelation of incorrect student number returns which prompted a substantial clawback of funds to the funding council.

Financial mismanagement, however, mostly reflects strategic failures which themselves derive from academic issues: the case of the incautious investment in new buildings arose out of an over-ambitious academic plan (Lancaster); the destabilization arising from the failure of a major department was the result of a system of wholesale academic and managerial devolution which gave the centre no locus to intervene when academic programmes were not working (Shattock and Rigby 1983); while cases of misreporting of student numbers tend to arise in universities failing to meet intake targets (South Bank University, London Metropolitan University). Even the mismanagement at Cardiff and Lancaster had antecedents in incautious academic strategies: the refusal to cut back academic programmes when the UGC was imposing budget reductions, in the case of Cardiff, and the wish to find an alternative mechanism to fund long term maintenance and some new capital developments so as to avoid cutting back on investment for the next RAE, in the case of Lancaster. In both cases misjudgement, lack of professionalism, and the absence of adequate financial control also played a large part.

These were among the more celebrated cases of institutional failure that attracted publicity in the UK but there have been others where misgovernance (Huddersfield, Portsmouth and Glasgow Caledonian Universities) or academic organizational failures (Thames Valley University) have caught the headlines. But there are also many institutions which have not faced failure in the technical sense but where academic decline has simply not been arrested. There are universities, for a variety of reasons, not punching their academic weight; there are other universities, ambitious to propel themselves into 'the top 10' which are anxious to improve their performance. Finally there are universities at the top who stay there in part because they are able to identify and turn round or eliminate failing activities so as to maintain a consistently high performing institution. There are some accounts in the literature as to why institutions hit the buffers (Shattock 1988; Segal Quince Wicksteed 1988) and there are accounts of how institutions handled the 1981–4 budget cuts (Shattock and Rigby 1983; Sizer 1987, 1988) or there are reports like the QAA's (Quality Assurance Agency for Higher Education) on Thames Valley (QAA 1998) or the reports on the Capsa disaster at Cambridge (Finkelstein 2001; Shattock 2001b) but there are few impartial reports on how institutions recovered, or were turned round.

Turning companies round

In the business world, however, there is a considerable literature about how companies were turned round often written by 'business gurus' or 'company doctors' who have, in their own words, done it on behalf of the shareholders (Dunlap 1996; Pete and Platt 2001; Sutton 2001). There are also popular business texts that offer analyses of failures and turnrounds (Peters and Waterman 1982; Grinyer *et al.* 1998). It goes without saying that turning round a university and a company are very different because the 'businesses' are very different: companies tend to have only two main objects – to make a profit, or to satisfy the shareholders – and the accounts provided by business gurus celebrate producing profitability, or shareholder value, but do not tell us whether what has been achieved is a quick fix or a long term recovery. But business has far fewer inhibitions in forcing quick changes of direction, and financial approaches in business, with acquisitions, private equity deals, flotations, mergers, sell offs and the ease of reducing and deploying staff, offer a range of options not available to university management.

In spite of this Dunlap's four major principles for success in turning round companies: 'get the right management'; 'pinch pennies'; 'improve the balance sheet by focusing the business'; 'get a real strategy for success', could with a certain adjustment represent some key headings for action in the university world. Indeed when he describes what he was told about the Scott Paper Company, around the rescue of which his book is based:

> This is acute. Its an overly bureaucratic organisation, spending too much money on the wrong things. It's so slow moving that it can't get out of its own way.
>
> (Dunlap 1996: 5)

It is not difficult to think of institutional parallels in the university world. *Mean Business* is an unappealing work, long on the macho style of its author and short on sophisticated business analysis, but it contains strategic insights about turning companies round which go beyond the 'chainsaw' nickname, which the author clearly enjoyed. In some ways it shows how different business life can be from the university world but in others it can offer cautionary messages to universities. Describing a major conglomerate with a large top-heavy headquarters staff it makes the point 'that everything ran smoothly because nothing was happening'. This is not a bad description of some universities whose structures seem to emphasize smoothly running administrative processes over the dynamism necessary to be competitive (the University B case study from Chapter 10, before the new vice-chancellor was appointed, provides an example). It argues convincingly that speed of reaction is an important element in bringing about change. Universities that react immediately and firmly to a poor RAE/REF result or a downturn in intake are much more likely to show an improvement next time than those that allow the process to extend over two or three years. One might balk at firing the whole management team, which seems to have been the approach that won Dunlap his sobriquet, but changing the management in significant ways in a university, whether in the centre or at the department level, and doing it quickly, is likely to be much more effective than simply supplementing individuals already in place with yet more staff and hoping the situation will improve. It also stresses that 'a real strategy looks at short term and at long term results', that 'you must have a direction that dictates what you do on a day-to-day basis. If your strategy is to have a global brand, what are you doing day-in, and day-out to develop it?' (Dunlap 1996: 100). In university day-to-day decision making over a whole range of disparate areas, whether about staff appointments at whatever level, the quality of student recruitment material or the appearance of the campus, must be geared to longer term success. In particular it requires a proactive approach to strategy:

> Look ahead ten years but don't expect or demand precise adherence to such a long-term vision. That approach will bankrupt you. Instead, set new goals along the way, adjust annual plans so they dovetail into new strategic directions. Review action plans daily, weekly, monthly and yearly to assess whether conditions have changed and whether it's time for you to shift in a different direction.
>
> Most companies are generally good in laying out a strategy. They think through developing products and the competitive market. Where they fail is in implementation. Walk into most businesses and they can show you a thick strategic plan, attractively bound and labeled. But just putting the plan together doesn't make it happen. You have to have follow-through and the discipline to implement your plan or to change it if it is not working. Most executives don't follow through enough. Or, they do it over such a long period of time that the competition beats them to the finish line.
>
> (Dunlap 1996: 100–1)

Universities may not need to review their actions daily or weekly, but his remarks about strategy and 'follow through' are highly relevant in a university context where the implementation of decisions can be notoriously weak.

Universities and the four Dunlap principles

Dunlap's four principles are deceptively simple, and the strength of his approach is that he makes it appear they are simple to put into practice in business. In universities they are certainly not simple both because of the legal complexities of university constitutions and because precipitate action may prove to be counterproductive in destabilized situations. The first principle, getting the right management team, is a good example of this. Universities in serious decline or actually failing will invariably have a management structure which is dysfunctional in important ways. At Cardiff, where dysfunctionality was endemic, the removal from the scene of the principal, the registrar and the bursar and the elevation to acting principal of the senior professor who had been the academic most critical of the previous regime together with the creation of a small operational group of more junior administrators until new appointments from outside could be made, served only to demonstrate that the institution was unable to rescue itself because the whole decision making structure had been infected by an inability to act without strong (perhaps better described as 'wilful') central direction. So a merger had to be arranged with an institution that was more effectively led.

In many such situations where huge communication gaps exist between central authority in the vice-chancellors' office and the academic community, the removal of the vice-chancellor from the scene without other compensatory changes produces only vacuum and drift because no new leadership cohort or structure can be found to fill the gap. Leadership or 'the right management team' requires legitimacy in a university context and, if it is to be effective in a destabilized institution, it needs to draw in members of the academic community. This is not just to ensure that decisions are taken that reflect academic thinking but because the academic community will only feel committed to difficult decisions if it believes that they have been taken by some of their own representatives. But putting that team into place will require, in the university context, both personal negotiation and a positive vote by a body like the senate or the governing body where different and contrary interests may be represented. In some universities the solution to decline is seen as either to appoint yet further managers for example additional quality managers or enhanced research offices, or more student recruiters, producing the overly costly and hierarchical bureaucratic management that Dunlap was so keen to remove, or alternatively, to remove or side-line all the professional managers and replace them in managerial positions with enthusiastic senior academics who lack the necessary professional experience and know-how to get things done. In both cases, therefore, changes in 'the management team' may accelerate decline rather than reverse it, although in the short run the changes may produce false expectations that decline is about to be arrested.

Even when institutional decline or failure is primarily academic in nature, lax expenditure habits are likely to be associated because a loss of rigour in academic matters usually replicates itself in matters of administration. Of course, the more institutional management itself becomes vested in a hierarchical structure and the more that executive powers are concentrated in a very few people the more likely it is that salary differentials will grow and other aspects of corporate lifestyles will become more obtrusive. The introduction of 'pinch penny' cost reduction schemes should offer more than simply reducing overheads and should re-introduce corporate disciplines and a proper sense of what De Geus has described as a conservative approach to finance (De Geus 1997) (see Chapter 3). Dunlap makes a particular point of the symbolism in company turnrounds of closing prestigious corporate headquarters and relocating them to a much smaller set of offices close to one of a company's major plants. Opportunities such as this are not likely to occur in most universities facing decline or failure but symbolic cutbacks in, for example, university corporate entertaining, the loss of special transport facilities or the added use of energy saving devices are often valuable in dramatizing the importance of adopting more frugal ways of living campus-wide. Frugality is not just a matter of symbolism, however, because turnrounds will always require the investment of new resources, whether to pay for voluntary redundancies or to buy new equipment to support successful groups or enterprises. Freeing up resources for investment represents a critical requirement for any turnround.

Reform and renewal in the academic heartland of a university must be the key to turning round failure or arresting decline, albeit this will not be achieved unless the institution's management is improved and funds can be found for new investment. If we adapt Dunlap's phrase 'improve the balance sheet by focusing the business' to 'reviewing academic strengths and weaknesses and deciding whether to reinforce strengths and rescue weaknesses or eliminate them' we can begin to identify the analogies. The process by which this is brought about, however, may determine the outcome because if it lacks credibility or is thought to be prejudiced or simply wrong headed it will excite opposition even from those who are not materially affected, and opposition in a university context may mean adverse votes in a senate meeting, representations to a governing body or refusal to implement at a departmental level. The 1980s produced a variety of approaches to institutional reviews ranging from the use of rhetorical language condemning 'extinct volcanoes in the common room' as a means of generating support for decisive action, to the creation of 'gang of four' exercises where an experienced group of disinterested academics were asked to interview weak academic units and propose appropriate action (Shattock 1982). Universities that did not respond vigorously in that decade tended to suffer more in the next. In the 1990s reviews became more sophisticated incorporating external advisers drawn from the membership of RAE or QAA panels;

as an alternative approach many institutions have relied on budgetary incentives where the decisions are devolved to faculties (or to deans) or direct to departments using a 'sticks and carrots' approach where a reduction in budget is intended to force changes and a reward system is designed to improve performance. Gioia and Thomas describe an approach, which has been adopted in more than one UK university, where the top management of a large public research university, seen to be failing to match changed conditions in the 1990s, based their programme of strategic change on a vision of becoming a 'top 10' public university, this becoming a slogan to rally institutional support (Gioia and Thomas 1996). The danger of such rhetoric, however, unless accompanied by action at all levels is that it has little impact at the micro level of the academic departments where, as we saw in Chapter 2, many of the critical day-to-day strategic decisions must be taken.

Except in crisis situations where special action may be required, there is no substitute for a regular review mechanism. Ambitious universities will always use RAE/REF results as a basis for departmental reviews and the elimination of weaknesses. But regular reviews of research performance, department by department, will be the norm in research intensive universities. Equally reviews of GCE 'A' level entry scores, retention rates, external examiners reports and the National Student Survey scores are necessary both as an audit on performance but also as a driver for improvement. The success of these measures depends on the climate in which they are undertaken and the organizational culture of the institution: they can be undertaken to satisfy self-regulation requirements of bodies like the QAA or can be manifestations of the competitive spirit which will produce over time better performance, higher league table rankings and an enhancement of reputation.

In the UK, a research intensive university – because of its dependence on a state funding mechanism in which approximately 80 per cent of the state's recurrent financial support is based on student numbers – needs to have a significant undergraduate population to provide a secure financial base. (By comparison MIT's or Princeton's first degree population is not much more than half that of Cambridge.) This has the benefit of forcing research intensive universities to take student recruitment and undergraduate teaching seriously and provides a disincentive to allowing research stars to withdraw from the teaching process. However, a research intensive university facing a decline in research ratings will suffer a disproportionate financial impact because any decline in research reputation will be given publicity in the published league tables and may be reflected in falls in student recruitment. Successful universities may be able to maintain recruitment to subject areas where there are national shortfalls in student numbers because they have a strong institutional brand, but universities perceived as being in decline will be placed under a double pressure in these subject areas where national trends may be accelerated by falling academic morale resulting from declining research performance. Evidence of this can be found in the closure of physics and chemistry departments where the costs of reinvigorating research has been made worse in the short term by shortfalls in student-related income. Thus the solution for a research intensive university facing a dip in performance must be radical if it is to be effective. By the same token a vigorous research intensive department that faces shortfalls in its student number targets will be threatened in a period of acute financial stringency and internal competition for resources by its university's inability to maintain uneconomic staffing levels in departments short of students.

Thus the solutions for a university facing a falling off in research performance must be multifaceted and decisive; once a university joins the down escalator, reversing the trend demands major action to turn the situation round. Unlike one of Dunlap's company turnrounds, turning round performance in a research intensive university cannot be achieved quickly: a period of two RAE cycles may be necessary, even if action is taken immediately RAE results are released. The two critical steps must be a searching review of every academic department, not just those that have most obviously declined, together with an assessment of the investment funding necessary to put matters right. The review has to look at the research performance and potential of every member of staff, the research grant income and the size and recruitment potential of the postgraduate population. The reason why the review must be so comprehensive is that even if the failing departments can be turned round (or eliminated) some departments that start the period looking strong may reveal evidence that their performance levels are not secure either because of ageing staff or long term trends in student choice, so that an overall institutional recovery could be further set back by problems in later years.

One of the most significant differences between a university and a company turnround are the problems surrounding staff. A decline in research performance is usually related to a falling off of individual staff research productivity. Normally once this sets in it is difficult for individuals to recreate the research enthusiasm necessary for its renewal, though there may always be special cases. It is relatively easy to identify high performers and low performers but deciding the longer term potential of those in between is much more difficult. But even when some tentative conclusions are reached they have to be consolidated with information about teaching needs and quality and student recruitment factors and with an estimate of the resources that may be available to procure voluntary redundancies and recruit new research active staff. This takes us to the financial aspects of turnround. Decline cannot be arrested and the institution cannot recover without a significant investment in new people and in persuading some existing staff to retire. Additional sums may also be necessary for equipment, refurbishment of academic premises or for improved marketing. Where a company can improve its productivity by cutting its overheads, a university must nearly always bring in new research active staff, probably at the senior end, to give new research leadership. Even when a university has the cash available to cover the redundancy costs it may need to keep the posts vacant for a year or more to generate the ability to bring in more research active replacements.

Closing a department may be a process which takes four or even five years to complete because of the need to provide teaching for the student cohorts already committed to the programme. So not only is the timetable for turning a research intensive institution round liable to extend over several years but throughout there are problems of institutional and departmental morale as staff retire and new staff are appointed. To carry it through an institution must show real determination, and must be prepared to act speedily both in conducting the review, acting on it and recruiting new staff. Above all it must maintain the morale of its staff and present a buoyant and positive image to the outside world, while it takes the necessary steps to revive its fortunes.

By comparison, turning round non-research intensive universities is less complicated because the key dimension of non-performance is likely to be student recruitment (although like Thames Valley University it might be the report of an external agency like the QAA). Generating cash for more effective marketing of the university may be necessary but is not likely to be sufficient on its own. Detailed reviews of curricula need to be accompanied by real surgery in areas where student recruitment looks unrecoverable together with divestment of related property assets in order to generate cash to cover the run down. But the turnround of a non-research intensive university must also address research issues and must establish some nodes of successful research, not only to raise morale internally and to establish a more positive external image but to ensure that the university remains competitive in its ability to attract staff. Once again the level of investment is the key: and unless the university has sizeable reserves such an investment is only likely to come from significant savings on staff costs.

In either case, the research intensive or the non-research intensive institution will do well to consider its estates and buildings and how they reflect its reputation and morale. Institutions in decline instinctively cut their maintenance budgets to make savings to prop up weak departments which it is hoped, against the odds, will somehow refashion themselves. They would be better advised to close the weak departments and use the money saved to refurbish the campus, thus raising the morale of students and staff and providing a better image for student recruitment. Too often academic decline and low morale is accompanied by impoverished campuses. Decline then feeds decline and can quickly turn into failure. In a period of financial stringency turning round institutions is made more difficult by the absence of resources for re-investment. It is not enough simply to reduce staff costs, but the savings from staff cuts must be used positively to bring in new faces to regenerate departments. Speed of action, robust decisions and unquenchable optimism are the essential characteristics of such a process.

This chapter has concentrated so far on looking at institutional declines from a central perspective, where committees in the centre review departments that are seen to be failing and call for changes. Universities are, as we have seen, a form of conglomerate and it is not the case that departments as the components of the conglomerate are only reformed by pressure from head office, the board or whatever other euphemism one chooses. On the other hand, departments are not just 'little universities' and, because they are broadly mono-disciplinary, their dynamics are very different. Academic reviews of research, annual staff appraisals or the assessment of teaching evaluation forms are conducted between staff who are both more knowledgeable and less impartial because they are in the same discipline than would be the case if they were conducted at an institutional level. Questions of seniority in the field both obtrude and can be helpful in untangling problems and providing opportunities. Challenging departmental strategies at departmental meetings may mean challenging a leadership group on whom one's promotion may rest. These potential tensions place a much higher premium on departmental leadership in a personal sense than might be the case for an institution as a whole. If a department is in decline it is clear that its head (or chair) has the major responsibility in improving its performance. Ramsden argues that: 'Evaluating, recognising and developing staff performance are the very essence of the academic leader's responsibilities' (Ramsden 1998: 205) and goes on to offer suggestions on performance management systems involving feedback, dealing with difficult staff, staff conflict and underperformance. He emphasizes the importance of 'ownership' of the system by the academic staff themselves (Ramsden 1998).

But to reverse decline, departmental heads must find resources to create new posts, and must then find appropriate people to fill them and carry their senior colleagues along with them in the process. Heads must also stimulate new activities or enable others to do so so as to change their department's focus and build new strengths. To be successful, heads must work closely with supportive central university authorities – new appointments will require new facilities and perhaps start-up funds; new activities, like new Master's programmes, need crash programmes to market them and perhaps special financial arrangements to launch them; retaining valuable staff who are being invited to move elsewhere may need individual reassurances as to their future promotion; persuading non-performing staff that they should be redeployed into administrative functions or that they should leave altogether will require extensive consultation as to the individual's and the institution's rights and responsibilities.

Heads of department who are going to lift the performance and rating of their departments are unlikely to be able to do it on their own, but will need support from senior colleagues and from the centre. Once again the importance of quick communication, speedy decision making and informal relationships within the institution must be emphasized. The task of the centre is to give the head all possible support including advice on how best to chart a course most expeditiously through university regulations and protocols. The task of the head is to convince his/her colleagues that improved performance will bring benefits of professional standing as well as additional resources. High departmental morale communicates itself to students as well as to competitor departments in other universities, and enhances colleagues' working lives. When it is translated into a whole institution it breeds a momentum which removes thoughts of decline or failure from the agenda.

It is an uncomfortable truth that the leadership and the management team that presides over decline, whether at institutional or departmental level, is not best placed to lead a turnround. Just as the business team which led a company into serious debt is not the one to pull it out again, so the dynamics of decline render attempts to stem the tide seem inappropriate or unconvincing when undertaken by those who can be deemed, however unfairly, to be responsible for the decline. Such dynamics also programme individual behaviour in particular ways so that simple changes at the top may be insufficient to implement the necessary change process. A new and energetic vice-chancellor whose ideas are constantly challenged by risk averse colleagues who are in positions where they can prevent them from reaching fruition will not be able to bring about sufficient change to turn an institution round unless these road blocks can themselves be removed. Similar considerations occur at departmental level.

Institutions or departments in decline are also not always best at making appointments to accomplish a turnround; too often the appointment will replicate the weaknesses of the predecessor because the appointing committee is itself so embedded in the situation and may be insufficiently aware of, or responsive to, the statistical and other evidence of decline to recognize the scale of the problem. So there are serious dangers that institutions in decline are caught in a spiral from which it is very hard to extract themselves. The external voice, 'the company doctor', may have a role to play in changing the culture providing the message he or she produces is clear, unvarnished, and cannot be misunderstood, and is delivered to all the main components of the institution's management. Whereas in companies a powerful board and a determined chief executive can force change, universities are much more dependent on individual commitment for their success; arresting decline or turning round failure requires political as well as managerial skills. Colleagues need to be convinced that decline or failure is actually happening and that the benefits of revival and renewal are worth the sacrifices that will be called for. Universities need to consent to such a process and endorse it; where they do not it may not take place.

A significant element in obtaining consent is to gain support for a strategy which is realistic and which indicates a timetable and manageable targets. An academic community is sceptical of rhetoric and self congratulation because it conflicts with those qualities of intellectual discrimination which are key components in the way academics are trained. A strategy for renewal and revival needs to be endorsed by senate/academic board, as well as by the governing body; to achieve this the academic case must be sufficiently robust to carry academic support, and in particular from those who will have the major responsibility for implementation. But in the modern, more financially driven system the academic case must be seen to be financially viable or it will not command support. The traditional separation of governing body business from academic concerns does not work in these situations; the academic community may be much more difficult to convince about a business plan for recovery than a lay dominated governing body. Finally, the strategy must have measurable targets whether in relation to student recruitment, staff numbers, research income, new buildings, refurbishment schedules or size of the surplus (or deficit) in the accounts. If institutional support is to be maintained, achieving or failing to achieve these targets must be reported on honestly and discussed openly; academic commitment will be dependent on the extent to which trust is maintained through the process. Without new investment a turnround is unlikely to be achieved, so that a key element in any strategy must relate to the source of the investment and how quickly it can be brought on stream. A business plan based simply on new income being generated from the existing staff complement and the existing range of activities will convince no one, and should not; what has to be done is to make real savings which will generate new resources to make the investments possible.

Mergers and strategic alliances

Dunlap's account of his rescue of Scott Paper concludes with its merger with a commercial rival, Kimberly-Clark, his argument being that now that the company had a strong balance sheet and a considerable cash flow the choice lay in whether to pay very large dividends to shareholders or use the cash to generate new business through acquisition. The selection of Kimberly-Clark was because it also made paper based products and its products were closely related, but not necessarily competitive, with Scott Papers'. In general, mergers and acquisitions in business have been shown to have a poor record of long term success: *Business Week* says that 50 per cent of mergers do not create added value for the acquirer and, according to *The Economist*, two thirds of mergers do not work (CIHE 2001). Kay says that over a 25 year period about half of company acquisitions were divested because, while the case for merger was usually to acquire new markets, the internal architecture of the companies did not fit (Kay 1993). For this reason alone mergers in higher education, as a way of improving performance or turning institutions round, must be regarded with caution. Higher education mergers have perhaps an unfairly good reputation in the UK because in the period of greatest activity, when polytechnics were taking over colleges of education, polytechnics were operating in an expanding market where mergers represented acquisitions that brought in new products which were complementary to existing activities; they offered bases for further growth in student numbers and attractive real estate premises, without the complication of having to consider the compatibility of research reputations. The conditions were very different then to what they are in 2010. In the 'old' university sector the success of the merger between Cardiff and UWIST also prejudiced thinking in favour of mergers. This merger was a success because the external pressures of finance and political will were strong enough to keep the merger on track during periods of difficulty; these conditions are less likely to recur without the replication of the driving force of a powerful chairman of the UGC.

Mergers re-emerged as an option for arresting institutional decline in higher education in the late 1990s in the light of the plethora of acquisitions and takeovers in the corporate sector in the economic boom years of that period. Perversely they have been seen as the solution to problems arising from public expenditure cuts consequent on the economic crisis of 2008–10. The drivers for corporate mergers are, however, very different from those usually found in universities: reducing costs in procurement, administration and marketing; eliminating overlaps and duplication of activities; gaining new markets; strengthening the core business through the synergy of the two operations; and removing competition or strengthening the company against commercial competition. Key factors in making such mergers a success according to the Committee for Industry and Higher Education (CIHE) are: a common vision at the top; cultural compatibility; speedy implementation; not accepting fudges; a clear managerial model; good internal and external communication; the elimination of nonperforming units; focusing staff on critical success factors and cutting overhead costs (CIHE 2001). On the other hand, these key factors are only rarely realized in the corporate world. McKinsey suggests that only 12 per cent of companies actually see an acceleration of their sales growth after three years because mergers slow the business down, key people are often lost, an uncertainty factor is introduced and managers can be distracted from what were previously clear business targets. Moreover there is no guarantee that merger will improve performance: 'most sloths remained sloths, while most solid performers slowed down' (London 2002). Deloitte and Touche analysed the 40 biggest investigations by their reorganization service practice and found that 57 per cent had a failed merger or acquisition as the chief cause of their problems (Knowles-Cutler and Bradbury 2002). Most mergers that fail did so because revenue growth stalled during integration and failed to recover afterwards. The Boston Consultancy Group lists seven reasons why corporate mergers fail:

- they underestimate the difficulty of post merger integration;
- they miss the strategic opportunities that merger seemed to offer;
- management concentrates on managing change rather than giving leadership;
- there is an assumption that a fair approach means equal treatment for all;
- the integration is under-resourced because the same approach is applied in each area;
- the belief that the organization cannot be stabilized until all the details are agreed;
- victory is declared too soon and the promised changes are not followed through.

(Monnery and Malchione 2000)

What can the university world learn from corporate experience of mergers? The first message is that the pressure for university mergers is more often from external than internal sources, and that the idea of a merger tends to enthuse management at the top of the institution more than academics because it has fewer obvious advantages and some definable disadvantages for the latter working in their departments. Cardiff was an exception here because although the pressure was mostly from external authorities and although the UWIST management was enthusiastic, the Cardiff academic community, although previously hostile to merger, decided that if merger could eliminate Cardiff's debts and provide a stable academic environment it was preferable to a continued independent but debt-laden existence. This emphasizes a second important point: unlike companies, universities are essentially bottom heavy organizations and the attitudes of academic staff who will bear the brunt of the changes have to be taken into account. The power of the academic community to destroy a merger proposed by senior management was demonstrated in 2002 by the UCL staff's reaction to the idea of merging with Imperial College. In a pre-1992 university academic support or opposition would be constitutionally voiced at the senate; dissent at the academic board of a post-1992 university would not carry the same constitutional weight. Even so, if a university governing body was to go ahead with merger without academic staff support, the merger, if it took place, would be unlikely to succeed. Harman, for example, found that 'if the settling down period is not managed relatively quickly and with super sensitivity, the impact of merger on morale and loyalty of staff can be devastating' (Harman 2002: 107). Again, organizational culture may be more important in universities than is the case in companies but even in companies, according to Buono and Bowditch, the task of coordinating and integrating different cultures:

> is one of the most demanding complex and problematic aspects of mergers and acquisitions ... [and] cultural orientations can significantly limit what organisational members are willing to accept and do in a merger.
>
> (Buono and Bowditch 1989: 162–3)

Organizational cultures can be obstacles to change or can be the glue that holds a badly managed university together; merging university cultures is a difficult task, and may leave uncertainties and frictions that handicap academic collaboration. 'Cultural conflict has proved to be the norm in the post-merger phase of most institutions' (Harman 2002: 108).

One of the drivers of corporate mergers is the opportunity to reduce overheads, particularly in central costs, but this can be more difficult in universities where it is the central staff that have to carry the full weight of implementing the merger and where a rundown of the staffing may have to be delayed. Inevitably this means that costs are not reduced quickly, which reduces the opportunity for investment in new projects or even paying for the costs of merger itself, and may impact seriously on the merged institution's bottom line. Indeed Curri, reviewing mergers in New South Wales, concluded that 'The lesson to be learned is that there is very little evidence restructuring higher education by itself produces greater efficiencies', rather it was more likely that 'the new organisation may become less efficient due to increased bureaucracy rather than more' (Curri 2002: 150). On the other hand, universities are not dependent on share prices and can therefore set longer targets than would be the case in a company, which would look for a quick market endorsement and for benefits for their shareholders. But in both worlds takeovers are easier and more likely to prove successful than mergers between equals, but even takeovers in the most favourable circumstances may not in the long term bring all the benefits originally anticipated. If takeovers from strength do not always translate into complete success, mergers undertaken out of weakness, or mergers intended to arrest decline or avert failure are much less likely to be successful in improving performance. Evidence suggests that university mergers can succeed but only if the management of the merger is decisive, if the costs of integration are not underestimated, if it is done quickly, if it can be made to produce real savings which can be reinvested in the merged institution and if it can be done under favourable conditions, preferably in a period of expansion.

It is inevitable that mergers will be disruptive, will distract key staff, will place the solution of long standing issues onto a back burner, will delay new initiatives and, in the short term, will prove to be a drain on recurrent and capital funds. Where a university is spread over several sites it may increase a sense of alienation between the centre and the academic community. If the academic staff cannot be persuaded that the long term benefits outweigh the short term discomforts then universities are best to resist the challenge. Mergers undertaken from strength may prove to be successful, mergers from weakness will almost certainly not. Even when mergers are undertaken from strength and are financially strongly supported like the merger of medical schools with Imperial and Kings Colleges and UCL, there is little evidence that they actually improve performance in the short term. Harman and Meek in a wide ranging international review conclude that 'few if any mergers are painless . . . it is generally agreed that it can take up to 10 years for the wounds to heal and for the new institution forged from previously autonomous identities to operate as a cohesive and well integrated whole' (Harman and Meek 2002: 4). The largest and most expensive merger in UK university history between the University of Manchester and UMIST might seem to be a case in point.

An alternative that is often suggested is a joint venture or a strategic alliance. Again commercial parallels are not encouraging. In business arrangements the most common joint ventures are the result of globalization where one company partners another in some other part of the world either to transfer technology, to get access to scarce resources or to obtain access to new markets. Mostly they are agreed for fixed periods but the record of success is not high: 'Although popular, they are also risky, and in point of fact most such ventures do ultimately fail. That is they never make any money, or they break down and have to be terminated, or they fail on both counts' (Witzel 2002).

The reasons for breakdown are twofold – lack of trust and lack of goal alignment. There is in practice little evidence to encourage the view that mergers or strategic alliances can turn institutions round. The complications and distractions of integration or of working partnerships between two organizations are such that institutions whose performance needs improvement are unlikely to be capable of the additional effort required to make these arrangements a success. Indeed it is more likely that they will accelerate decline.

Institutional responsibility

The solution to arresting decline must continue to rest in the institution's own hands but the task is formidable because it requires an institution to accept that it must take disagreeable steps, probably over quite a long period, before it can see success. Universities are unlikely to attempt this unless they have an organizational culture which empowers them to do it, or they appoint a new vice-chancellor who can drive them to it, or some external agency stimulates them to do it. Lay governors have the power and the responsibility to call for such action but have shown little sign of having the determination to do so. The problem about institutional decline in higher education is that so many factors are involved, so many are interrelated and mutually dependent. Attacking the problem of falling research productivity will not be solved simply by persuading non-research active staff to retire. University activities are multidimensional, and addressing one dimension only will rarely succeed. Holistic organizations need to be addressed holistically if we are to change or improve them, and this requires a multifaceted approach.

It is a truism that it is a great deal easier to maintain and improve the performance of an institution than to arrest its decline and produce a recovery. If there is one incentive that can be offered to institutions it is that the process of turn round is so difficult to achieve, so risky and so fraught with painful decisions that it is infinitely preferable to make the necessary sacrifices to identify and prevent decline before it occurs. Where a drop in performance is identified whether in one department's research or another department's fall in student numbers the moral is to act quickly and decisively before weaknesses in one area transmits itself to others. In a competitive world at least half the universities in the system are actively trying to improve their performance; relaxation or loss of institutional ambition will soon reflect not only in published data but in the climate of the institution. Once that climate begins to change remedial action is necessary.

Managing retrenchment

A wholly different situation occurs when a major income stream either ceases to flow altogether or is greatly reduced and retrenchment becomes necessary to ensure institutional survival. In this case one cannot fault the university; it does not represent a management failure but a shock to the system which would have been hard to anticipate; universities are labour intensive. Since between 50 per cent and 60 per cent of university expenditure is on academic staff and some 70 per cent overall on total staffing any retrenchment scenario is bound to involve a reduction in staffing numbers.

In 1981 the university system overall was cut by about 17 per cent (including the impact of the decision to remove the subsidy for international students) but the cuts were differential in that the UGC inserted decisions to reduce student numbers differentially both to reflect academic quality judgements and to emphasize science and technology fields over humanities and social sciences. Sizer's study referred to above (Sizer 1987) describes how universities coped, and on the whole coped very successfully, with the necessary retrenchment but one must remember that they were greatly assisted in doing so by the provision of a generous early retirement scheme. The removal of tenure in 1987 would make that otiose in Treasury minds for any future scenario. A comparable study (Hardy 1996) describes how Canadian universities coped with serious budget reductions between 1981–2 and 1985–6. Both studies emphasize the importance of transparency and the need to engage the academic community fully in the rationale of the exercise. Hardy, in particular, shows how universities that opted for a very top down approach were less successful in the conduct of the operation than universities that were committed to a high level of academic participation in decision making. However, in both the Sizer and Hardy accounts it is clear that those universities which did engage their academic community in the exercise had a tradition of 'shared governance'. It is unlikely that such a tradition can be created overnight, or that it will be an effective mechanism for long, if it is attempted simply to manage a crisis, so perhaps a first conclusion for any consideration of managing retrenchment is that those universities which have maintained an organizational culture that stresses academic involvement in decision making will be advantaged providing they do not resile from previous practice. It was noticeable that London Guildhall University, which faced radical retrenchment in the 1990s owing to the conjunction of the expiry of a number of property leases in central London, conducted the readjustment of its budget entirely through its governing body. Since the University was actually also a company it was inevitable, of course, that the governing body as the company board would play a very large role, but the nature and history of its post-1992 constitution would have made it inherently unlikely that its organizational culture would have permitted any other option.

In approaching severe retrenchment, caused by whatever external events, every institution is differently circumstanced and has assets, vulnerabilities and issues particular to itself. Nevertheless there are some basis principles which can be applied:

- However steep the budget reduction necessary to restore the bottom line a university should undertake its short term adjustments in the context of its longer term priorities and strategic objectives. Budget reductions should reinforce the institution's strategic vision not conflict with it. Panic driven or unplanned opportunist cuts may significantly delay recovery. Indeed retrenchment may provide an opportunity to realize strategic objectives which might be more difficult to achieve in a steady state funding situation by providing the excuse to eliminate weaker programmes or departments which might otherwise be hard to terminate. Universities that handle retrenchment effectively can often emerge stronger.

- Apply reductions selectively; spreading them equitably over the whole institution weakens the whole institution. Recovery will come about through the efforts of successful departments, research centres and groups: an 'equal misery' approach will handicap them and delay recovery.

- Look for savings in terms of specific items, that is particular large facilities or programmes the elimination of whose running costs will make a difference to the budget. Try to remove the whole budget line, not just reduce it. This may change the shape of the university somewhat (e.g. closing the swimming pool or a full undergraduate programme) but will protect the core activities.

- Central authorities are often not best placed to see where a variety of budget reductions can be made or may have closed minds in relation to certain issues. Invite suggestions from the whole university community. One effective practice is to establish small groups of young academics and administrators (and therefore not part of the decision making establishment) to investigate particular operations with a remit to offer suggestions for 5 per cent, 10 per cent or 15 per cent savings or compensating gains in income.

- Review the whole range of university activities to see where new income can be raised (the Warwick 'Save half, make half' slogan of the 1981 cuts). Perhaps the swimming pool, for example, can be saved from mothballing by a new charging policy? Canvass ideas widely about income generation: universities are full of creative people some of whom may see this as an opportunity to do something they have always half wanted to do.

- Recognize that investment will nearly always be necessary to achieve change, whether it is to start an income generation project or to eliminate a facility or programme. Starving projects because of short term budget pressures will render them less achievable and will reduce the commitment of those charged to carry them out.

- Set targets and timelines for achieving budget cuts and ensure they are accepted by the senate/academic board as well as by the governing body; make regular reports of progress to relevant bodies and invite discussion.

- Be resolute in implementation; being decisive creates a momentum for further action.

- Link planned budget reductions firmly with the five year financial plan so that their impact on future years can be judged; ensure that there is a body, normally a finance committee of the governing body, which is not engaged in the day-to-day process of identifying savings, but which owns the financial plan and can take a detached view on the progress being made to reach budgetary targets.

- View merger with another institution as a counsel of last resort; mergers that are euphemisms for takeovers can work (as at Cardiff) but will be undertaken primarily for the benefit of the acquiring institution, not for the institution losing its identity.

Retrenchment on a significant scale puts a severe test on leadership and organizational culture. What experience we have from the 1980s suggests that some universities have actually benefited from the experience because they were able to rise to the challenge but that these were an exception. Austin's brilliant eye witness account of managing retrenchment at Manchester demonstrates how difficult achieving budget reductions consensually can really be (Austin 1982). For most institutions it must be a damage limitation exercise; measurement of success in managing it can only be undertaken some years after the event.

12

Managing universities for success

This chapter summarizes the main findings of the book. It emphasizes the importance of the concept of the 'strengthened steering core' and the role of the executive in implementation and day-to-day management. It lists four characteristics of company success and compares them with university success. Finally, it argues that successful university management is underpinned by a belief in institutional autonomy and should be exercised not from the top down but through a continuous dialogue between the centre and the operating units.

Cardinal Newman, in a lecture for the School of Science in the new National University of Ireland, wrote:

> Among the objects of human enterprise . . . none higher or nobler can be named than that which is contemplated in the erection of a university. To set on foot and to maintain in life and vigour a real university is . . . one of those greatest works, great in their difficulty and their importance on which are deservedly expanded the rarest intellects and the most varied endowments.
>
> (Kerr 1976: 368)

Newman himself, frustrated by ecclesiastical conservatism, was not as effective in the practical matters of running a university as in writing or speaking about it but his words remind us that universities do not run themselves and that university management requires some of the most able people in the university to be involved in it. Preceding chapters have emphasized:

- That teaching and research represent the core business of universities and that those universities that excel in these areas also tend to attract the best qualified students and lead the field in industrially supported research or in extending the boundaries of the university in social and economic activities; that universities are strongly differentiated in their levels of performance and that it is possible to identify those that perform consistently better than the rest.

- That maintaining a climate of intellectual vibrancy and the encouragement of academic entrepreneurialism makes a more important contribution to the 'management' of the core business than compliance with quality driven processes or the top down direction of research.

- That there are no absolute predictors of what makes a university successful, whether age of foundation, location or disciplinary base, although these factors may make a large contribution; institutional management in its broadest sense makes a critical contribution both to creating success and to maintaining it.

- That managing universities is a holistic process; the functions of a university are closely interlocked and mutually dependent so that a weakness in one function can affect others and strengths in key functions can be mutually reinforcing; recognizing the integrated nature of university management is a key to success.

- That the maintenance of financial stability is an important component in achieving academic success but this can only be attained in the modern period from a diversified funding base in which the state does not provide the major proportion of the income; to manage this financial literacy must be widely distributed and a degree of fiscal puritanism should be encouraged.

- That collegiality is a more effective management tool for success in the core business of teaching and research than managerial direction.

- That academic departments represent the essential building blocks of a successful university and that structures which relate departments directly to the centre of the university without intermediary layers provide shorter lines of communication and speedier decision making.

- That the character and composition of a 'strengthened central steering core' will be one of the determinants of institutional success; leadership is essential but distributed, rather than charismatic or personal leadership will be the most likely to produce sustainable high institutional performance.

- That good governance makes a positive contribution to institutional success when the lay element in governance, the executive and the academic community work closely together; on the other hand progress will be inhibited if one of these elements becomes over dominant.

- That the widening social and economic roles of universities essential to their well-being in modern society imposes increasing burdens of complexity and coordination on central university management; the successful prosecution of many of such activities will depend on the recruitment of professionals from non-university environments, and the extent to which their contribution can be integrated into a central university framework of policy objectives will determine the impact they have on the university's mission.

- That institutional reputation and image is a far more important corporate asset than many universities realize; building and sustaining a corporate reputation demands investment and long term commitment but more than pays for itself in market success.

- Ambition is a key to success but institutional ambition must be translated into all those activities which are essential components of institutional performance: the appointment of outstanding staff, whether academic or administrative; investment in new ventures, and in all aspects of institutional life; an ambitious university will not accept second best; a reputation for institutional dynamism can become a self-fulfilling prophecy for staff and students.

- That one of the strongest incentives to maintaining and improving institutional performance is that the process of arresting and reversing decline is so difficult and painful to achieve; quick remedial action is required when any element of performance is seen to dip.

- Retrenchment forced by external circumstances should be approached on the basis of reinforcing existing strategies not being deflected from them; universities that have a tradition of 'shared governance' should use it to the full to set targets and timelines; they should be resolute in implementation.

The strengthened steering core

Institutional management is much more than management by a subset of individuals within a university; like leadership it must be distributed throughout the institution. Nevertheless it will rest, at the highest level, on the hub of a close working partnership between a group which we can follow Clark and call the 'strengthened steering core': a very small number of lay members of the governing body, the vice-chancellor, the governing core of the academic community and the senior administrators. This group will be central to decision making and to implementation. Their working relationships, the way they resolve tensions between competing interests, their attitudes to environmental pressures, their shared understanding of the institution's central objectives and their confidence in their capacity to read situations, take risks, back new ventures and reach decisions quickly will have a huge impact on the university's ability to sustain its forward momentum. The relative contribution of each category of member of such a group is critical to the group success. The lay members, probably the chairman of the governing body, the chairman of the finance committee and perhaps one other senior member, need to protect the institution from undue risk, to serve both as impartial interrogators of new ideas and as a source of encouragement to realizing them and to be interpreters of the way the external environment is moving. They will be unlikely to initiate developments but ultimately their judgement will be closely involved in decisions about large investments of university resources in them. They must also carry the confidence of the governing body and be willing to exercise leadership in piloting through controversial developments which they are convinced will succeed. The senior academics, pro-vice-chancellors and deans and other senior colleagues must be able both to reflect and lead academic opinion and individually to champion academic initiatives and/or to ask searching questions about them, as well as to run the day-to-day academic processes of institutional self governance. They will not back off from 'constructive confrontation' over policy initiatives with which they do not agree either with the vice-chancellor or any of their colleagues, lay or academic, but they will be loyal to due process if the initiatives survive scrutiny. They will reassure a senate or academic board critical of decisions taken at speed to meet externally imposed timetables. Meantime the vice-chancellor must not only lead the process, chair the senate/academic board and the central steering group and guide the governing body, but must introduce his or her own initiatives as well as selecting, from among the initiatives that come up around the university, which to support and see through to fulfilment. In all this the vice-chancellor's key support and analytical back up on policy must be the registrar and the senior professional officers in finance, buildings, human resources and so forth.

The administration

Critically for success, it will be the administration which organizes implementation as well as being responsible for much of the day-to-day management of the university. In universities where there is a unitary administrative structure, the registrar becomes, in effect, the chief operating officer of the university responsible both for the efficiency of the day-to-day management of the university and for the coordination of the preparation of data relevant to policy decisions. The linkages between policy, management and implementation are extremely close in universities: policies grow out of management practice and from evidence that arises either from data collection or from day-to-day administration and may be altered by the process of implementation; workable policies rarely spring fully developed from a single new idea unconnected with past experience. If we believe with Mintzberg that strategy is best developed incrementally, that it 'emerges' and is 'evolutionary' rather than being the result of formal planning procedures, then the efficiency and effectiveness of day-to-day management is doubly important. The university that is quick off the mark in dealing with management issues, that is systematic but responsive in routine administration matters, and that contrives to present itself well to the outside world in all circumstances, however adverse, will offer a rich seed bed for incremental initiatives because the very effectiveness of its management style will drive events, create opportunities and attract invitations to submit bids for new projects: the newly appointed lecturer, chosen from a large and excellent field, will be encouraged to submit grant applications quickly and, when successful, will be provided with space, equipment and technician support; an up-to-date and efficient library will markedly improve a student's learning experience; an effective system for capturing financial and other information will speed up decision making and improve financial performance. Effectiveness in running services, innovation in developing them and decisiveness in correcting mistakes contributes a great deal to the development of a 'can do' organizational culture extending throughout the institution.

A key contention of this book is that management makes a difference and represents a major component of university success. Institutional management must be interpreted broadly and its most important elements have been described. However, we cannot ignore the contribution to the process of those staff who are described as 'administrators' but who, for the most part are actually managers – the professional managers, to distinguish them from the rest. The training and formation of this group of staff for senior positions is as important as the parallel process for young academic staff. First, they should be selected with care (not casually on the basis of a single interview); second, their academic or professional qualifications should be such that they can work on equal terms with their academic colleagues; third, their preparation over time for senior positions should include a well balanced workload of policy related and day-to-day administrative related duties with changes in responsibilities every two or three years; and fourth, their working environment should be robust and should encourage initiative and debate. A registrar should take personal responsibility for the career development of university administrators whether under his/her direct control on the centre or located in devolved academic structures. Too often the spark is driven out of able young administrators by imposing on them a monotonous diet of administrative detail in specialist jobs year on year, so that as they progress up a ladder of competence the qualities of initiative, flexibility and lateral thinking which are necessary in senior management positions are stifled. The more administrators lack intellectual confidence the more they are likely to lose sympathy with the *mores* of academic life as they grow older. The greater the intolerance or lack of understanding the more a split can appear between administrative and academic cultures to the disadvantage of the institution itself; a university where trust has broken down between these two communities is gravely handicapping itself when decisions have to be taken and particularly when they have to be taken quickly, or on trust.

The characteristics of sustained success

De Geus in his book *The Living Company* (1997) cites four characteristics of companies that have sustained success over long periods all of which apply to universities. The first is their sensitivity to the environment and particularly to societal considerations. The administrative community is especially important here through its understanding of funding mechanisms, its engagement with external policy communities and their membership of sector-wide professional associations. The second is their sense of cohesiveness and of identity:

> case histories repeatedly showed that strong employee links were essential for survival and change. This cohesion around the idea of 'community' meant that managers were typically chosen for advancement from within; they succeeded through the generational flow of managers and considered themselves stewards of the long standing enterprise. Each management generation was only a link in a long chain.
>
> (De Geus 1997: 6)

This could be regarded as controversial – organizations, notably universities, make appointments from outside to refresh their activities; too many internal appointments may lead to complacency and mediocrity; a department that appoints too many of its own PhDs to academic posts is likely to be accused of inbreeding. Nevertheless universities that grow their own talent, whether in academic or administrative life (providing the growing takes place in an atmosphere of excellence, competition and ambition) build a sense of institutional coherence and an institutional culture which can be very valuable in confronting external challenges. The young lecturer who has risen, in successive promotions, to a personal chair or the young administrator who has been promoted to a senior rank have networks they can consult with; they will understand the decision making processes, and they can anticipate how their institution will react to opportunities. In successful universities, they will know what has to be done to achieve success and they will expect those responsible to act accordingly; their futures are quite heavily invested in them doing so. In weak institutions the opposite can be the case, where even positive actions can be undermined by the scepticism of staff 'who have seen it all before'.

A third characteristic, perhaps less unusual in universities than in companies, is a willingness to tolerate experiment and idiosyncratic approaches either to organizational structures or to tackling particular issues. Universities need not be organizationally tidy to be successful; they need to encourage the structures which fit disciplines best and which provide the right kind of focus for good research or for student learning. An interdisciplinary school drawing in academics from different departments to deliver a broad undergraduate degree, or a research institute that encompasses more than one department in order to bring together researchers in a common field, or an idiosyncratic but successful one person research centre should all be able to coexist with traditional departmental structures.

The fourth and final characteristic is conservatism in regard to financial management. Here, universities like De Geus's companies should practise frugality rather than extravagance, neither entertaining lavishly and ostentatiously nor borrowing to fund projects that cannot cover the repayments themselves, nor paying salaries to their vice-chancellor and other senior colleagues at levels which distance them radically from their academic colleagues. Financial conservatism, though unfashionable, husbands resources so that occasionally an institution can pursue options not available to competitors or can take the kind of calculated leap forward that moves it into a higher division. It also creates a culture of parsimony in regard to minor expenditure which staff quickly buy into.

Good management in universities thrives when it can draw on a shared past of achievements, of risks taken which have paid off, of taking difficult decisions on important issues without breaking a tradition of senate reaching its conclusions consensually, of surviving budget cuts, of managing through breakdowns and misfortunes, of pulling together packages which attract major academic figures to the university, of closing down an activity without recrimination or of surviving retrenchment with morale intact. These events offer texts or corporate memories on how to manage future issues and give the managers, whether academic or administrative, vice-chancellors or chairs of governing bodies, the confidence to take risks that other universities might flinch from and to assume that the culture of the institution is sufficiently cohesive to sustain high speed decision making over complex issues when external pressures require it. Financial security or the availability of significant reserves should be important in generating institutional confidence, but in practice they often build a resistance to taking risks. (A review of the size of departmental reserves in almost any university will illustrate how reluctant the academic community can be to spend funds accumulated for the proverbial rainy day.) Universities are much more willing to take positive, even risky decisions, if they have developed the habit of doing so and if they have a momentum of decision making which carries the institution forward from one initiative to another.

Underpinning successful university management is a belief in institutional autonomy. Clark refers to 'stand up' universities or 'self reliant' universities as institutions which have created for themselves a corporate culture and a defined way of managing themselves which marks them out as having an identity and a mode of operation which is not state dependent, even if the institutions are significantly state funded. In almost any higher education system where institutions are in receipt of substantial state funding there are hidden pressures which can weaken institutional autonomy: formula funding can produce replications of state created formulae in institutional resource allocation models; financial stringency can encourage every institution to bid for funds from every new state funded initiative; accountability pressures can impose rigidities in internal academic and financial structures increasing bureaucratic layers and inflexible managerial hierarchies; and the absence of a diversified income base can create a dependency culture which mimics the latest twists and turns of state policies. Such universities may be technically autonomous but it is in fact a 'derived' autonomy which commands little loyalty from the staff. Successful universities, on the other hand, have a 'self directed' autonomy which enables them to establish goals intrinsic to their own ambitions, to establish resource allocation criteria to fit their own aspirations, to resist the automatic bidding culture, to accommodate accountability rules within academic structures that grow out of the management of academic disciplines, modes of teaching, and research environments and to merge state and non-state income streams to match the needs of the institution. They develop a shape and an organizational culture which reflects their inner purposes.

University management in a situation of 'derived' autonomy is reduced to administering or imposing external rules and pressures, and to defending such rules and pressures to an academic community whose role is to respond to them. By contrast 'self directed' autonomy is created by a university community empowered by a corporate culture that has a secure identity. University management in this culture is inclusive, it is strongly reflective of bottom-up initiative but it recognizes the importance of coordination and prioritizing at the centre. One of its main tasks is to protect the academic community, as far as it can, from externally imposed rules and pressures in order that it should not be distracted from concentrating in the most effective way it knows how on the core business of teaching and research. Successful university management represents not an imposition from the top but the outcomes of a continuous dialogue between the centre and the operating units combined with realistic implementation skills and a drive to success. No university can sustain success unless it is equipped with a management style which mirrors its ambitions and commands the trust of its community.

Appendix

Notes to Tables 1, 2 and 3

Table 1

RAE results 1986	scores of 'outstanding' = 5, 'above average' = 4, 'average' = 3, 'below average' = 1.5
RAE results 1989	as published in the *Financial Times*, 26 August 1989
RAE results 1992	as published in *The Times Higher Education Supplement*, 18 December 1992
RAE results 1996	as published in *The Times Higher Education Supplement*, December 1996, adjusted to reflect the proportion of staff entered in the RAE
RAE results 2001	as published in *The Times Higher Education Supplement*, 14 December 2001, adjusted to eliminate small or specialist institutions
RAE results 2008	as published in *The Times Higher*, December 2008, adjusted to eliminate small or specialist institutions

Table 2

O'Leary, J. and Cannon, T. (1994) *The Times Good University Guide 1994–1995*. London: Times Newspapers.

O'Leary, J. and Cannon, T. (1995) *The Times Good University Guide 1995–6*. London: Times Newspapers.

O'Leary, J. (ed.) (1996) *The Times Good University Guide*. London: Times Newspapers.

O'Leary, J. (ed.) (1997) *The Times Good University Guide 1997*. London: Times Newspapers.

O'Leary, J. (ed.) (1998) *The Times Good University Guide 1998*. London: Times Newspapers.

O'Leary, J. (ed.) (1999) *The Times Good University Guide 1999*. London: Times Newspapers.

O'Leary, J. (ed.) with Hindmarsh, A. Kingston, B. and Loynes, R. (2000) *The*

Times Good University Guide 2001. London: Times Newspapers in association with PricewaterhouseCoopers.

O'Leary, J. (ed.) with Hindmarsh, A. and Kingston, B (2002) *The Times Good University Guide 2003*. London: Times Newspapers in association with PricewaterhouseCoopers.

O'Leary, J. (ed.) with Hindmarsh, A. and Kingston, B. (2003) *The Times Good University Guide 2004*. London: Times Books.

O'Leary, J. (ed.) with Hindmarsh, A. and Kingston, B. (2004) *The Times Good University Guide 2005*. London: Times Books.

O'Leary, J. (ed.) with Hindmarsh, A. and Kingston, B. (2005) *The Times Good University Guide 2006*. London: Times Books.

O'Leary, J. (ed.) with Hindmarsh, A. and Kingston, B. (2006) *The Times Good University Guide 2007*. London: Times Books.

O'Leary, J. with Exeter Enterprises (2007) *The Times Good University Guide 2008*. http:// extras.timesonline.co.uk/gug/gooduniversityguide.php

O'Leary, J. with Kennedy, P. and Horseman, N. (2008) *The Times Good University Guide 2009*. London: Times Books.

O'Leary, J. with Kennedy, P. and Horseman, N. (2009) *The Times Good University Guide 2010*. London: Times Books.

The Guardian University Guide 2001, *The Guardian*, 22 May 2001

The Guardian University Guide 2002, *The Guardian*, 28 May 2002

The Guardian University Guide 2003, *The Guardian*, 20 May 2003

The Guardian University Guide 2004, *The Guardian*, 24 May 2004

The Guardian University Guide 2005, *The Guardian*, 19 April 2005

The Guardian University Guide 2006, *The Guardian*, 2 May 2006

The Guardian University Guide 2008, *The Guardian*, 1 May 2007

The Guardian University Guide 2009, *The Guardian*, 1 May 2008

The Guardian University Guide 2010, *The Guardian*, 12 May 2009

The Sunday Times League Table 1999, *The Sunday Times*, 8 November 1998

The Sunday Times League Table 2000, *The Sunday Times*, 19 September 1999

The Sunday Times League Table 2001, *The Sunday Times*, 17 September 2000

The Sunday Times League Table 2002, *The Sunday Times*, 16 September 2001

The Sunday Times League Table 2003, *The Sunday Times*, 15 September 2002

The Sunday Times League Table 2004, *The Sunday Times*, 14 September 2003

The Sunday Times League Table 2005, *The Sunday Times*, 12 September 2004

The Sunday Times League Table 2006, *The Sunday Times*, 2 October 2005

The Sunday Times League Table 2007, *The Sunday Times*, 10 October 2006

The Sunday Times League Table 2008, *The Sunday Times*, 23 September 2007

The Sunday Times League Table 2009, *The Sunday Times*, 21 September 2008

The Sunday Times League Table 2010, *The Sunday Times*, 13 September 2009

Kingston, B. (2007) *Good University Guide 2008*, http://www. thecompleteuniversity guide.co.uk/single.htm?ipg=8642, featured in the *Independent*, 30 July 2007.

Kingston, B. (2008) *Complete University Guide 2009*, *The Independent*, 24 April 2008.

Kingston, B. (2009) *Complete University Guide 2010*, *The Independent*, 30 April 2009.

Table 3

The Times Good University Guide (as for Table 2 above)

References

Abreu, M., Grinevich, V., Hughes, A., Kitson, M. and Ternmouth, P. (2008) *Universities, Business and Knowledge Exchange*. London: CIHE.

Aitken, R. (1966) *Administration of a University*. London: University of London Press.

Angluin, D. and Scapens, R.W. (2000) Transparency, accounting knowledge and perceived fairness in UK universities' resource allocation. Results from a survey of accounting and finance, *British Accounting Review*, 32: 1–42.

Annan, N. (1999) *The Dons*. London: HarperCollins.

Armstrong, P. and Fletcher, P. (2004) Securitization in Public Finance, *Public Money and Management*, 24(3): 175–92.

Ashby, E. (1963) *Technology and the Academics*. London: Macmillan.

Audretsch, D.B. (2002) *Entrepreneurship: A Survey of the Literature*. Brussels: Commission of the European Communities.

Austin, D. (1982) Salva sit universitas nostra: a memoir, *Government and Opposition*, 17: 469–89.

Bain, G.S. (2003) Bain's basics for smooth university operators, *Times Higher Education Supplement*, 8 August.

Baldridge, J.V. and Okimi, P.H. (1982) Strategic planning in higher education: new tools or gimmick? *AAHE Bulletin*, 35(b): 15–18.

Bank Boston (1997) *MIT: The Impact of Innovation*, A Bank Boston Economics Department Special Report. Boston, MA: Bank Boston.

Becher, R.A. and Kogan, M. (1992) *Process and Structure in Higher Education*. London: Routledge.

Becher, R.A. and Trowler, P. (2001) *Academic Tribes and Territories*. Buckingham: Open University Press/SRHE.

Bennett, B. (2002) The new style boards of governors – are they working? *Higher Education Quarterly*, 56(3): 287–302.

Benneworth, P. and Sanderson, A. (2009) The regional engagement of universities: building capacity in a sparse innovation environment, *Higher Education Management and Policy*, 21(1): 131–46.

Bett Report (1999) *Independent Review of Higher Education Pay and Conditions* (the Bett Report). London: HMSO.

Birnbaum, R. (2000) *Management Fads in Higher Education*. San Francisco, CA: Jossey Bass.

Birnbaum, R. (2004) The end of shared governance: looking ahead or looking back, *New Directions for Higher Education*, 127: 5–22.

Birnbaum, R. (2007) No world class university left behind, *International Higher Education*, 47 Spring.

Bolden, R., Petrov, G. and Gosling, J. (2008) *Developing Collective Leadership in Higher Education, Final Report*. London: Leadership Foundation.

Bryan, L.L. and Joyce, C.T. (2007) *Mobilizing Minds: Creating Wealth from Talent in the 21st Century Organization*. Maidenhead: McGraw-Hill.

Buono, A.R. and Bowditch, J.L. (1989) *The Human Side of Mergers and Acquisitions – Managing Collisions Between People, Cultures and Organisations*. San Francisco, CA: Jossey Bass.

Burn, I. (ed.) (2003) The new Vice-Chancellor outlines the future, *Reading: reading*, University of Reading.

Cadbury Report (1994) *Report of the Committee on the Financial Aspects of Corporate Governance* (the Cadbury Report). London: Gee Professional Publishing.

Campbell, A. and Goold, M. (1988) Adding value from corporate headquarters, *London Business School Journal*, Summer.

Castells, M. and Hall, P. (1994) *Technopoles of the World, The Making of 21st Century Industrial Complexes*. London: Routledge.

Charles, D. (2003) Universities and territorial development re-shaping the regional role of universities, *Local Economy*, 18: 7–20.

Chatterton, P. and Goddard, J. (2000) The response of higher education institutions to regional need, *European Journal of Education*, 35(4): 475–96.

CHERI (Centre for Higher Education Research and Information and Hobsons Research) (2008) *Counting what is Measured or Measuring what Counts?* HEFCE 2008/14.

Chester, J. and Bekhradnia, B. (2009) *Oxford and Cambridge: How different are they?* Oxford: Higher Education Policy Institute.

CIHE (Committee for Industry and Higher Education) (2001) *Cooperation and Collaboration: Some Private Sector Experience*. London: CIHE.

Clark, B.R. (1998) *Creating Entrepreneurial Universities*. Oxford: IAU Press/Pergammon.

Clark, B.R. (2004) *Sustaining Change in Universities*. Maidenhead: Open University Press.

Claverly, P. and Goyder, M. (2001) *Employee Ownership in Tomorrow's Company*. London: Centre for Tomorrow's Company.

Codling, A. and Meek, V.L. (2006) Twelve propositions on diversity in higher education, *Higher Education Management and Policy*, 18(3): 31–54.

Cohen, M.D. and March, J.G. (1974) *Leadership and Ambiguity*. New York: McGraw-Hill.

Collins, J.C. (2001) *Good to Great*. London: Century.

Collins, J.C. and Porras, J.I. (1994) *Built to Last: Successful Habits of Visionary Companies*. London: Century.

Collinson, M. and Collinson, D. (2006) *'Blended Leadership': Employee Perspectives on Effective Leadership in the UK Further Education Sector*. Leicester: Centre for Excellence in Leadership.

Committee of Vice-Chancellors and Principals (1985) *Report of the Steering Committee on Efficiency Studies* (the Jarratt Report). London: CVCP.

CUC (Committee of University Chairmen) (1995, 1998, 2000, 2006) *Guide for Members of Governing Bodies of Universities and Colleges in England, Wales and Northern Ireland*. London: HEFCE.

Curri, G. (2002) Reality versus perception: restructuring tertiary education and institutional organisational change – a case study, *Higher Education*, 44(1): 133–51.

David, F.R. (1996) *Strategic Management*. Englewood Cliffs, NJ: Prentice Hall International.

DBIS (Department for Business, Innovation and Skills) (2009) *Higher Ambitions: The Future of Universities and the Knowledge Economy*. London: HMSO.

De Geus, A. (1997) *The Living Company*. Boston: Harvard Business School Press.

Deem, R., Hillyard, S. and Read, M. (2006) *Knowledge, Higher Education and the New Managerialism*. Oxford: Oxford University Press.

DEFS (Department for Education and Skills) (2003) *The Future of Higher Education*, CM5735. London: HMSO.

DES (Department for Education and Science) (1991) *Higher Education: A New Framework*, CM1541. London: HMSO.

Di Maggio, P.J. and Powell, W.W. (1983) The iron cage revisited: institutional isomorphism and collective rationality in organizational fields, *American Sociological Review*, 48(2): 147–60.

Dill, D. and Soo, M. (2005) Academic quality, league tables and public policy. A cross analysis of university ranking systems, *Higher Education*, 49(4): 103–25.

Docherty, T. (2008) *The English Question*. Sussex: Academic Press.

Donaghue, S. and Kennerley, M. (2008) Our journey towards world class: leading transformational strategic change. Paper delivered at the OECD/IMHE General Conference, Paris, 8–10 September.

Douglas, J.A. (2007) The entrepreneurial state and research universities in the United States: policy and new state-based initiatives, *Higher Education Management and Policy*, 19(1): 95–132.

Doyle, P. (1998) *Marketing Management and Strategy*. Englewood Cliffs, NJ: Prentice Hall.

Doyle, P. (1999) From the top, *The Guardian*, 30 January.

Drabenstott, M. (2008) Universities, innovation and regional development: a view from the United States, *Higher Education Management and Policy*, 20(2): 43–58.

Dunlap, A.J. (1996) *Mean Business*. New York: Times Business, Random House.

Dutton, J.E. and Dukerich, J.M. (1991) Keeping an eye on the mirror: the role of image and identity in organizational adaptation, *Academy of Management Journal*, 34: 517–54.

Etzkowitz, H. and Kemelgor, C. (1998) The role of research centres in the collectivisation of science, *Minerva*, XXXVI (3): 271–88.

Etzkowitz, H. and Leydesdorff, L. (1998) The endless transition: a 'Triple Helix' of university-industry-government relations, *Minerva*, XXXVI (3): 203–8.

Etzkowitz, H. and Webster, A. (1998) Entrepreneurial science: the second academic revolution, in H. Etzkowitz, A. Webster and P. Healey (eds) *Capitalizing Knowledge*. Albany, NY: SUNY Press.

Evidence Ltd. (2009) *Monitoring Research Concentration and Diversity: Changes Between 1994 and 2007*. London: Universities UK.

Fazakerley, A. and Chant, J. (2009) *Sink or Swim? Facing up to Failing Universities*. London: Policy Exchange April.

Ferlie, E., Ashburner, L., Fitzgerald, L. and Pettigrew, A. (1996) *The New Public Management in Action*. Oxford: Oxford University Press.

Finkelstein, A. (2001) Capsa and its implementation. Report to the Audit Committee and the Board of Scrutiny. Part A: Processes and Decision-making, *Cambridge University Reporter*, CXXXII (6): 157–71.

Florida, R. (2001) *The Rise of the Creative Class*. New York: Basic Books.

Fombrun, C.J. (1996) *Reputation: Realizing the Value of Corporate Image*. Boston: Harvard Business School Press.

Garvin, D.A. (1993) Building a learning organization, *Harvard Business Review*, 71(4): 78–91.

Geiger, R.L. and Creso, M.Sa. (2008) *Tapping the Riches of Science. Universities and the Promise of Economic Growth*. Cambridge, MA: Harvard University Press

General Board, Cambridge (1974) *Report of the General Board on the Long Term Development of the University*, No. 4884, 17 December.

Ghoshal, S. and Bartlett, C. (1993) *The Individualised Corporation*. London: Heinemann.

Gibbons, M., Limoges, C., Nowotny, H. *et al.* (1994) *The New Production of Knowledge*. London: Sage.

Gioia, D.A. and Thomas, J.B. (1996) Identity, image and issue interpretation: sensemaking during strategic change to academia, *Administrative Science Quarterly*, 41(3): 370–98.

Goddard, J. (1999) How universities can thrive locally in a global market, in H. Gray (ed.) *Universities and Wealth Creation*. Buckingham: Open University Press.

Goddard, J. and Puuka, J. (2008) The engagement of higher education institutions in regional development: an overview of the policies and challenges, *Higher Education Management and Policy*, 20(2): 11–42.

Goodall, A.H. (2009) *Socrates in the Boardroom. Why Research Universities Should be Led by Top Scholars*. Princeton: Princeton University Press.

Green, J., Rutherford, S. and Turner, T. (2009) Best practice in using business intelligence to determine research strategy, *Perspectives*, 13(2): 48–55.

Grinyer, P.H., Mayes, D.G. and McKiernan, P. (1998) *Sharp Benders: The Secrets of Unleashing Corporate Potential*. Oxford: Blackwell.

Gueno, A. (1998) The internationalisation of European universities: a return to medieval roots, *Minerva*, XXXVI (3): 253–70.

Gunaseka, C. (2006) Universities and associate regional governance: Australian evidence in non-core metropolitan regions, *Regional Studies*, 40(7).

Habermas, J. and Blazek, J.R. (1987) The idea of the university: learning processes, *New German Critique* (41) Spring–Summer.

Hamel, G. (2007) *The Future of Management*. Boston: Harvard Business School Press.

Hampel Report (1998) *Committee on Corporate Governance, Final Report*. London: Gee Professional Publishing.

Hardy, C. (1996) *The Politics of Collegiality*. Montreal and Kingston, London and Buffalo: McGill-Queen's University Press.

Hardy, C., Langley, A., Mintzberg, H. and Rose, J. (1983) Strategy formation in the university setting, *Review of Higher Education*, 6(4): 407–33.

Harman, K. (2002) Merging divergent campus cultures into coherent educational communities: challenges for educational leaders, *Higher Education*, 44(1): 91–114.

Harman, K. and Meek, V.L. (2002) Introduction to special issue. Merger revisited: international perspectives on mergers in higher education, *Higher Education*, 44(1): 1–4.

Harris, S. (2002) Beware the celebrity CEO trap, *Financial Times*, 24 July.

Haslam, S.A., Platow, M.J., Turner, J.C. *et al.* (2001) Social identity and the romance of leadership: the importance of being seen to be 'doing it for us', *Group Processes and Intergroup Relations*, 4: 191–205.

Hayes, R.H. (1985) Strategic planning – forward or reverse? Are corporate planners going about things the wrong way round? *Harvard Business Review*, 63(6): 111–19.

Hazelkorn, H. (2007) The impact of league tables and ranking systems on higher education decision making, *Higher Education Management and Policy*, 19(2): 70–87.

Hazelkorn, H. (2009) Rankings and the battle for world class excellence: international strategies and policy choices, *Higher Education Management and Policy*, 21(1): 40–55.

HEA/GENIE Centre for Excellence in Teaching (2009) *Reward and Recognition of Teaching in Higher Education Interim Report*. London: HEA.

HEFCE (1999) *Performance Indicators in Higher Education*, HEFCE Report December 99/66. Bristol: HEFCE.

Higgs, D. (2003) *Review of the Role and Effectiveness of Non-Executive Directors*. London: HMSO.

Hodges, L. (2009) Trouble at the top: Malcolm Gillies' departure from City University has revealed an intense relationship between governors and vice-chancellors, *The Independent*, 13 August.

Hogan, J. (2005) Should form follow function? Changing academic structures in UK universities, *Perspectives: Policy and Practice in Higher Education*, 9(2): 49–57.

Howell, J.M. and Shamir, B. (2005) The role of followers in the charismatic leadership process: relationships and their consequences, *Academy of Management Review*, 30(1): 96–112.

Huisman, J. (2007) Images and words: how do UK universities present themselves on the internet?, in B. Stensaker and V. D'Andrea (eds) *Branding in Higher Education: Exploring and Emerging Phenomenon*. Amsterdam: EAIR.

Jarzabkowski, P. (2002) Centralised or decentralised. Strategic implications of resource allocation models, *Higher Education Quarterly*, 56(1): 5–32.

Jarzabkowski, P. (2003) Contradiction and coherence: managerial contributions to strategic activity. Aston Business School Working Paper RP0305. Birmingham: Aston University.

JM Consultancy Ltd (2005) *The Costs and Benefits of External Review of Quality Assurance in Higher Education*. Bristol: HEFCE/Universities UK/Standing Committee of Principals.

Jobbins, D. (2002) The rating game, *Times Higher Education Supplement*, 20 September.

Johnson, G. (1995) *University Politics. F.M. Cornford's Cambridge and his Advice to the Young Academic Politician*. Cambridge: Cambridge University Press.

Kantor, R.M. (1995) *World Class: Thriving Locally in the Global Economy*. New York: Simon and Schuster.

Kaplan, R.S. and Norton, D.P. (2001) *The Strategy Focussed Organisation: How Balanced Scorecard Companies Thrive in the New Business Environment*. Boston: Harvard Business School Press.

Kay, J. (1993) *The Foundations of Corporate Success*. Oxford: Oxford University Press.

Kekale, J. (1998) The field of possibilities and academic leaders, *International Journal of Educational Leadership*, 1(3): 237–55.

Kekale, J. (1999) Preferred patterns of academic leadership in different disciplinary (sub) cultures, *Higher Education*, 37: 217–38.

Keller, G. (1983) *Academic Strategy: The Managerial Revolution in American Higher Education*. Baltimore, MD: Johns Hopkins Press.

Kelly, J. (2001) Oxbridge shows that college system puts it in a league of its own, *Financial Times*, 7/8 April.

Kelly, J. (2002) Cambridge high-tech industries call for resumption for fast train service into London, *Financial Times*, 14 May.

Kerr, C. (1991) The new race to be Harvard or Berkeley or Stanford, *Change*, May/June.

Kerr, I.T. (ed.) (1976) J.H. Newman *The Idea of a University*. Oxford: Oxford University Press.

Kets de Vries, M.F.R. (2002) Beyond Sloan: trust is at the heart of corporate values, *Financial Times*, 2 October.

Keynes, J.M. (1936) *The General Theory of Employment, Interest and Money*. Cambridge: Cambridge University Press.

Kirp, D.L. (2003) *Shakespeare, Einstein and the Bottom Line: The Marketing of Higher Education*. Cambridge, MA: Harvard.

Knight, M. (2002) Governance in higher education corporation: a consideration of the constitution by the 1992 Act, *Higher Education Quarterly*, 56(3): 276–86.

Knowles-Cutler, A. and Bradbury, R. (2002) Why mergers are not for amateurs, *Financial Times*, 12 February.

Lambert, R. (2003) *Lambert Review of Business-University Collaboration, Final Report*. London: HMSO.

Lawton Smith, T. (2003) Universities and local economic development: an appraisal of the issues and practices, *Local Economy*, 18(1): 2–6.

Leslie, D.W. and Fretwell, E.K. (1996) *Wise Moves in Hard Times*. San Francisco, CA: Jossey Bass.

Lockwood, G. (1987) The management of universities, in R.A. Becher (ed.) *British Higher Education*. London: Allen and Unwin.

Lockwood, G. and Fielden, J. (1973) *Planning and Management in Universities*. London: Chatto and Windus.

London, S. (2002) Secrets of a successful partnership, *Financial Times*, 6 February.

Lundvall, B.A. and Johnson, B. (1994) The learning economy, *Journal of Industry Studies*, 2: 23–42.

McCormack, A.C. (2002) Bringing the Carnegie classification into the 21st century, *AAHE Bulletin*, January.

McNay, I. (1999) Changing cultures in UK higher education: the state as corporate market bureaucracy and the emergent academic enterprise, in D. Braun and F-X Merrien (eds) *Towards a New Model of Governance for Universities?* London: Jessica Kingsley.

McNay, I. (2002) Governance and decision making in smaller colleges, *Higher Education Quarterly*, 56(3): 303–15.

Mahroum, S. (1999) Global magnets: science and technology departments in the United Kingdom, *Minerva*, XXXVII (4): 379–90.

Maitland, A. (2003) Reputation: you only know what it's worth when it lies in tatters, *Financial Times*, 31 March.

Marginson, S. (2009) The knowledge economy and higher education: a system for regulating the value of knowledge, *Higher Education Management and Policy*, 21(1): 20–39.

Marginson, S. and Considine, M. (2000) *The Enterprise University*. Cambridge: Cambridge University Press.

Marsh, P. (2002) A guide to the winners and losers, *Financial Times*, 16 May.

Merton, R.K. (1988) The Matthew Effect II, *Isis*, LXXIX: 606–23.

Midgley, S. and MacLeod, D. (2003) Vice-squad, *Guardian Education*, 1 April.

Milgrom, P. and Roberts, J. (1995) Complementarities and fit: strategy, structure and change in manufacturing, *Journal of Accounting and Economics*, 19(2).

Mintzberg, H. (1979) *The Structuring of Organizations*. Englewood Cliffs, NJ: Prentice Hall.

Mintzberg, H. (1994) *The Rise and Fall of Strategic Planning*. London: Prentice Hall.

Mintzberg, H. and Walters, J.A. (1985) Of strategies, deliberate and emergent, *Strategic Management Journal*, 6: 257–72.

Monnery, N. and Malchione, R. (2000) Seven deadly sins of mergers, *Financial Times*, 2 March.

Moodie, G.C. and Eustace, R.B. (1974) *Power and Authority in British Universities*. London: Allen and Unwin.

Morley, L. and Aynesley, S. (2007) Employers, quality and standards in higher education: shared values and vocabularies or elitism and inequalities?, *Higher Education Quarterly*, 61(3): 229–49.

NCIHE (National Committee of Inquiry into Higher Education) (1997) *Higher Education in the Learning Society* (The Dearing Report). London: HMSO.

O'Leary, J. with Hindmarsh, A. and Kingston, B. (2002) *The Times Good University Guide 2003*. London: Times Books in association with Pricewaterhouse Coopers.

Owen, G. (2000) The secrets of corporate survival, *Financial Times*, 28 August.

PACEC (Public and Corporate Economic Consultants) (2008) *Higher Education Innovation Fund Round Four Institutional Strategies. Overview and Commentary*. HEFCE 2008/35.

Parkes, Sir E. (1980) Address by the Chairman of the UGC to the Committee of Vice-Chancellors and Principals. CVCP Archive, 24 October.

Pete, C. and Platt, H. (2001) *The Phoenix Effect – Nine Revitalizing Strategies No Business Can Do Without*. London: John Wiley & Sons.

Peters, T.J. and Waterman, R.H. (1982) *In Search of Excellence*. New York: Harper and Row.

Pettigrew, A.M. and Whipp, R. (1991) *Managing Change for Competitive Success*. Oxford: Blackwell.

Pettigrew, A.M., Whittington, R., Van der Bosch, F. and Volberda, H. (1999) Change journeys: processes, sequences and complementarities. Paper presented to the Academy of Management Annual Conference, Chicago, 9–11 August.

Porter, M.E. (2003) The economic performance of regions, *Regional Studies*, 37(6/7): 549–78.

QAA (Quality Assurance Agency for Higher Education) (1998) *Special Review of Thames Valley University*. Gloucester: Quality Assurance Agency.

QAA (2008) *Annual Report*. Gloucester: Quality Assurance Agency.

Quin, J.B. (1985) Managing innovation: controlled chaos, *Harvard Business Review*, 63(3): 73–84.

Ramsden, P. (1998) Managing the effective university, *Higher Education Research and Development*, 17(3): 347–70.

Ramsden, P. (2000) *Learning to Lead in Higher Education*. London: Routledge.

Rhoades, G. (1990) Political competition and differentiation in higher education, in J.C. Alexander and P. Colony (eds) *Differentiation Theory and Social Change*. New York: Columbia University Press.

Rowe, P. (ed.) (1997) *The University of Lancaster: Review of Institutional Lessons to be Learned 1994–96*. Lancaster: The University of Lancaster Press.

Schoenberger, E. (1997) *The Cultural Crisis of the Firm.* Oxford: Blackwell.

Schofield, A. (2009) *What is an Effective and High Performing Governing Body in UK Higher Education?* London: Leadership Foundation and CUC, para. 2.23.

Schwarz, S. (2003) Can you pinpoint your boss? *Times Higher Education Supplement,* 7 March.

Searle, J. (1972) *The Campus War.* London: Penguin.

Segal Quince Wicksteed (1988) *Review of the Financial Situation and Prospects of the University of Aberdeen. A Report to the University and to the University Grants Committee.* Cambridge: Segal Quince Wicksteed.

Shattock, M.L. (1982) How should British universities plan for the 1980s? *Higher Education,* 11: 193–210.

Shattock, M.L. (1988) Financial management in universities: the lessons from University College, Cardiff, *Financial Accountability and Management,* 4(2): 99–112.

Shattock, M.L. (1994) *The UGC and the Management of British Universities.* Buckingham: Open University Press.

Shattock, M.L. (1997) The managerial implications of the new priorities, *Higher Education Management,* 9(2): 27–47.

Shattock, M.L. (2001a) The academic profession in Britain: a study in the failure to adapt to change, *Higher Education,* 41(1–2): 27–47.

Shattock, M.L. (2001b) Capsa and its implementation. Report to the Audit Committee and the Board of Scrutiny. Part B Review of University Management and Governance Issues Arising Out of the Capsa Project. *Cambridge University Reporter,* CXXXII (6): 177–205.

Shattock, M.L. (2002) Re-balancing modern concepts of university governance, *Higher Education Quarterly,* 56(3): 235–44.

Shattock, M.L. (2006) *Managing Good Governance in Higher Education.* Maidenhead: Open University Press.

Shattock, M.L. (ed.) (2009) *Entrepreneurialism in Universities and the Knowledge Economy.* Maidenhead: Open University Press.

Shattock, M.L. and Becker, R. (2006) *The London School of Hygiene and Tropical Medicine – A Case Study.* www.EUEREK.info

Shattock, M.L. and Rigby, G. (1983) *Resource Allocation in British Universities.* London: SRHE.

Sizer, J. (1987) *Institutional Responses to Financial Reductions within the University Sector,* Final Report to the DES. London: DES.

Sizer, J. (1988) British universities responses to events leading to grant reduction announced in July 1981, *Financial Accountability and Management,* 4(2): 79–98.

Smith, D., Adams, J. and Mount, D. (2007) *UK Universities and Executive Officers: The Changing Roles of Pro-Vice-Chancellors.* London: Leadership Foundation.

Snow, C.P. (1934) *The Search.* London: Victor Gollanz.

Sporn, B. (1999) *Adaptive University Structures.* London: Jessica Kingsley.

Standard and Poor's (2003) *Higher Education Changing by Degrees: University Credit Ratings.* Standard and Poor's.

Sutton, G. (2001) *The Six Month Fix – Adventures and Rescuing Failing Companies.* Chichester: John Wiley.

Taylor, J. (2006) Big is beautiful: organisational change in universities in the United Kingdom: new models of institutional management and the changing role of academic staff, *Higher Education in Europe,* 31(3): 251–73.

Temple, P. (2009) Teaching and learning: an entrepreneurial perspective, in

M.L. Shattock (ed.) *Entrepreneurialism in Universities and the Knowledge Economy.* Maidenhead: Open University Press, pp. 46–92.

Temple, P. and Shattock, M.L. (2007) What does 'branding' mean in higher education?, in B. Stensaker and V. D'Andrea (eds) *Branding in Higher Education: Exploring an Emerging Phenomenon.* Amsterdam: EAIR.

Temple, P. and Whitchurch, C. (eds) (1989) *Strategic Choice. Corporate Strategies for Change in Higher Education.* Reading: CUA.

Tierney, W. (2008) *The Impact of Culture on Organisational Decision Making.* Sterling, VA: Stylus.

Tight, M. (1999) Do league tables contribute to the development of a quality culture? Football and higher education compared. Paper presented at the EAIR Conference, Lund, Sweden, 22–5 August.

Tomkins, R. (2002) Coca-Cola still world's most valuable brand, *Financial Times,* 27/28 July.

Tomlin, R. (1998) Research league tables: is there a better way? *Higher Education Quarterly,* 52(2): 204–20.

University of Oxford (1964) *Report of a Commission of Inquiry Under the Chairmanship of Lord Franks* (the Franks Report). Oxford: University of Oxford.

University of Oxford (1997) *Report of a Commission of Inquiry, Supplementary Volume* (the North Report). Oxford: University of Oxford.

Van Vught, F. (2008) Mission diversity and reputation in higher education, *Higher Education Policy,* 21: 151–74.

Volberda, H.K. (1998) *Building the Flexible Firm: How to Remain Competitive.* Oxford: Oxford University Press.

Watson, D. (2006) New labour and higher education, *Perspectives: Policy and Practice in Higher Education,* 10(3) and 10(4): 92–6.

Watson, D. (2009) The dark side of institutional research, *Perspectives,* 13(3): 71–5.

Watson, D. and Amoah, M. (2007) *The Dearing Report Ten Years On.* London: Bedford Way Papers.

Weick, K.E. (1976) Educational organisations as loosely coupled systems, *Administrative Science Quarterly,* 21: 1–19.

Whittington, R., Pettigrew, A.M., Peck, S., Fenton, E. and Conyon, M. (1999) Change and complementarities in the new competitive landscape, *Organisation Science,* July: 583–600.

Witzel, M. (2002) *Financial Times,* 17 August.

Woodfield, S. and Kennie, T. (2007) Top team structures in UK higher education institutions: composition, challenges and changes, *Tertiary Education and Management,* 13, 4 December: 331–48.

Zemski, R., Weger, G.R. and Massy, W. (2006) *Re-making the American University: Market Smart and Mission Centred.* New Brunswick/London: Rutgers University Press.

Index

The Society for Research into Higher Education

The Society for Research into Higher Education (SRHE), an international body, exists to stimulate and coordinate research into all aspects of higher education. It aims to improve the quality of higher education through the encouragement of debate and publication on issues of policy, on the organization and management of higher education institutions, and on the curriculum, teaching and learning methods.

The Society is entirely independent and receives no subsidies, although individual events often receive sponsorship from business or industry. The Society is financed through corporate and individual subscriptions and has members from many parts of the world. It is an NGO of UNESCO.

Under the imprint *SRHE & Open University Press*, the Society is a specialist publisher of research, having over 80 titles in print. In addition to *SRHE News*, the Society's newsletter, the Society publishes three journals: *Studies in Higher Education* (three issues a year), *Higher Education Quarterly* and *Research into Higher Education Abstracts* (three issues a year).

The Society runs frequent conferences, consultations, seminars and other events. The annual conference in December is organized at and with a higher education institution. There are a growing number of networks which focus on particular areas of interest, including:

Access	FE/HE
Assessment	Graduate Employment
Consultants	New Technology for Learning
Curriculum Development	Postgraduate Issues
Eastern European	Quantitative Studies
Educational Development Research	Student Development

Benefits to members

Individual

- The opportunity to participate in the Society's networks
- Reduced rates for the annual conferences
- Free copies of *Research into Higher Education Abstracts*
- Reduced rates for *Studies in Higher Education*

- Reduced rates for *Higher Education Quarterly*
- Free online access to *Register of Members' Research Interests* – includes valuable reference material on research being pursued by the Society's members
- Free copy of occasional in-house publications, e.g. *The Thirtieth Anniversary Seminars Presented by the Vice-Presidents*
- Free copies of *SRHE News* and *International News* which inform members of the Society's activities and provides a calendar of events, with additional material provided in regular mailings
- A 35 per cent discount on all SRHE/Open University Press books
- The opportunity for you to apply for the annual research grants
- Inclusion of your research in the *Register of Members' Research Interests*

Corporate

- Reduced rates for the annual conference
- The opportunity for members of the Institution to attend SRHE's network events at reduced rates
- Free copies of *Research into Higher Education Abstracts*
- Free copies of *Studies in Higher Education*
- Free online access to *Register of Members' Research Interests* – includes valuable reference material on research being pursued by the Society's members
- Free copy of occasional in-house publications
- Free copies of *SRHE News* and *International News*
- A 35 per cent discount on all SRHE/Open University Press books
- The opportunity for members of the Institution to submit applications for the Society's research grants
- The opportunity to work with the Society and co-host conferences
- The opportunity to include in the *Register of Members' Research Interests* your Institution's research into aspects of higher education

Membership details: SRHE, 76 Portland Place, London W1B 1NT, UK. Tel: 020 7637 2766. Fax: 020 7637 2781. email: srheoffice@srhe.ac.uk
world wide web: http://www.srhe.ac.uk./srhe/
Catalogue: SRHE & Open University Press, McGraw-Hill Education, McGraw-Hill House, Shoppenhangers Road, Maidenhead, Berkshire SL6 2QL. Tel: 01628 502500. Fax: 01628 770224. email: enquiries@openup.co.uk –
web: www.openup.co.uk

Related books from Open University Press
Purchase from www.openup.co.uk or order through your local bookseller

ENTREPRENEURIALISM IN UNIVERSITIES AND THE KNOWLEDGE ECONOMY

Michael Shattock

- How entrepreneurial are European universities? Perhaps more than is generally realised.
- What are the factors that encourage entrepreneurialism to flourish in research, technology transfer, teaching, regional engagement and internationalization?
- How do different kinds of HEIs – comprehensive, specialist, regional or private – address these issues?
- What are the conditions which stimulate or inhibit the "academic intrapreneur"? And in what forms does entrepreneurialism contribute to the knowledge economy?

This book, which is the product of a major EU funded research programme and is based on twenty-seven institutional case studies, attempts to offer answers to these questions through a series of cross national thematic studies. It considers how national systemic characteristics in financial arrangements, human resource management and institutional governance impact on entrepreneurialism and suggests ways in which individual initiative can be released and universities freed up to make their contribution to the EU Lisbon Strategy.

Contents

List of case studies / List of abbreviations / Lists of tables, figures and charts / Preface / Entrepreneurialism and organisational change in higher education / Finance and entrepreneurial activity in higher education in a knowledge society / Research, technology and knowledge transfer / Teaching and learning: an entrepreneurial perspective / Human resource management and the generation of entrepreneurialism / Governance, organizational change, and entrepreneurialism / Entrepreneurialism and Private Universities / Entrepreneurialism and the internationalisation of higher education in a knowledge economy / Impediments, inhibitors and barriers to university entrepreneurialism / The dilemmas of the changing university / Entrepreneurialism and the knowledge economy in Europe: some conclusions from the study / Appendix: A statistical overview / Index

2008 216pp
978–0–335–23571–1 (Paperback)
978–0–335–23570–4 (Hardback)

THE QUESTION OF MORALE
MANAGING HAPPINESS AND UNHAPPINESS IN UNIVERSITY LIFE

David Watson

- Why is so much discourse about contemporary higher education structured around (real and imagined) unhappiness?
- How does this connect with the realities of life within (and just outside) the institutions?
- Does it matter, and, if so, what should we be doing about it?

There is a comforting tale that heads of higher education institutions (HEIs) like to tell each other. "Go around your university or college," they say, "and ask the first ten people who you meet how their morale is. The response will always be 'rock-bottom'. Then ask them what they are working on. The responses will be full of life, of optimism and of enthusiasm for the task in hand." The moral of the story is that the two sets of responses don't compute; that the first is somehow unthinking and ideological, and the second unguarded and sincere.

The thesis of this book is that the contradictory answers may well compute more effectively than is acknowledged: that the culture of higher education and the mesh of psychological contracts, or "deals," that make it up make much of the current discourse about happiness and unhappiness in contemporary life look simplistic and banal.

Based on historical, sociological and philosophical analysis, this book explores the complex issue of happiness in university life, offering some challenging and optimistic answers to the questions it has posed.

Contents

2009   184pp
978–0–335–23560–5 (Paperback)
978–0–335–23559–9 (Hardback)